"Religion" in Theory and Practice

NAASR Working Papers

Series Editor: Brad Stoddard, McDaniel College in Westminster, Maryland.

NAASR Working Papers provides a venue for publishing the latest research carried out by scholars who understand religion to be an historical element of human cognition, practice, and organization. Whether monographs or multi-authored collections, the volumes published in this series all reflect timely, cutting edge work that takes seriously both the need for developing bold theories as well as rigorous testing and debate concerning the scope of our tools and the implications of our studies. NAASR Working Papers therefore assess the current state-of-the-art while charting new ways forward in the academic study of religion.

Published:
Method Today: Redescribing Approaches to the Study of Religion
Edited by Brad Stoddard

Forthcoming:
Constructing "Data" in Religious Studies: Examining the Architecture of the Academy
Edited by Leslie Dorrough Smith

"Religion" in Theory and Practice

Demystifying the Field for Burgeoning Academics

Russell T. McCutcheon

SHEFFIELD UK   BRISTOL CT

Published by Equinox Publishing Ltd.

UK: Office 415, The Workstation, 15 Paternoster Row, Sheffield, South Yorkshire S1 2BX

USA: ISD, 70 Enterprise Drive, Bristol, CT 06010

www.equinoxpub.com

First published 2018

British Library Cataloguing-in-Publication Data

A catalogue record for this book is available from the British Library.

ISBN-13   978 1 78179 682 5   (hardback)
          978 1 78179 683 2   (paperback)
          978 1 78179 684 9   (ePDF)

Library of Congress Cataloging-in-Publication Data
Names: McCutcheon, Russell T., 1961- author
Title: "Religion" in theory and practice : demystifying the field for
   burgeoning academics / Russell T. McCutcheon.
Description: Sheffield, UK ; Bristol, CT : Equinox Publishing, Ltd, [2018] |
   Series: NAASR working papers
Identifiers: LCCN 2017049758 (print) | LCCN 2018022071 (ebook) | ISBN
   9781781796849 (ePDF) | ISBN 9781781796825 (hb) | ISBN 9781781796832 (pb)
Subjects: LCSH: Religion--Philosophy. | Religion--Study and teaching.
Classification: LCC BL51 (ebook) | LCC BL51 .M47645 2018 (print) | DDC
   200.7--dc23
LC record available at https://lccn.loc.gov/2017049758

Typeset by JS Typesetting Ltd, Mid Glamorgan

Printed and bound in Great Britain by Lightning Source UK Ltd., Milton Keynes and in the USA by Lightning Source Inc., La Vergne, TN

Contents

This book is dedicated to my big sister, Sylvia,
who helped to instill in me an appreciation for reading

Introduction

> After finishing *Entanglements*, I was left with only one pressing, unanswered question: Where are other books of this stature intended to support early career scholars? The volume is an effective academic mythmaking, by Lincoln's standards, but it is an even more productive demystification of the field for burgeoning academics. (Cooper 2017: 301)

So ended Travis Cooper's review of my 2014 collection of essays (also published by Equinox)—a set of eighteen responses and rejoinders that I've written, over about a twenty-five-year period. For whether in journals or at academic conferences, I've been lucky enough to have had the opportunity to engage (sometimes spar) with a wide variety of colleagues, and though few of these pieces likely rise to the level of counting as rigorous research—at least in the eyes of many in the field—it struck me that these uncollected pieces (a couple of which were unpublished) were worth pulling together. But to add a little more to the book I decided to write original and substantial introductions to each chapter (with a self-conscious nod to a past reviewer who asked for more information on the provenance of each piece in one of my earlier essay collections). And because the settings and implications of each response struck me as possibly being relevant to earlier career scholars, that's who I decided to make my intended audience as I wrote these introductions, hoping that my sense of those past situations, along with what I saw to be at stake and the strategies employed in the debate, might be handy to someone who, like me when I wrote the first of the pieces collected in that book (which dates from 1990, when I was a doctoral student), was newer to the game.

I had no idea how the book would be received—well, come to think of it, I guess I had my suspicions. For, as with some of my past publications, I admit that I anticipated reviews—if such a volume was lucky enough to even be reviewed—something like Brian Collins's brief book note (sent to me by my publisher) published eventually in *Religious Studies Review* (2017): it curiously notes only the hardback edition's price (which is indeed four times the price of the paperback—but, yes, there has always been a $26.95 paperback edition of the book); it mistakenly claims that all of the pieces had been previously published (two main chapters, along with all of the introductions, had not been—in fact, by my count, about 55,000 of the book's 127,500 words were previously unpublished); it portrays me as disingenuous and employing faux naiveté in the essays (something readers will, of course, judge for themselves but, yes, I do indeed use rhetoric in my writing, as do all writers); and it concludes with:

> But eighteen McCutcheon essays in a row soon begin to yield diminishing returns. (Collins 2017: 44)

That all this could be packed into an approximately 380 word book note was an impressive feat. Though I admit that I sincerely hope that a publisher will one day use one of Collins's lines from that book note—"McCutcheon is a gifted essayist"— on a promotional blurb.

So, with that one reader's response in mind, one that conformed to how I could see some readers judging the book, you can imagine my surprise when a far longer and more detailed review in *Religion* also came to my attention. I remember once reading that Eliade claimed not to read or respond to his critics,[1] but I try to read most replies or reviews that come to my attention—it seems the collegial thing to do, given that we all inhabit this discourse whose boundaries are under debate. As exemplified in the book note cited above, my work has certainly had its share of harsh comments over the years but Cooper's review, which also has some critical things to say, stood out for me; for, as a doctoral student himself, he was among the people to whom the book had been purposefully aimed. The review therefore pleased me a great deal, I must admit, for here was an early career scholar making a strong statement about people at my stage—for whether my writings on such topics as professionalization and the state of the field proved correct or useful to such a reader he certainly recognized (as is evident from the opening quotation, above) the need for a genre focused on providing frank feedback from the other side of the divide. (To be sure, any number of things constitutes that divide, e.g., professor/student, employed/unemployed, tenured/untenured, fulltime/ contingent, etc.) For in any structured setting (i.e., higher education is an institution, after all), where agents are not in control of most levers, any opportunity to make plain where choices might actually have effect strikes me as a something worth publicizing, so that other agents can also work to take full advantage of their chances. And, whether other readers like it or not, that was the rationale of collecting the pieces together in the book Collins and Cooper each reviewed so very differently—so differently, in fact, that, looking them both over as I write this introduction, I tend to think that (taking reader response theory seriously) it tells me far more about them, and each of their specific situations within our institution, than it tells me anything factual about the book they reviewed.

Given that I'm under the impression that there may be other readers out there like Cooper (i.e., proactive early career scholars, working on Ph.D.s or, having defended their dissertations, working on gaining a toe-hold on a Humanities job market that's been terribly imbalanced for decades and shows no time of improving any time soon), I decided to put together this current set of essays; I feel it necessary to draw explicit attention to the fact that four of my own following chapters are re-published, though all have been rewritten to varying degrees (including an opening note, in each chapter, on the occasion of its composition and/or publication). The remaining six chapters in Parts I and II are new, though I briefly make use of material I've published online in three of those (something noted in each essay that draws on this material).

The title of the book, and its internal structure, should make plain that, like *Entanglements*, I'm hoping that this book gets into the hands of the same readers (my subtitle comes straight from Cooper, by the way), for while section one offers some of my broader and more recent thoughts on the current state of the field (addressed in three of four previously published pieces that I'm not sure have come to many readers' attention), the six chapters included in section two each select a specific professional location to examine—from such sites as the introductory course and our professional associations to the problem of contingent labor, the challenge of talking about what a scholar of religion actually does, and even where we elect to publicize our writing. One doesn't have to agree with my thoughts on any of these issues, of course, but I'm hopeful that everyone who flips through the book would agree that each of these sites deserves careful attention (i.e., whatever stand you take you at least know that they each warrant our taking a stand rather than just overlooking them as either nonexistent issues or someone else's problem). After all, as the last chapter makes evident, departments don't invent themselves and certainly don't keep running of their own inner momentum. That there are far more sites in the profession that deserve extended comment should go without saying—for a variety of practical reasons, this volume only tackles a few. Perhaps, in response to Cooper's call, we will see more seasoned authors addressing those other sites in the future. One can only hope.

There is, of course, a third and final part to the book, in which my own writing recedes considerably to the background by merely providing a pithy opening for others to have their own say; in this part, collected and published together, are the twenty-one responses originally commissioned by Matt Sheedy (while he was managing the blog for the *Bulletin for the Study of Religion*) to my own "Theses on Professionalization" (McCutcheon 2007). Given that my theses were written and published a decade ago, just prior to the most recent worldwide economic collapse that, once again, pulled the rug out from under the humanities job market, I welcomed his interest, a couple years ago, to invite a wide variety of early career scholars to reflect on the relevance of what, ten years ago, I thought doctoral students/early career scholars ought to bear in mind as they thought ahead toward that time when they'd be looking for work and transitioning roles in our field—and so we return to the topic of agents working to take full advantage of their satiation (not knowing where it will all go, of course).

That such pre-professionalization is a problem—whereby people who are not yet in a profession are nonetheless judged and then ranked by the criteria of the profession, as if newly minted Ph.D.s should already have peer review publications, plenty of teaching experience, and maybe even a single-authored book or two, etc.—goes without saying; but, like it or not, and due to factors well beyond any individual's control, it is now a fact of life and won't likely be changed any time soon or without consider effort to organize and then persuade taxpayers and governments to think differently about how we now fund higher education. (For, at least where I live and work, there was a day when education was considered a social good worthy of our collective investment, unlike today when, in many cases, significant portions of the total costs are transferred from the state to students and their families.) In fact, it has been this way for some years (for a few decades, actually), though there's an argument to be made that in the past decade things have ramped up considerably, at least in such areas as publicly funded education in a variety of liberal democracies. That some currently early-career scholars fail to understand that the problems they have inherited were decades in the making, and that some who are now ready to retire were not always as fortunate as they might now appear, and that some who now occupy those senior positions fail to understand the unique pressures faced by graduate students today, facing a job market (and thus a future) that increasingly relies on low cost contingent labor, means to me that it can't be a bad thing to establish and thereby try to promote an occasion for scholars across generations to join ranks and, together, think through not only some of the problems that we face but also some of the solutions, or at least strategies, that might be within an individual's reach. So seeing these replies posted individually online struck me as beneficial, yes, and even though their original appearance helped start a few social media conversations, that does not strike me as sufficient.

So I'm pleased that Matt was game to organize and introduce the responses that make up Part III of this book, which we have called "In Praxis," thereby tipping our hat to the rather engaged manner in which theory and practice intermix when we find scholars reflecting on the institutional conditions of their own labor. I'm also very pleased that all of the original authors, each of whom occupies a rather different site in academia than I did when writing those theses, let alone than I do now (and some of whom occupy different positions today than when these were first posted a couple years ago), were up to revising their pieces for publication in this volume. Let's hope that this sparks a little more conversation on professional topics that are immensely important to all of us in higher education—especially conversations (and then action!) between not just supervisors and graduate advises but among members of graduate committees and especially between department chairs, graduate directors, and their deans, since these are the institutional actors who, in varying ways, have access to the levers of power, and who are thus in a position to help address these issues in a longer term, structural manner.

Before closing, let me also add that, as with some of my previous works, I've once again elected to publish with Equinox Publishers; just as happened when working on *Entanglements* for Equinox, I'm now also working on revisions to a second set of essays which, just as happened before, is destined for another European publisher. (In 2014 it was a set that came out with Brill; now I am happy to be publishing my first book with Walter de Gruyter.) The fact that some presses will only publish in hardback (at least initially, with the softcover coming out, if at all, after the first year or two that the book is in print) meant for me that the cost of such volumes would more than likely prohibit the readers I hope to reach with this book from ever obtaining it for themselves, should they wish. So, while extremely happy seeing my other work contracted by other academic publishing houses, I'm also eager to see that Equinox—whose reputation for cutting edge books is now well established, I would argue—continues to be interested in my writings. In fact, I still have a copy of the letter that I originally wrote to Janet Joyce, in the early 1990s, when I was an instructor at the University of Tennessee and when she was an acquisitions editor at what was then Pinter,[2] suggesting an anthology series that I hoped to establish and edit. Since then we've worked together on a lot of projects and have collaborated on getting a large number of other authors into print (many of whom were publishing their first chapter or book, as is the case with some contributing to the final section of this very book); Janet has not only been supportive and trusting of my judgment but has also understood the importance of affordable and thus accessible softcover books that represent non-dominant positions in the academic study of religion. So I'm flattered to find myself once again among her authors at Equinox—a press that, from its establishment, has had a sustained impact on the field and which has now published many of the people whom I consider to be central to its reinvention.

Notes

1 "… for many years now I haven't read what is written about me," as he wrote on January 8, 1979 (Eliade 1990: 2).
2 Cassell bought Pinter in 1995, only to be purchased itself by Continuum, and then Continuum by Bloomsbury some years later (which is how some of my early work has come to bear a Bloomsbury imprint today).

References

Collins, Brian (2017). "Book Note on *Entanglements: Marking Place in the Field of Religion*," *Religious Studies Review* 43/1: 44. https://doi.org/10.1111/rsr.12787

Cooper, Travis W. (2017). "Review of *Entanglements: Marking Place in the Field of Religion*," *Religion* 47/2: 298–301. https://doi.org/10.1080/0048721X.2016.1209050

Eliade, Mircea (1990). *Journal IV, 1979-1985*, trans. Mac Linscott Rickets, epilogue by Wendy Doniger. Chicago, IL: University of Chicago Press.

McCutcheon, Russell T. (2007). "Theses on Professionalization," in Mathieu E. Courville (ed.), *The Next Step in Studying Religion: A Graduate's Guide*, 41–45. London: Continuum.

—— (2014). *Entanglements: Marking Place in the Field of Religion*. Sheffield: Equinox Publishing.

Acknowledgments

Although occasional blog posts have, at times, been drawn upon in preparing this volume (which are all cited at the appropriate places throughout and discussed explicitly in the final chapter), earlier versions of some of the following chapters were originally published in the places listed below; I therefore wish to express my gratitude to each publisher for allowing them to appear here in their new forms.

Chapter 1 was the Afterword to Aaron Hughes (ed.), *Theory in a Time of Excess: Collected Papers from the NAASR 2015 Conference*, 191–202. Sheffield: Equinox Publishers, 2016.

Chapter 2 was the Afterword to Christopher Cotter and David Robertson (eds.), *After World Religions: Reconstructing Religious Studies*, 183–196. New York: Routledge, 2016.

Chapter 3 was a chapter entitled "Criticisms, Debates, and Futures: The Sociology of Religion and Social Theory," in William B. Parsons (ed.), *Social Religion, Macmillan Interdisciplinary Handbooks: Religion*, vol. 2: 179–196. New York: Macmillan, 2016.

Chapter 6 was an essay entitled "A Baker's Dozen of Choices in the Introductory Class," in Forum: Crafting the Introductory Course in Religious Studies (plus four invited responses), *Teaching Theology and Religion* 19/1 (2016): 80–89.

Finally, the responses to my own "Theses on Professionalization" all originally appeared, in earlier form (beginning in 2015), as posts at the blog of the *Bulletin for the Study of Religion*.

Part I

In Theory

This attention to category formation and genealogies, I submit, is where theory—properly calibrated and deployed—ought to fit within the academic study of religion.

Aaron Hughes, in *Theory in a Time of Excess* (Equinox Publishers, 2017)

Chapter 1

Feast *and* Famine in the Study of Religion[1]

The volume in which this essay first appeared, as an afterword, resulted from a program that marked the North American Association for the Study of Religion's thirtieth anniversary and which appropriately opened with Luther H. Martin and Donald Wiebe's co-written history of the association. That I was working toward earning my M.Div. degree back in 1985 and still a couple years away from becoming a graduate student in religious studies at the University of Toronto (where I studied under Wiebe), back when they, along with, Tom Lawson, first came up with the idea to establish NAASR, and that I was still several years away from my involvement in *Method and Theory in the Study of Religion* (which later became NAASR's official journal), made the opportunity of writing this essay, three decades later, which reflects on the state of the field, and NAASR's place in it, rather significant to me. For despite whatever disagreements some of us within NAASR may have had over the years concerning what we might profitably mean by method and theory (on this see McCutcheon 2014: ch. 1), it's fair to say that the institutional space created by the efforts of those who established NAASR, not to mention the now worldwide discourse that *MTSR* has helped to promote, has provided me with much of the operating conditions of my own career. For, long before helping to set the theme for NAASR's (and thus this volume's) 2015 meeting (along with Aaron Hughes, Willi Braun, and Craig Martin), I attended a NAASR session at my very first American Academy of Religion/Society of Biblical Literature conference back in 1992 (held in San Francisco that year) and the second conference paper listed on my CV was one presented at a NAASR session in 1995. (In fact, my first was a paper presented, as part of a panel on Benson Saler's work, in Mexico City earlier that same year, at the congress of the International Association for the History of Religions [IAHR], of which NAASR is a regional member society.) And it was because of NAASR's initiative that *MTSR*'s then editors (Willi Braun, Darlene Juschka, Arthur McCalla, and myself) met, at that same 1992 conference in San Francisco, with a representative of Mouton de Gruyter, which had been persuaded (presumably by Don and Luther) to be interested in acquiring the journal, thereby beginning the transition from a periodical completely edited and produced by graduate students just twice a year to what it has become today: one of the premier international peer review quarterlies in our field. And when *MTSR* was unceremoniously let go by Mouton de Gruyter, just five years later (a decision, I'm told, that still grates on the minds of people at the press), NAASR once again rose to the occasion and ensured that Brill's editors understood the opportunity that had just been presented to them. That *MTSR* has since those days been successively and successfully led by several different editors, all unrelated to the journal's founding at the University of Toronto (e.g., Jeff Ruff, Matt Day, and now Aaron Hughes and Steven Ramey), that it recently celebrated its twenty-fifth anniversary with a "best of" volume in what was then its newly inaugurated supplements book series with Brill (Hughes 2013), and that NAASR itself has now passed the thirty year mark tells us, I think, much about the viability of the alternative that these two sites still offer the field—and I say "still" because it seems to me that, despite some in the study of religion claiming that we are now somehow "post-theory," i.e., that we have come through the fires of the 1980s and 1990s methodological controversies and are now the better for it (see Hughes 2017 for more on this), the issues that have long animated both the journal and NAASR are still as relevant now as ever.

And this was the very topic that prompted the theme to NAASR's 2015 meeting (Theory in a Time of Excess"). For just what is the enduring relevance of an organization devoted to promoting explicit and sophisticated reflection on our tools and both the motives that animate our work, as well as the ends it serves,[2] if everyone in the field today claims that they too are a theorist (something made plain from many early career CVs today, which [presumably as a result of method and theory courses being established, as required in many of their programs, over the past decade or two] now list "method and theory" as being among most people's specialties)? Given that NAASR's subsequent year's conference theme (for 2016) was "Method Today," with major papers on description, interpretation, comparison, and explanation, along with responses (for the papers form this conference see Stoddard 2018), it should be evident that the consensus within the organization is not to close-up shop, in response to that question of relevance, and hang up a "Mission Accomplished" sign. There are those in the field who might think this would be a reasonable response, however; for given that few in our field talked openly or approvingly about this thing called theory thirty years ago yet nearly everyone today seems to see him or herself as a theorist, suggests that the issues that NAASR and its members (or at least its sympathizers—a group more than likely far larger than actually dues paying members) have been promoting have had an effect, inasmuch as a veritable feast of theoretical alternatives now seem to present themselves in the academic study of religion (i.e., from cognitive science to empathically studying what some refer to as "religion on the ground"). But the question remains as to just what this effect has been—for it would not be difficult for some to hear that the span of theoretical choices that I just named fails to identify comparable approaches and thus they might conclude that there is instead (as in in the past) only a light sprinkling of theory in the field today, one that hardly quenches an appetite. What's more, this at least minimal role for theories of either religion or the very category "religion" could be understood as merely being an inoculation against the threat of there being more; that is, upon closer examination of the work of many of those who claim to work in theory it becomes evident that longstanding assumptions about religion being an obviously important, deeply felt human universal remain, unscathed despite a generation of academic critique, and, at least for many, the role of theory is still seen as some sort of secondary add-on that, much like cooking with seasonings, one uses sparingly and only as needed, in hopes of not overpowering the main ingredients that were there long before the spices were brought to the table. But, should one instead think that theory provides the enabling conditions of any intellectual pursuit—that these things we call theories orient us, as scholars, and provide the basis for definitions which, in turn, enable us to distinguish and demarcate items in the world as worth paying attention to or not (i.e., definitions are just theories in miniature)—then the problem in the field today is that more people need to be aware *that they've been theorists all along*, even when they're simply describing the world around them. For even the religion on the ground and lived religion people, who aim to study religion in its authentically local and personal instances (or so they might claim)—those who strike me as simply updating and rebranding an old phenomenological approach (inasmuch as their work examines meaning being embodied, as opposed to essences being manifested)—*operate with a set of assumptions about what religion is and does*; for somehow they know what to describe and what to ignore. This tells me that they have a theory, though, sadly, it is one that is largely unrecognized and thus unacknowledged, as if their viewpoint was instead in lockstep with reality on the ground, in real people's real lives—as if scholars don't wear any lenses when they look at the world.

Contrary to this fantasy of immediate presence, I would argue that without an *a priori* way *explicitly* and *self-consciously* (both key points if we're to call ourselves scholars) to narrow our gaze, focus our attention, and thereby delimit the spectrum of possible points of interest one will quickly find that there is far too much in the world in need of description. In a move not unrelated to how Wiebe, when my teacher, would try to get me just to identify how many books were on the shelves of his office, in Trinity College, in a move presumably designed to establish that, contrary to my newly acquired postmodernist tendencies, there were such things in the world as disinterested facts. But instead, I now simply ask students (who have dropped by my office to discuss such topics, much as I myself had once done to my own professors) if there's any data in my office. It's a mess and houses plenty of books, of course, much as you'd expect from a university professor, but it is also filled with plants, and old typewriter, disorderly piles of stuffed file folders not to mention filing cabinets, a variety of framed pictures and documents, and quite a variety of trinkets from either my travels (e.g., a mug from this or that university or name badges from a variety of conference, that hang on a bookshelf hook much as a series of ski passes might adorn a winter coat) or tokens left by former students. (Aside: our Department secretary has a master key, after all, and periodically she lets students sneak into my office to leave little surprises for me, such as the romance novels scattered throughout the shelves, the wild-eyed Nicolas Cage cut-out heads that appear all over the room or which are now taped to my horizontal blinds [making their sudden appearance only when I close them], or the *papier-mâché* dinosaurs that adorn my shelves.) Sooner or later, and after looking over the whole room, the student will play my game and name something—say, my desktop computer or maybe one of the fridge magnets from around the U.S. that adorn my filing cabinets. (Yes, they're from a student who periodically mails them to us from her travels around the continent.) My next move in this chess game is to ask *why* that particular item *stood out for them*, in hopes of doing two things: (i) getting them to become self-conscious as to the (seemingly unthinking) criteria and interests they used in order to single that one item out from the background noise of my hectic office and (ii) moving them to a position that can entertain that, contrary to what I just wrote above, nothing in the room "stood out" of its own accord, i.e., the mugs and magnets do not have agency (they do not *stand* out) but, instead, these things became an item of discourse because of the student's own interests, assumptions, etc. So, contrary to how this pedagogical parlor trick might have been used on me when I was a student (and it was always the occasion for a lively exchange with Wiebe, to be sure—something we talk about to this day), I've repurposed it to make evident how implicated we each are in animating the world around us with the *appearance* of curious and thus significant things—curious and significant *to us*, that is, for this specific reason and at that particular moment. Come back another day or adopt a different stance, and something else will undoubtedly "stand out." For surely the University of Alabama's heating and cooling maintenance crew entering my office will pay attention to rather different things than will the interior design major or business student stopping by during office hours—and none will likely care (or even "see") that there's a box of Shreddies on my shelf, from a former student who, several years ago, mailed it to me from Vancouver. But enter a fellow Canadian ex-pat who grew up eating that "crisp and crunchy cereal, that's good to eat [good to eat] ..." and, well, that old jingle will likely come to their mind and we'll end up growing nostalgic and lamenting that such things as Coffee Crisp chocolate bars are not available in the U.S. What's more, that the historic building in which I have my office—built not long after the campus was burned down by northern troops, in the closing days of the U.S. Civil War—bears the name of our university's second president, Basil Manly Sr. (serving from 1837 to 1855), a man also known as one who advocated for the institution of slavery, will surely attract the attention of some visitors long before ever stepping foot in my office.[3]

With my office still in mind, consider another practical example: I have four potted Peace Lilies in my office—a gift from the late William Doty, the well-known myth scholar who retired from our Department within a month or two of my arrival, back in 2001. He had a green thumb, as they say, and was involved in volunteering at the local arboretum—his office and home reflected this interest—and so he gave me some plants to liven up what was then my sparse, newly arrived office. I've had them ever since and periodically water them, of course, along with the other vines that I have atop bookshelves, but there are also times when, I confess, I've been negligent and so, sometimes, they don't look so good. So one day, in the middle of a meeting with a student who was enrolled in one of my 100-level introductory courses, talking over his test performances, he just sort of leapt up from his seat, mid-sentence, and went behind me—I hadn't realized that he had been glancing for my shoulder for a while, at two of the scruffy-looking plants. As he expertly began pruning the dried, dead leaves from the plants, tossing them in my office garbage can, he told me that he just couldn't resist doing this, since his family was involved in the flower business, supplying plants to businesses and offices. It was a great example of how prior interests made something in the space (that I'd long overlooked, to their detriment) noticeable—so much so that he just had to do something about it, thereby paying far more attention to the plants than the conversation we were having concerning his tests. (The plants looked far better when he was done and, yes, he pulled up his grade in the course.)

But a further point remains to be made: although I think that this is how signification *always* works—i.e., that the world does not come pre-packaged for our passive enjoyment—if we happen to be the type of people known as scholars then we likely shouldn't just impulsively leap into action, trimming and grooming some part of reality that we're drawn to, for some inexplicable reason, for among our jobs (again, as scholars) is to clearly identify those interests and assumptions as best we can and then to make them as explicit and public as possible, organizing it all into what we'll just call a theory, that (i) directs our gaze, (ii) makes it possible to see something as more or less interesting to us (i.e., as an object of inquiry or datum), and, most importantly perhaps, (iii), inasmuch as it is explicit, invites our peers to call us to task by inquiring as to the warrant for, or implications of, what it is that we do.

This was a point, at least as I read him, nicely made by the philosopher of science, Karl Popper, in a passage I've quoted before, when he reports having asked his students, without elaboration or further instruction, simply to observe (i.e., to use a method of analysis). Concerning that episode, Popper writes as follows:

> The belief that science proceeds from observation to theory is still so widely and so firmly held that my denial of it is often met with incredulity. I have even been suspected of being insincere—of denying what nobody in his senses would doubt.
>
> But in fact the belief that we can start with pure observation alone, without anything in the nature of a theory is absurd; as may be illustrated by the story of the man who dedicated his life to natural science, wrote down everything he could observe, and bequeathed his priceless collection of observations to the Royal Society to be used as evidence. This story should show us that though beetles may profitably be collected, observations may not.
>
> Twenty-five years ago I tried to bring home the same point to a group of physics students in Vienna by beginning a lecture with the following instructions: "Take pencil and paper; carefully observe, and write down what you have observed!" They asked, of course, what I wanted them to observe. Clearly the instruction, "Observe!" is absurd. (It is not even idiomatic, unless the object of the transitive verb can be taken as understood.) Observation is always selective. It needs a chosen object, a definite task, an interest, a point of view, a problem. And its description presupposes a descriptive language, with property words; it presupposes similarity and classification, which in their turn presuppose interests, points of view, and problems. (Popper 1962: 46)

Updating Popper, I think of the difference between, say, Narrative Clip—a small, wearable camera that automatically takes a picture of your world every thirty seconds—on the one hand, and, say, an Instagram photo on the other. Whereas the former, attached perhaps to the lapel of your coat, for example, documents impassively and unfailingly, recording every single raw and uncomposed, uncropped setting that happens to be in front of it, with no editorial input ("Capture authentic video and photos effortlessly" their website says), the latter produces highly crafted, filtered images based on preferences that are applied, in hindsight, to the selected photo—making evident that choice (i.e., selection) and interest play a fundamental role in the latter (though it may not be as apparent, we must recognize that, in the case of the former, human agency plays no less a role, of course, since the camera didn't purchase itself or attach itself to your coat, let alone to the front, etc.). So, from one we get breathtakingly dazzling images of oddly vibrant sunsets while the other produces hundreds, even thousands of supposedly authentic (but more than likely uninteresting) photos of undecipherable things, such as whatever it was that the camera happened to snap as you took your coat off and threw it over a chair. That this little camera is called Narrative is a bit ironic, if you stop to think about it, for only by means of a subsequently spun, developmental tale would the disparate photographed moments of a life become part of a story; for, at the level of unending thirty second photographs, there is no narrative arc to the day but, instead, just the monotony of disconnected, raw happenings.[4]

Looking through library shelves or doing fieldwork are much the same, I'd argue: without a clearly and publicly stated reason for going there and thus a way to pay attention to just some of the things you find, it is an endless series of disconnected happenings of no consequence.

That too few in our field seem to recognize that, as the late Jonathan Z. Smith once quipped, "one wears eyeglasses when one gazes at these naked facts" (Smith 2007: 76), is the enduring problem of the field;[5] I take it that this naturalization of what are really happenstance or ad hoc interests explains the resistance I often encounter to historicizing the category religion itself, inasmuch as we all just seem to know that some things are (or ought to be) religious. I therefore often find scholars (who have evidently never read Popper, though they profess to have read Smith...) whose descriptive language is used as if it comes with no preconditions or implications; that is, as if it is assumed to be a natural fit with whatever it is used to name (despite a couple generations of anthropologists problematizing the notion of ethnography's impassionate neutrality). For example, I rarely find an explicit theory of myth or ritual but, instead, simply see things in the literature called myths (that the observer somehow just knows to be tales in distinction from all of the other stories) and actions called rituals (that are somehow clearly different from the seemingly meaningless habits that fill our days)—distinctions usually presumed to be rooted in some necessary quality or inherent feature of the item rather than in the contingent eye of the beholder. And so it seems to me that the distance between recognizing that our work is possible because of prior interests (that exist at a distance from the so-called lived reality of the people whom we study) as well as the technical terminology that we develop in pursuit of those interests, on the one hand, and, on the other, those who carry out their work as if their claims passively document self-evident realities outside themselves constitutes the landscape of our field's enduring debates.

Come to think of it, it's a distinction nicely captured in Bruce Lincoln's straightforward definition of religion, which he proposes in the second of his (I would hope) now well-known thesis on method:

> Religion, I submit, is that discourse whose defining characteristic is its desire to speak of things eternal and transcendent with an authority equally transcendent and eternal. (Lincoln 1996: 225)[6]

As we've often seen in the history of our field, when studying people who themselves aim to speak with a legitimacy attributed to such an authorized domain, there is a temptation for scholars themselves also to claim that authority for themselves and their own scholarly claims—as if this or that action or item just ought to attract our attention; in such cases, the if/then conditional of scholarly discourse—one I'd say Lincoln goes on to characterize as "that discourse which speaks of things temporal and terrestrial in a human and fallible voice, while staking its claim to authority on rigorous critical practice"—is dropped; for here there is presumed to be no theory, no lenses, and thus no posited (dare I say necessary?) gap between scholarly interest and matters of fact or actual state of affairs (thus, speculations on the motives and intentions of actors are repeatedly made in our field, as if hardly speculative, let alone the many totalized claims made by colleagues about this thing called the universal human condition). And so, rather than making clear the posited starting point and set of assumptions that provide the ground upon which a claim can be made, followed then by the implicit "If you grant to me all this, then here's what I make of this or that ..." (which, I'd further maintain, carries with it an invitation to test those assumption's utility, i.e., what do you think about what it allows me to say about the world?), scholarship takes on the form of assertion or proclamation, since its first principles are portrayed as needing no argumentation, since there's nothing conditional or contingent about them; rather, unlike that student trimming my plants who at least explained his actions in the light of prior interests, such speakers act as if their claims are in lockstep with reality itself—as if whatever a student happens to see as interesting in my office necessarily must also attract the attention of anyone else who walks in the door.

So those who mean by theory some sort of secondary step after an obviously significant thing "catches their eye" (thereby standing out of its own agency, perhaps?)—even those who claim an interest in rigorous explanatory theorizing sometimes presume the self-evidency of their datum (and who then also understand theory only as what they use to explain its already-present existence or function)—seem to fail to acknowledge what I take to be Popper's point: that a prior, happenstance and thus contingent set of interests was needed to make something in the world "stand out" as worth talking about, making it worthwhile to dig, for example, through the archives or travel to the other side of the world in order to examine it in greater detail. Simply put, some "it" doesn't proactively catch our eye but, instead, our eye catches it![7] So the challenge of theory, then, as I would describe it, is to historicize what is portrayed as self-evident and thereby to make plain our starting points—for, not unlike Klondike gold miners of old, our work as scholars is premised on staking a claim, defending it, and then getting busy within the ad hoc domain that our claims makes possible.

But, I'd add, that not just every claim and just any set of prior interests counts as part of the discourse of the academy is important to consider—I recall again the definition of History, as opposed to Religion, offered by Lincoln (the upper-cases are his). In my reading it's a distinction informed by Roland Barthes's 1957 Preface to *Mythologies*, where we read about what he characterizes as his motivation for writing the pieces collected in that volume:

> In short, in the account given of our contemporary circumstances, I resented seeing Nature and History confused at every turn, and I wanted to track down, in the decorative display of *what-goes-without-saying*, the ideological abuse which, in my view, is hidden there. (Barthes 1972: 11)

Staking itself instead on, as Lincoln puts it, "rigorous critical practice," what we might as well just call an historical discourse, one that contributes to the academic pursuit that I understand the study of religion to be, always keeps the contingency of the if/then conditional in view, mindful that nothing goes without saying (for then we wouldn't say it, now would we?); for the critically minded scholar whom I have in mind presumes that there is no outside of history and thus no final resting place where our work will be done—"it's turtles all the way down" is the shorthand some have come to use for this position (something referenced in my final chapter)—and thus that, despite what the people we may study might claim, there is also no absolute origin or ultimate end to scholarship. For with each new set of eyes or ears that appear on the scene there also come new interests (i.e., the data of my office are as innumerable as are its visitors). What we therefore have to take into account is situation and context, along with the interested observers arriving with questions that are more than likely alien to the interview subject or which have been previously unasked of an artifact—what we might otherwise name as a generic object that those very interests have already plucked from the obscurity of Trotsky's "dustbin of history" to make it into an item worth our time.

But, as I said, I find too few in the field interested in defining theory in this way and thus, despite the so-called reflexive turn, few seem open to scrutinizing their own position as a scholar and the contributions they offer to making the world seem interesting. Instead, as already noted, theory is assumed only to be a subsequent step, only sometimes used to explain religion itself.

In looking for a contemporary and easily described example of this problem, I came across a post at the Wabash Center for Teaching and Learning in Theology and Religion's blog, entitled "Integrating Theory and Research in the Undergraduate Islamic Studies Classroom"; it reflects on the challenge of using theory in courses where students expect an emphasis on a descriptive approach; for, as Caleb Elfenbein (2016) writes in his opening line: "More often than not, it seems, students register for courses on Islam [not to mention any number of the other world religions, I would add] wanting to learn 'stuff.'" But, as he then goes on to elaborate, "if we don't spend time really developing theoretical frameworks for understanding that stuff, then are we ultimately doing much more than presenting curiosities, intellectual knick-knacks?" This is a crucial point, of course, but given how I usually find this notion of theory being used in our field, I admit to a suspicion when reading comments such as these, for I'm inclined to wait for the other shoe to drop by, for instance, later learning that everything but religion needs such theorizing. And, sure enough, despite soon after rightly warning his readers that "[w]ithout explicit and sustained theorization, we create the mistaken impression that information stands on its own," it turns out that not religion or the idea of a tradition are theorized but, instead, only the idea of "the public" requires such treatment. Accordingly, an undergraduate course entitled "Being Muslim in America," in which the aim is for "students ... to consider the conditions in which Muslim communities have been or sought to be included or excluded from broader American public life," invites students "to spend some time figuring out what exactly 'public life' means, which requires us to ... theorize."

Now, as one who has spent some time thinking through the way that our own society employs the rhetorically effective private/public distinction (see, for example, various essays in *The Discipline of Religion* as well as *Religion and the Domestication of Dissent*: McCutcheon 2003, 2005), I am hardly unsympathetic toward those wishing to have students examine what it is that differing senses of "public life" can accomplish for social actors, but it was the following line that confirmed the suspicion mentioned above, for it made plain that while the environment in which religious things may take place need theories, religion is itself somehow exempt; for he writes: "There is a rich body of literature analyzing the place of religion in public life ..." (Elfenbein 2016). We see here what I would characterize as an untheorized, folk notion of religion as being something originally private (an experience or feeling, perhaps) that is initially set apart from the public domain and which only then interacts with it in some secondary manner; it is a well-known, philosophically idealist conception of religion, akin to some sort of private emotion or disposition, that, in my assessment, informs much of the literature on "religion in public life"; for if, instead, we theorized the very category religion as an inevitably public, socio-rhetorical term that some actors use to name, distinguish, and thereby manage elements of their social world, then the phrase "religion in public life" would be heard as redundant and unhelpful, for the fact that this or that claim, action, or organization *is called* religious (either to be privileged or critiqued—classification has a variety of effects, after all) would itself be seen as the trace of a prior social situation.

Now, of course one may counter that my critical reading here is overly ambitious; in support of it, I note that, a little further into the blog post, we find a no less philosophically idealist social theory:

> By the time we got to the end of the session we had come to the conclusion that what [Michael] Warner means by a "text" [in the reading for that day's class] is really *an expression of an idea*—in any medium—that grounds a common experience of some kind for people. *This common experience is then what generates a public.* (Elfenbein 2016; italics added)

Perhaps best exemplified in the much earlier work of William James, scholars simply reproducing the presumption than private inner states (also called such things as ideas or faith) are the primary ground of public domains (such as texts and actions or groups and institutions) leaves unexamined the way in which certain social circumstances are legitimized *as if* they originated from a pre-political, personal realm. The problem, then, is that binary pairs—i.e., private/public—are often *not* treated by scholars *as a binary* and, instead, one pole (in this case privacy, such as our common, folk conception of the self as *expressing* private meanings into the secondary, public realm) is naturalized while only the other (the so-called public) is historicized. The effect of this strategically useful, partial theorization, of course, is that traditional understanding of religion as a privileged experience or pure, interior disposition that is only subsequently projected outwardly (where it is prone to misinterpretation and pollution, to recall James's classic approach) is employed as if it was necessarily accurate, and thereby reinforced. For, contrary to this idealist approach, there are others (some of whom are represented in the selections included in Martin and McCutcheon 2012, for example) who would see not common experiences as generating a public but quite the other way around. Case in point: as I've noted on previous occasions, without the vocabulary and grammar taught to each of us by others, who were themselves parts of even more prior institutions not of their own making, none of us would be *experiencing* the thing we commonly call *meaning* that we take to be within this text (i.e., meaning, despite what we usually think, is a social phenomenon, inasmuch as it results from prior situations).

So despite the fact that he concludes by noting that his "students did a great job locating varied 'texts' that sought to include or exclude American Muslims from public life," the trouble is that this understanding of theory leaves unexamined not just the thing that we call religion, but, more specifically, how the identity "American Muslim" is itself *constituted*; instead, we look only at how it is *expressed* in this or that setting. According to this model of what it means to theorize, then, both are presumed to be prior, coherently existing things that only interact, in some secondary manner, with the world, i.e., are Muslims included or excluded from public life? The more interesting theoretical question, I'd argue, is to examine how (along with asking *by whom* and *in what occasions*) certain groups of people are constituted *as* Muslim in this or that setting. For my presumption is that this particular identity is not a naturally occurring fact but, instead, is operationalized by various people in different manners and at different times.

I think here of then candidate for the Republican party's nomination, Donald Trump; in response to a speech by President Obama—in which Obama had said, in his December 6, 2015, speech from the Oval Office:

> Muslim Americans are our friends and our neighbors, our co-workers, our sports heroes—and, yes, they are our men and women in uniform who are willing to die in defense of our country …

—Trump tweeted as follows, on the same day:

> Obama said in his speech that Muslims are our sports heroes. What sport is he talking about and who? Is Obama profiling?

In response to this tweet, a number of news outlets (as they typically do in response to now President Trump's tweets) began fact checking and listing all of the Muslim sports stars in American history, going so far as to note that Trump himself had won the Muhammad Ali Entrepreneur award in 2007 and even met the famed boxer at the event. But my guess is that such retorts entirely miss the point, for at the time of composing the tweet, African Americans or members of the Nation of Islam were probably not what Trump (or whomever manages his Twitter account—if, indeed, it is someone other than him) had in mind as constituting "a Muslim." My point was nicely evidenced in the parodies that followed the controversy, at least for some, of Beyoncé's 2016 Super Bowl halftime appearance (in which her dancers' costumes referenced the look of the Blank Panthers), as well what was then her new single, "Formation" (released just the day before). The parodies of reactions to both lampooned many white Americans' apparent shock at realizing that the singer herself was African American (inasmuch as they heard her music to explicitly engage what they saw to be racially charged topics, such as featuring the Black Lives Matter movement);[8] this nicely illustrates that the idea of the Other is not an inherent quality as much as it is a subject-position ascribed to oneself by others (with a nod here, of course, to Louis Althusser's notion of interpellation). To return to my point: the interesting question may not be which conditions allow Muslims to be included in public life (an approach that naturalizes a notion of being Muslim, as if ones Muslim identity was a constant and uniform possession), but, rather, *which conditions do or do not constitute various people as Muslims—for whom, in what situation, and to what effect.*

The problem, then, with how many members of the field use theory is that it dehistoricizes the very thing that we might instead be scrutinizing as an historical, and thus human, act. For as Elfenbein (2016) concludes, "applying a theory heightened their [i.e., his students'] capacity to learn about and reflect on the conditions of public life for American Muslims," but, judging by the blog post on this class exercise, at no time did it examine the constitution of that very identity itself—instead, it seems to have been taken as a given—let alone tackle the implications of conceiving of it as a specifically *religious* identity about which we, as scholars of religion, ought to have something to say. (Whether this is done at other points in the course is something that I, of course, do not know.) And so, when this way of understanding theory is used, an exercise in *applying* theory ends up also being an exercise in *limiting* theory by ensuring that students understand that only certain things need to be examined or, better put, not all things are the discursive products of prior curiosities, assumptions, interests. After all, something that predates theory is the thing to which we subsequently apply it, no?

Because this is the way in which I see many of our peers to be theorizing it strikes me that NAASR's role, as a scholarly organization with a specific focus, is now as relevant as its founders thought it was thirty years ago (i.e., if by theory we mean to develop analyses of religion as a mundane element of the human, rather than just offering accounts of some interior dimension's inter-actions outside the so-called believers' hearts and minds). Most recently, I think of Amy Paris Langenberg's use of Mary Douglas's work on purity systems as a positive, counterexample for the field, inasmuch as Langenberg draws upon the anthropologist's theory to make sense of (i.e., to see as comparable to examples from other groups[9]) diverse pollution taboos and rituals, on the one hand, and the production of social and gendered identity in classical Indian texts, on the other—specifically those regulations involving blood taboos, as she terms them, associated with menstruation (Langenberg 2016). The result of her use of Douglas is a conclusion separate from how elite insiders might have understood their own texts and injunctions for, following Douglas's understanding of the need to study total systems of purity (i.e., think here of how Douglas explained the role of the Levitical dietary codes), Langenberg makes novel claims about these practices—exemplifying that theory allows us to produce new knowledge about the world that is not constrained by the way the people we happen to study see the world. For, *if* you grant to her Douglas's theory on the social function of pollution taboos, *then* this is what we can now say about disparate texts not previously understood as related. That much of the issue of the *Journal of the American Academy of Religion* in which Langenberg's article appears is devoted to rather different, normative topics in the field (as some have sadly come to expect from this journal) makes her essay exemplary of a marginal but nonetheless important position in the field.[10]

And it is just such a position that, in my reading, NAASR aimed to represent and encourage back in 1985; it's an old position, to be sure, that (though we now differ from them in many regards) dates to our intellectual predecessors in the late nineteenth century (if not even earlier—at least according to the late Sam Preus): that those things some people privilege as religions can be productively studied by non-participants, doing so cross-culturally and comparatively, and then ana-lyzed as accomplishing mundane (but not unimportant) things; and it is a posi-tion that I maintain is no less in need of representation and encouragement now, notably in the work of a newer generation who agree that religion isn't really about religion—especially when we still find such scholars as Wilfred Cantwell Smith being appreciatively cited in the field and such figures as Rudolf Otto called a "theorist of the holy."[11] So the themes of these recent NAASR conferences, all focused either on ways of theorizing religion today or the tools needed to carry out this work,[12] as a still relevant dispatch from one edge of the field, sampling issues and conversations that ought to have an impact far wider than the panels where they initially took place. And in doing so, readers should note that many of the participants in those conferences were rather early in their academic careers when they first wrote and presented their papers (several were doctoral students at the time, in fact, along with a variety of early-stage assistant professors), which suggests to me that this is an edge to which we will continue to pay attention; I'm therefore looking forward to seeing even more intellectually provocative devel-opments in the near future. For the scarcity of theory in our field, at least as I believe we should understand this term, will hopefully not continue to character-ize the field for too much longer.

Notes

1 As described in the opening lines, this essay was originally written to conclude a collection of essays from the 2015 annual meeting of NAASR, whose panels that year—chaired by Aaron Hughes, who also edited the proceedings (Hughes 2017)—were all devoted to what some of us see to be the problem of the prominence yet marginalization of theory in the field today. The conference discussions were particularly productive, in my opinion, inasmuch as the event involved four, rather different, major papers (by Jason Blum, Merinda Simmons, Claire White, and Matt Bagger), that were each pre-distributed and then only summarized at the session, followed by multiple responses from a variety of early career colleagues. This annual meeting format was productive enough that it was followed by NAASR in 2016 and in 2017.

2 As its mission statement notes, NAASR aims to "encourage the historical, comparative, structural, theoretical, and cognitive approaches to the study of religion among North American scholars; to represent North American scholars of religion at the international level; and to sustain communication between North American scholars and their international colleagues engaged in the study of religion" (see https://naasr. com/about-2, accessed June 25, 2017).

3 See the 2006 article in our local newspaper, where it is noted that the two slave graves on campus, which were marked for the first time in 2004, contain the remains of slaves whom Manly owned; see www.tuscaloosanews.com/news/20060407/ slavery-marks-universitys-past (accessed June 25, 2017).

4 Gordon Bell's (b. 1934) noted experiments in so-called life-logging (i.e., Microsoft's "My Life Bits" project)—documenting everyone moment and sound from a life via wearable devices—also comes to mind as one example.

5 See my own "In Memoriam: Jonathan Z. Smith (1938–2017)" (posted on January 5, 2018, at http://rsn.aarweb.org/articles/memoriam-jonathan-z-smith-1938%E2%80%932017) for a tribute to Smith, who passed away on December 30, 2017. That his work has had a tremendous influence on my own, despite having never studied with him, should indicate the importance of reading and writing as an academic.

6 It may or may not be surprising to learn that a number of the undergraduate and even graduate students who routinely find me on social media, to start up a conversation about their frustrations with the field, are not aware of Lincoln's "Theses on Method."

7 The passive voice so easily enters our discourse—correction: we so often find it useful to use the passive voice—that we often overlook the active work its doing for us, as I at first did when writing this very sentence's opening, before adding the above aside.

8 I have in mind Saturday Night Live's skit, from February 13, 2016, entitled "The Day Beyoncé Turned Black"; view it at www.nbc.com/saturday-night-live/video/ the-day-beyonce-turned-black/2985361 (accessed March 18, 2016).

9 "[H]ere I take the view that, at least for now, more is to be gained from viewing Buddhist impurity as a total system normative for social reality and comparable to ritual impurity systems in other religions than in focusing on how it is unique and specific" (Langenberg 2016: 164).

10 For instance, a set of papers, originally from a roundtable at the 2013 meeting of the American Academy of Religion, published in this same issue of *JAAR* and devoted to defending various sense of normativity in Islamic studies scholarship, was the focus for a recent critical essay of own; see McCutcheon (2017).

11 On my former claim, see the previous *JAAR* editor's inaugural editorial (*JAAR* 79/1 [2011]: 4–5) or some of the above-mentioned papers on normativity in Islamic Studies

(*JAAR* 84/1 [2016]). On the latter, this is a claim made by Robert Orsi in his own chapter, "The Problem of the Holy," in his edited volume, *The Cambridge Companion to Religious Studies* (2011: 86); see also his podcast discussion on this same topic, in which he characterizes Otto—the German Lutheran theologian—as a "theorist of religion" within the opening moments of the interview: www.religiousstudiesproject.com/podcast/robert-orsi-on-rudolf-otto (accessed March 17, 2016).

12　Following the focus on theory and then on method, NAASR's 2017 meeting's focus was on the data that we, as scholars, study; see Smith (forthcoming) for the papers from this session.

References

Barthes, Roland (1972). *Mythologies*, trans. Annette Lavers. New York: Hill & Wang.

Elfenbein, Caleb (2016). "Integrating Theory and Research in the Undergraduate Islamic studies Classroom." Retrieved from http://wabashcenter.typepad.com/teaching_islam/2016/03/integrating-theory-and-research-in-the-undergraduate-islamic-studies-classroom.html (accessed March 18, 2016).

Hughes, Aaron W. (ed.) (2013). *Theory and Method in the Study of Religion: Twenty Five Years On.* Supplements to *MTSR* vol 1. Leiden: Brill. https://doi.org/10.1163/9789004257573

—— (2017). "Introduction," in Aaron W. Hughes (ed.), *Theory in a Time of Excess: Beyond Reflection and Explanation in Religious Studies*, 1–10. Sheffield: Equinox Publishers.

Langenberg, Amy Paris (2016). "Buddhist Blood Taboo: Mary Douglas, Female Impurity, and Classical Indian Buddhism," *Journal of the American Academy of Religion* 84/1: 157–191.

Lincoln, Bruce (1996). "Theses on Method," *Method and Theory in the Study of Religion* 8: 225–227. https://doi.org/10.1163/157006896X00323

Martin, Craig and Russell T. McCutcheon (2012). *Religious Experience: A Reader.* Sheffield: Equinox Publishers.

McCutcheon, Russell T. (2003). *The Discipline of Religion: Structure, Meaning, Rhetoric.* New York: Routledge. https://doi.org/10.4324/9780203451793

—— (2005). *Religion and the Domestication of Dissent, or How to Live in a Less Than Perfect Nation.* New York: Routledge.

—— (2014). *A Modest Proposal on Method: Essaying the Study of Religion.* Leiden: Brill.

—— (2017). "Identifying the Meaning and End of Scholarship: What's at Stake in Muslim Identities?" *Culture and Religion* 18/2: 34–48. https://doi.org/10.1080/14755610.2017.1301973

Orsi, Robert (ed.) (2011). *The Cambridge Companion to Religious Studies.* Cambridge: Cambridge University Press. https://doi.org/10.1017/CCOL9780521883917

Popper, Karl (1962). *Conjectures and Refutations: The Growth of Scientific Knowledge.* New York: Basic Books.

Preus, J. Samuel (1987). *Explaining Religion: Criticism and Theory from Bodin to Freud.* New Haven, CT: Yale University Press.

Smith, Jonathan Z. (2007). "The Necessary Lie: Duplicity in the Disciplines," in Russell T. McCutcheon (ed.), *Studying Religion: An Introduction*, 74–80. Sheffield: Equinox Publishers.

Smith, Leslie Dorrough (ed.) (forthcoming). *The Architecture of the Academy: Processes, Institutions, and Power in the Academic Study of Religion.* Sheffield: Equinox Publishers.

Stoddard, Brad (ed.) (2018). *Method Today: Redescribing Approaches to the Study of Religion.* Sheffield: Equinox Publishers.

Chapter 2

Utility and Limits: On the World Religions Paradigm[1]

Indeed, I've often argued when teaching in the social science Core that, if I could only have the first week of Chemistry 101, my job would be infinitely easier because at least we would have raised the possibility that one wears eyeglasses when one gazes at these naked facts. (Smith 2007: 76)

In Prague in 2006, the members of the International Astronomical Union (IAU) voted, as part of their 26th General Assembly, on two resolutions that, unlike the work accomplished at most scholarly conferences, made the headlines.[2] The first was Resolution 5A: Definition of "Planet." They agreed, by a resounding majority (so much so that the votes didn't even need to be counted) that a planet is an object that (1) orbits the sun, (2) has enough mass so that its own gravity can ensure that it maintains what they call "hydrostatic equilibrium" (in layman's terms, it stays round), (3) has cleared the path of its own orbit of smaller orbiting bodies, and (4) is not itself a satellite of another planet (ruling out our moon, for example, from being a planet). There were also some other parts of this resolution, such as creating the new category of "dwarf planet"—a celestial body that meets all the criteria of a planet but one: it has not sufficiently cleared its orbit of neighbors. As mentioned above, the astronomers who comprise this international group voted on a second noteworthy resolution that year, this one passing with 237 votes for and 157 votes against (with 17 abstentions). Called Resolution 6A: Definition of Pluto-Class Objects, it dealt explicitly with what made this all news to people like you and I: in light of the other resolution, Pluto—that merely 1,400-mile-wide planet with several moons of its own, finally discovered in 1930 after being long predicted to exist (prior to its discovery it was just called, in suitably sci-fi terms, Planet X), and whose orbit takes it to the furthest edge of our solar system—*was not a planet*. And just like that, we no longer had 9 planets but, instead, 8 so-called "classical planets," a variety of newly minted "dwarf planets,"[3] along with everything else floating around out there in our local night sky (i.e., what they named "small solar system bodies").

What may be even more curious to those who are troubled to find that the so-called facts of science are open to debate and, yes, democratic votes where a simple majority wins, is that about an additional 11,000 members of the IAU[4] were *not* present for the 237 to 157 vote that prompted us not only to recalibrate how we understand the night sky but also which forced publishers to issue new editions of their science textbook. How would those absent astronomers have cast their ballot if they had attended the conference or stayed for the business meeting (lending new meaning to the old saying that the world is run by those who go to the meetings)? Might Pluto still be a planet?[5] But there are other things that could attract our attention about this recent episode in cosmic classification; for, as far as I can tell, no one seems to be able to agree on what counts as a planet's "neighborhood" let alone how free of debris it must be in order to be judged sufficiently cleared (i.e., how small does something have to be to count as debris worth noticing and thus tracking?). After all, not only does every so-called shooting star that briefly streaks across the night sky signify an invader into our planet's neighborhood (that it's "shooting" means we've cleared it out of our way, I guess)—something that got a little too close to us for its own good (come to think of it, why does the path even have to be cleared to count as a planet?)—but, as mentioned above, there's plenty of objects that we call moons (another question: how big does something have to be before we stop calling it "debris"?) cluttering up the orbits of lots of planets—we have one, of course, whose reflection of the sun lights up our night sky, but Jupiter has 67 varying sized objects orbiting it that we call not orbiting debris (to be cleared) but moons (to be studied); in fact, it even had a monolith orbiting it in the 1968 film *2001 A Space Odyssey* (for whatever reason, it was Saturn, not Jupiter, in Arthur C. Clarke's 1968 novel that was developed alongside the movie). And, come to think of it, Saturn is literally ringed with what we estimate to be billions of objects, thought to range from just a centimeter to 10 meters in size, but that hardly counts as an unclear orbit for what, I guess, we somehow are already certain to be obviously or self-evidently a planet ...

Not unlike the certain knowledge we once had, for almost a hundred years, that Pluto was not only one of the ancient Greek names for the god of the underworld (named in early texts as Zeus's brother Hades) but also the name of a planet—a rather tiny, extremely distant planet but, yes, a planet all the same.

Another aside: did you know that Ceres—the ancient Roman goddess of agriculture, which also names an object orbiting in what we now know as the asteroid belt between Mars and Jupiter, first seen in 1801 by the Italian astronomer and Roman Catholic priest, Giuseppe Piazzi (1746–1826)—was originally classed as a planet, but, by the mid-nineteenth century, was demoted to an asteroid (a term for "star-like" objects, coined around 1802)? And did you also know that the larger ones were once called planetoids (what we now know as dwarf planets)? Did you also know that for much of human history, stretching from antiquity to the European Middle Ages, the sun was, yes, also understood to be a planet? (Of course Nicolaus Copernicus's [d. 1543] critique of the so-called geocentric, or Ptolemaic, view of the universe, with the earth presumed to be its center, put an end to that.) And, further, did you know that, as our star-gazing methods have become increasingly refined and sophisticated, we understandably keep finding more and more stuff out there, some of it an awful lot like what we already knew to exist (like Eris, for instance, the roughly Pluto-sized object first spotted in 2005 and which, as you may be able to predict, played a role in prompting scientists to recalibrate their definitions, for if Pluto is a planet, then why not Eris ...?). And so, with each technological advance (i.e., improvement in our methods), we are put in the position of either continually expanding the number of planets whose names, many poached from ancient Greek and Roman gods, we teach school children or, instead of seeing this list as open-ended, seeing it as a delimited family, which then requires the creation of whole new, and more easily expanded, subtypes (e.g., asteroids, dwarf planet, trans-Neptunian objects—the latter of which are also now called, with a nod to the classificatory conundrum presented by Pluto, plutoids) into which we can place the miscellany of those newly found objects that, in our estimation, fail to match up to our planetary prototypes.

In 2006, the members of the IAU took the latter path, thereby declaring the canon of planets to be closed.

And voila, headlines about Pluto that once read, "Scientists Spy Planet Hunted for 25 Years: Astronomers Believe It's Big and Cold" (*Chicago Daily Tribune*, March 14, 1930) were replaced by signs at a September 1, 2006, protest that read "Size Doesn't Matter" (taking place at New Mexico State University, at which colleagues of the late Clyde Tombaugh [1906-1997], who is credited with discovering Pluto, contested the IAU's vote from just a week before); and now, Pluto is no longer a planet—at least for some. For others, such as those of us who grew up knowing— that's right, not believing or thinking or assuming, but *knowing*—that there were nine planets, we'll always have a soft spot for that careful little object, so far out there in space, that crosses Neptune's path but never collides with it.

The moral of the story? Assumptions, criteria, judgments, debates, votes, social interests, and, yes, technological advances, all determine not only how we talk about the world but how we arrive at a sense of a world worth talking about.

Contrary to how we normally think of science, as dealing with the objective, cold hard facts of the case, all of these contingent and thus negotiable historical factors therefore make possible our ability to devise and authorize a system, a structure, that helps us to make sense of the world, such as, in this one case, describing and thereby understanding those twinkling things in the night sky— and, as a result, understand something about our own place in a cosmic pecking order. But who would have thought that such certain knowledge about the heavens, let alone who we are in relation to it, would hinge on a vote where the vast majority didn't show up?[6] For now you don't have to be a conspiracy theorist speculating on secret sound stages and actors dressed in astronaut suits to come to hear the seemingly simple, straightforward statement "We landed on the moon" as being far more than just an idle description of an obvious or disinterested fact. After all, should we propose another resolution and hold another vote, making the moon a planet instead, then 1969 might have marked not a "moon landing" but, rather, our inaugural adventure in interplanetary travel, making current hopes to get to Mars in the near future somewhat redundant.

But now for the question that some, or all, readers are likely asking themselves: what has all this got to do with the study of religion?

Like our definition of "planet," the "world religions" category that now catches some people's attention in the field—whether to defend or critique its use—performs a service, for it is now part of our modern conceptual grid, a pair of those eyeglasses that Smith mentions in the epigraph with which this chapter opened, that we daily use not just to make sense of *the* world but, more specifically, *our* specific world—doing so in a very particular and always self-beneficial manner; for it is a conceptual and thus organizational tool that a particular group of people (those people being *us*) have developed as a way of making sense not of objects in the heavens but items in their social orbit (or, more specifically, to arrange the people in it, the ones who are said to "have a religion" or "to be religious"), so as to understand themselves in light of the relations they could establish with near or distant others (for these two are interconnected, of course—who I am, and who I'm like, is just code for who I'm not and from whom I differ, and vice versa). They've done this by placing select actions, associations, symbols, and claims (and in that placement that groups things together *as* religious or not, we have all the evidence that we need for seeing the world as composed of the choices and distinctions that have been made by invested social actors) into highly controlled, structured relations with each other, relations of similarity and difference, much as our predecessors once decided that Pluto, though small and distant, was sufficiently like Mercury and our own home here on the Earth to be a classed a member of the family of planets—a judgment which, as we've seen, can be changed, all depending on who shows up to vote, and which can also prompt a reaction, such as a series of online petitions, inviting us to wonder when it might be returned to the planetary ranks. After all (with an even more recent classificatory headline in mind), despite paleontologists deciding in the very early twentieth century that the well-known *Brontosaurus* (you know, the one Fred Flintstone slides down when the whistle [correction, bird] blows to end the work day at the quarry?) was, in fact, not a distinct genus whatsoever, but a mistakenly classified species of *Apatosaurus*, some[7] now argue that what scholars have ever since been calling *Apatosaurus excelsus* really ought to just be renamed *Brontosaurus* once again.

The bones haven't changed, of course, but, like lens-grinding advances that presented to our ancestors' senses more and more celestial objects in need of names as well as a place not in the universe but in *their* representations and schemes, the way we identify, study and then classify them has changed; this is also nicely evident in the case of those newly named dwarf planets: classification is therefore all about us, the classifiers ("classification is a political act!" as students in our Department once phrased it) and their continually changing practical situations (i.e., their interests, priorities, and technologies). And so, contrary to commonsense, it is not driven by the need to fit or account for the so-called stable or obvious facts on the ground (or in the sky), which makes all the more interesting that our changing definitions for what counts as a planet seem, in an unplanned way, to have much to do with where we got that word "planet" in the first place: from ancient Greek, meaning "to wander."[8] For those so-called concrete, objective facts—i.e., what's worth paying attention to and what can just be overlooked altogether—turn out to be the products of our own meandering, contingent (read: historical) definitions and the situations that produced them. So while the objects we name may themselves wander, our criteria for what counts as something worth watching and tracking are dependent on other changeable factors, making evident that they wander as well.

But, come to think of it, this seemingly self-evident opposition between facts and lenses, between things and our possibly skewed viewpoint of them—the old distinction of subject and object—is part of the problem we have to reconsider if we take classification (whether applied to stars or people) seriously as both an inevitable cognitive and socio-political act. Take Pluto for example yet again; just as was the case with, as we say, "discovering" Neptune, we only knew to go looking for Planet X because of a hypothesis we had concerning our observations of other planets (in the case of finding Neptune it was observations, from the early nineteenth century, of what seemed to be deviations of Uranus's orbit and in the case of what eventually was named Pluto it was subsequent observations of Neptune's orbit failing to conform to our predictions of what it ought to be doing out there in the dark). Lacking those observations (and the technological means to make them) and without a systematically arranged set of assumptions (aka a theory of how objects of mass move and, more importantly, affect each other's movements), no one would have gone looking for Planet X—like that tree falling in the forest with no one around to witness its demise, it didn't exist for us and was therefore not an item of discourse. It only became something worth looking *for* (long before something worth looking *at*) once we devised a way to imagine it, making the it, the object, of the observing subject the product of our own imaginations and thus our ability to distinguish (to return to another earlier example) what will now count as *this* ancient beast's petrified remains as opposed to those of *that* one; lacking the criteria, without the theories and assumptions, and thus in the absence of the curiosity we feel to resolve anomalies in how the world appears once we arrange it however we might, we just have piles of indistinguishable bones (making evident that no matter how closely we look at the so-called archeological facts in the ground, we can't make sense of them without those *a priori* categories); but *with* the criteria, *with* the attempt to explain why things don't fit together as *we* think they should, we suddenly again have the *Brontosaurus* in our museums and textbooks (at least those taking evolutionary theory seriously) and we are compelled to search for whatever object of mass that *might* be out there causing what we see as that unexplained wobble in Neptune's orbit. But until the moment when we can imagine their existence (long before ever even having a name for them, let alone see them) and thereby obtain a point of purchase that allows us to draw an imagined boundary or establish a fictive relationship, the objects that we only later come to take for granted—so much so that we end up anachronistically assuming that they were there all along, like the Americas prior to Europeans setting sail west, as if they were just patiently waiting to be discovered by those early explorers—were not part of our system of knowledge, were therefore not an "it" that could be named or could *attract* our attention (and there we see the subject/object distinction reintroduced, as if the subject's disinterested gaze is irresistibly drawn to objects due to their own gravitational pull and not, instead, due to *our* assumptions, *our* need to resolve what *we* see as anomaly, and *our* technological innovations).

So it's not so much about the way we look at the world, about a viewpoint that we happen to have that can be critiqued in light of how it does or does not fairly represent the world as it really is, but, rather, about the way we create the impression of a world worth looking at. At least considering that we wear eyeglasses when looking at the naked facts is, as the epigraph suggests, an important first step, but pressing this considerably further (as Smith's use of "at least" suggests he was certainly game to see happen) means that we need to take seriously that without our prescription lenses there's nothing to see. And when that *we* who are actively constituting our world is expanded to include the imaginative acts of the very people we're studying—for, unlike celestial bodies that remain silent when we decide what they are or are not, the human bodies that we, as scholars, name and group together or distinguish from one another, end up talking back to us and have interests, investments, and goals of their own, and thus are engaged in their own strategic groupings and identifyings—it makes our effort to say who is or is not a Hindu or a Jew, and which tales are myths and which are history, so much more complex than the astronomical analogy with which I've set this chapter's table.

But again, I should ask: what has all this got to do with studying religion?

It is likely the same question posed by my students when, in my own introductory course on the study of religion, we spend a class discussing a short, but significant nonetheless, 1893 U.S. Supreme Court judgment on whether a tomato is a fruit or a vegetable,[9] sooner or later also citing D. G. Burnett's fascinating book, *Trying Leviathan* (2007), devoted to an 1818 New York state federal course case on whether a whale is a fish or a mammal. That we classify to establish and manage relationships and identities might be obvious but, that issues of power and rank are woven into the very fabric of the classificatory act may not be so evident—not, that is, until, as a newly arrived visitor rushing to make a connecting flight, you stand before a sign in the customs area of any international airport that distinguishes citizens from aliens (with the line for the former being infinitely shorter than the latter's). Or until we learn that under the U.S. Tariff Act of 1883 all imported vegetables were taxed while imported fruits were not. (Is not the tomato a fruit, botanically speaking? Could you leverage a return of the duty you paid on the tomatoes that you brought in from the West Indies by means of an argument anchored in botany rather than in their popular use?) Or perhaps once we understand that there might be an incentive to try to recoup the import tax paid on the whale oil your early nineteenth-century ships brought to port once we question whether the longstanding tax on fish oil ought to apply to those sea creatures that, at least in Europe two centuries ago, were being dissected systematically for the first time, to reveal just how unfish-like they were on the inside. (There was no tax on importing mammal oil, after all.) That much of my course is a subtle argument to treat naming something *as* religion, seeing something *as* a world religion, as no more or less mundane a moment, and thus no less intertwined with practical issues of power and identification, as these other examples might escape some students, but I'll guess not many; for once we address issues of tomatoes and whales (and that's where we learn of the judge's interest in a stipulative definition, by the way, for he wasn't concerned with what tomatoes *really were* but, instead, what they would be for purposes of trade and tariff) we soon turn our attention to the U.S.'s Internal Revenue Service's ongoing efforts to define what counts as a church—a specific type of non-profit organization, for purposes of taxation.[10] And not long after that we end up considering something like the host of news articles, that, depending on what is going on in the world, appear almost daily, on whether this or that "radical" group is, say, legitimately Muslim or not. In fact, keeping in mind the variety of classificatory moments and boundary calls that, collectively, constitute our field (e.g., at what historical point does Buddhism become something other than Hinduism and if Jesus was actually a Jew then what do we make of talk of Christian origins?), I'd go so far as saying that the story of Pluto is directly relevant to any course on world religions since such a course is actually a study in classificatory ingenuity and thus a class on the utility—or, dare I say, lack of—of what was originally a late-nineteenth century way of dividing up the world and identifying oneself within it (e.g., "they are/are not like us because..."). That the global divisions we know as modern nation-states date from around the same time should make clear that just because it is old doesn't make it old fashioned our outdated, but if we see classification as an all too historical, and thus situated, human act, then we ought not only to be curious about the ramifications of cutting the cake this way rather than that (as was evident in those 237 for and 157 votes against at the IAU), but also in asking whether any of these particular slices, as time honored as they may appear, suit our tastes today.

So why do we persist in thinking a distinct part of human action is or is not religious? Why do we think the globe is organized in terms of large, international groupings—making them, perhaps, the first transnational corporations—called world religions? Why are they so good to think with—even today?

After opening this chapter with a tale of planetary identities and then briefly touching not just on ambiguous dinosaurs but also on tomatoes (the versatile fruit that we use as a vegetable) and what we now confidently know to be seafaring mammals (despite all of our predecessors knowing with certainty that whales were just big fish), I'm hoping some readers have already started asking these questions for themselves, becoming interested in such things as whether our views on a category's shortcomings are linked to the number of things able to gain admission to the grouping. For example, do we criticize a textbook for not having a chapter on primitive religion, or what we later re-classed as tribal religions, and what was eventually reformulated as the now more acceptable primal or small scale or what some may now even term indigenous religions? Or, instead, can we entertain being curious not about how we either encourage or police entrance to the world religions club, thus quibbling over what's worth calling or being treated as a world religion, but, instead, shift the ground entirely and study why such a "member's only" club exists in the first place? Such a shift would have us studying whose interests are served by continually tinkering with the admission criteria. For while private golf clubs across the U.S. have increasingly debated whether to admit members who were different from their (in most cases) exclusively white male founders and present owners, what exactly has been accomplished by opening membership to more diverse groups? Sure, the board of directors may have been expanded, which is likely a noble goal to many, but it is not difficult to imagine someone whose interests were, say, economic rather than gendered or racial, and thus a person who would see the very existence of class-based private associations as the curious item worth studying, rather than investing our energy in advocating for expanding the membership to yet other no less affluent groups.

Case in point: will the recent two-volume *Norton Anthology of World Religions* (Miles 2015) attract debate on its editor's possibly controversial choice to include *only* five entries—Hinduism, Buddhism, Daoism, Judaism, Christianity, Islam—*or* will the controversy be that in the year 2015 a major publisher has invested its time and resources in producing a classroom anthology that reauthorizes this conceptual holdover from the height of the colonial era?[11]

What's noteworthy about debates over the category world religions is that it nicely exemplifies divisions over which of the two preceding options to pursue; for while some are interested in the implications of even thinking that there are such coherent and distinct things as world religions, let alone religion itself, others seem to be rather invested in that discourse and, accordingly, are mainly concerned with addressing the level of inclusion/exclusion evident in its uses (i.e., for some, the problem with "world religions" is that we define it too narrowly and they merely wish to include more under the umbrella). It's as if members of the latter grouping were voting on whether Pluto was or was not a planet, debating the limits of the family and thereby assuming that there just are, or ought to be, such things as planets and that our job, as scholars, is to arrive at the definitive list, while those in the former group strike me as more akin to those 17 abstentions in that astronomical exercise in democracy, a move that could be understood as registering ones dissent from assuming that some cognitive tool, such as "world religions," ought to be used to create the impression of cross-cultural unity and shared identity among otherwise diverse people. And so, much like that 2006 IAU meeting, where the disagreements over the pros and cons were represented alongside those exempting themselves from having to make the choice, I see much the same debates and maneuvers taking places in our field—with some simply fine tuning the world religions paradigm by offering better ways to study the real religion of ever more people's lives or of the past, while yet others are trying to figure out ways to make the designation itself their object of study.[12]

Finding this debate today in our field suggests to me that it is at a rather interesting moment in its history; for it is not difficult to imagine such abstentions—I think here of Teemu Taira's (2016) interest in a discursive analysis of the very act of using the world religions category, *however it is defined*—would not have been represented at all since they were hardly heard in the academy of that day. (Did we even call something in our field "discursive analysis" back then?) Sure, some could cite Wilfred Cantwell Smith's work, from as far back as the early 1960s, when he criticized our use of the category religion by historicizing the word itself. But I don't think that it takes too close a reading of Cantwell Smith's work to understand that his criticism was concerned with the inadequacy of the word *to convey the deeper significance of what he claimed to be the prior, inner, personal, and thus immaterial no-thing called faith*, which he then distinguished, in typically idealist fashion, from observable and changeable *traditions* that scholars relying on nothing but our five ordinary senses have no choice but to study—don't think you're studying religion's source and true meaning just because you've described a ritual, recited a myth, or understood a set of ecclesiastical rules, he might as well have said, for (in a typically phenomenological manner) the timeless essence (*the faith of men* [sic], as he called it) is not to be conflated with its various historical and thus tangible and limited manifestations. And so we arrive at a moment when (in a move reminiscent of Friedrich Schleiermacher's [d. 1834] much earlier rhetorical distinctions, not to mention William James et al.) original and immaterial faith was strategically differentiated from subsequent action, yet another handy division of labor (much like subject/object or private/public, let alone citizen/foreigner, etc.) that lives on to this day, being but one variation on the now popular "I'm spiritual, not religious" stance that some now use to authenticate, and thereby authorize, themselves in distinction from others. That there's nothing novel or unique about this bold attempt to individuate is the great irony, of course (as demonstrated in a later chapter); in fact, this contradiction is among the few things that makes such claims interesting to study.

It is this very ability to see an author, such as Cantwell Smith, as being involved in authorizing a position, a situation, perhaps even a speaker, by how he framed, divided, ranked, and thereby talked about the world, rather than reading him as talking dispassionately, descriptively, about some obviously existing and thus real sentiments and affectations in the world, which marks what is new in our field—and, rather than being discouraged at the ambivalence present in the current field, I find it encouraging that at least some colleagues find this to be an approach worth adopting.

But, like all orbits, I must now return to the opening to this chapter, since Pluto and Neptune have even more relevance for classificatory debates in the study of religion; for economic advantages and technological advances led not only to discovering more and more objects in the sky (prompting us to redefine "planet" as a regulatory mechanism that governs the economy of newly found objects) but such advantages and advances also made possible sailing ships with ever-increasing range and thus more and more ambitious expeditions ensued, funded by private and public wealth's search for even more wealth, setting off for the known world's periphery from a variety of centers of power and knowledge across Europe. This was an ambitious exercise of the people who, for a few centuries, had already quite successfully been refining that ancient Latin word *religio*, for purposes that were hardly religious (at least as we today define and use that term). For instance, the terms sacred and secular have a long history, of course, but, contrary to how many now tell this story, we'd be in error to assume that all along they were specifically *religious* concepts, just as we today use them (i.e., even the Latin antecedents of the modern world "religion" aren't religious); instead, we might avoid self-serving anachronism in our history writing by assuming that they simply functioned as a conceptual grid to distinguish the domains and thus duties of officials in a specific institution we call the Church (who should themselves be understood not as specifically religious people, working in a specifically religious institution, but, rather, as officials of one among many social institutions that composed what we know as the medieval European world): some worked within "the world" or "among their generation" (from the Latin *secularis*), as in a parish priest (aka ritual specialist), as opposed to those who were themselves "set apart" from the world and thus carrying out duties inside the walls of the institution itself, say, living and working within a convent or a monastery (as in how people once referred to a monk as "a religious"). Thus, while these terms are deeply embedded in our discourse on religion today, we would be well advised to see them as once simply naming a practical division of labor within a specific institution. (Something they still do today, perhaps?) How they were then gradually resignified and spiritualized so as to seem to mean a deeply personal, private affection that transcends time and space—a use that functions as a no less practical division of labor today—is then the interesting question.[13]

But keeping in mind those technological wonders that we once called sailing ships and celestial navigation, in the moments of contact that ensued ("contact" being a euphemism for all sorts of scenarios that unfolded once those ships came ashore all across the so-called New World or the Mystic East) the local and known was inevitably used (by all parties) as the model to assimilate information on the distant and the unknown—we today, in the European intellectual tradition, happen to have just inherited the results of one side's deliberations, of course, making our preoccupation with religion an historical accident. And, like our necessarily wandering definition of planet, so too those early explorers', traders', soldiers', and missionaries' understandings of what was sufficiently like them also changed over time (e.g., the term "Orient" keeps moving eastward, from once being used to name what we now call the Middle East to now designating the so-called Far East), all of which was prompted by increasingly bold journeys over land and water, repeated greetings, trade, conquest, and yes, even subjugation and domination. So, as David Chidester told us some time ago (1996), we would be wise to consider not only our term "religion" but also the later "world religion" to develop from out of this particular historical confluence, always keeping in mind the practical reasons for and effects of classification. This awareness might in turn prompt us to look anew at those late nineteenth-century scholars who first coined *Wereldgodsdiensten*, in Dutch, and *Weltreligionen*, in German, both of which were in contradistinction from what they thought to be merely ethnic or national religions (which, for whatever reason, had failed to find what these scholars understood as worldwide converts beyond their own original kin groups), the ones who first identified just two members of the world religions family (read: world class)—Christianity and Buddhism (Masuzawa 2005: 108–109). But since then the category has spread worldwide while being repeatedly repurposed—as with all language, mind you—and, like the family of planets, the world religions kin group has steadily grown, regularly assimilating the newly familiar, and ending up so large today that any world religions map will now inform you, as if conveying neutrally and thus innocently descriptive information, that every human being on the globe can be plotted somewhere within this now universal taxonomy—in fact, even atheists are now regularly placed on such maps, perhaps because (thanks in part to the late Ninian Smart) some now see that thing we call a worldview as the genus of which religion is but one of several species. And so now, much like astronomers working out the details of dwarf plants vs. asteroids, many scholars of religion are working to make this classification scheme more precise and total ("If it names a deeply trans-human trait then shouldn't we expect to see it everywhere?"), so that it is truly able to encompass everything, past and present; for where the was once just two world religions as opposed to a host of local or national religions there's now lived religions and global religions, major or international religions as opposed to folk religions, elite versus popular, vernacular, material, and embodied religions, and, of course, there's those the sociologists have recently grouped together as "the Nones" who scholars of religion seem to feel compelled to study as a group, despite these people's adamant claims, via their answers to just a couple questions on questionnaires, that they have no religious affiliation whatsoever.

And so we arrive at a moment when a taxonomy originally developed about 150 years ago, used to identify those who some Europeans once thought shared a sufficient amount of their own globalizing ambitions, in distinction from those who were merely local and presumably unambitious (and thus no threat?)—it was, after all, an us/them device—has become so successful in helping us to deal with what Jonathan Z. Smith once called the "explosion of data" that attended the imperial exercise (Smith 1998: 275) that, like stargazers using their now self-evident grids, many of us can't imagine *not* talking about the world religions, however defined, as not just constituting coherent, trans-national communities of people (e.g., the Taoists, the Zoroastrians, etc.) but also as naming deeply human, universal characteristics and timeless motivations shared by all social actors. Case in point: "Muslim and Hindu Riots Turn Deadly ...," began the *Daily Mail* headline on September 8, 2013, reporting on a conflict in the Indian state of Uttar Pradesh; we seem unable to make sense of the world, and thereby understand, as readers of newspapers, why people do whatever it is we see them doing, without these designations and the deep motivations we imagine them to signify—or, rather (and is this why the category continues to be used?), dropping it would mean that we'd have to entertain using alternative systems to make that sense and, because that might risk understanding human action as motivated by something other than timeless affinities and the stands we assume people take on existentially Big Questions, we more than likely prefer to group people in this old manner, as if knowing that the eighteen-year-old Tenzin Choezin is a *nun* and thus a *Buddhist* will provide newspaper readers with essential information as to why, in early February of 2012, they may have seen a news photo of her on fire in Aba Prefecture (also known as Ngawa) in the western Chinese province of Sichuan (a region that, historically and culturally, might also be termed Tibetan). Knowing something instead about the complex relations between modern China and the nation we once called Tibet (or what, since 1965, has been renamed by the Chinese government as the Tibetan Autonomous Region), and thereby making sense of what strikes us as a shocking, graphic event by referencing historically specific and continually changing geo-political situations, likely prompts us to talk about a very different set of relations and identities when confronting the shocking image of that burning woman. But, as I argued two decades ago with regard to how scholars write about what we generally name as "self-immolation" (McCutcheon 1997), for those unwilling, for whatever reason, to take issues of difference, conflict and conquest into account in their studies, those who are unable to make the Copernican shift that some colleagues now see to be a viable option in our field, there is something to be gained by continuing to understand human behavior by devising a few epicycles[14] to help make an old scheme work, continually coining some new subspecies (such as how we got from heathens to primitives and eventually to indigenous religions), publishing lightly revised editions of decades old textbooks, continuing to offer these courses to undergrads, and thereby drawing upon the world religions model to make sense of the world and our place in it.

But my hope is that more of us in the academic study of religion can learn something from the arc of Pluto's rise and fall as a planet—if nothing else, at least to see that it is *we* who do the classifying, revealing such acts to be choices of agents whose situations are governed by wide structures as well as local interests. If so, then despite disciplinary divisions the Humanities and the so-called soft sciences might be understood to share much with the natural sciences and we may come to see scholars in all of these areas to be equally invested in devising taxonomies to make sense of that part of the world that they find curious; that is to say, despite their sometimes overly confident claims about reality, none are studying obviously existing items and none are free of *a priori* assumptions, but, instead, as a group they are all implicated in fabricating the places where they carry out their own work. That few in our field seem to recognize this, instead seeing objectively existing Sikhs and Christians whose compelling doings each seem to produce a gravitational field all their own, thereby demanding our careful description and comparison, turns out to be little different from the tendency in the hard sciences, from where so many of our world religions enrollees come (at least in the U.S. where so many of our students first stumble across our field as an elective that satisfies a Core Curriculum, or General Education, breadth requirement). But if what we're teaching these diverse students in our world religions courses are not just the names and dates that these students are probably focused on but, instead, subtly demonstrating to them how scholarship happens, how historically situated people make sense of their settings by naming and distinguishing and ranking, then perhaps there's something to be gained by making reference to astronomy in one of our classes, or making reference to botanic classification and perhaps using a Chemistry experiment in distillation, in which we boil away the water to see what remains, as a way to explain what we mean by reduction in the study of religion. For it seems to me that, at the end of the day, we ought to be teaching our students (especially in such broad, lower level surveys as a world religions course) not just names and dates specific to our material but skills that are relevant across the disciplines, skills that are useful in unanticipated settings, skills such as how social actors make the worlds they happen to find themselves in—complete with twinkling lights in the sky and people making references to immaterial beings who govern their fates—sensible and thus habitable. And one of those skills is always being on the look-out for the grids any group, including scholars themselves, impose and then authorize, those historically and culturally discrete systems of order that sanction interests but also produce anomalies when released into the wild of an unruly world. "World religions" is one such imposed structure that, of course, has uses (whether one agrees with them or not), but like anything with utility, it likely also has a limited shelf-life and thus an expiration date. Are our students aware of this or has the designation taken on such a life of its own that we, its makers, fail to recall that we find religions in the world only because we're the ones who have defined them in such a way that enables us to go looking for them?

And so, to conclude by returning one last time—slowly and elliptically, perhaps, but returning nonetheless—to where we started: if some in our field could teach just the first week of not just the Chemistry 101 class, where students are introduced to what seems to them to be eternal principles, but also the omnipresent survey of world religions that is still taught by so many of our colleagues, or maybe have the luxury of inserting a crafty forward into the surely planned umpteenth edition of Mary Pat Fisher's *Living Religions*, then our job as scholars and teachers would be infinitely easier because, as Jonathan Z. Smith rightly observed, "at least we would have raised the possibility that one wears eyeglasses when one gazes at these naked facts." For the students might then learn that not only the textbook "participates in the construction of the objects it references" but they and their instructor do as well (Baldrick-Morrone et al. 2016: 40).

Notes

1 Originally invited as the afterword to a multi-author collection of essays (Cotter and Robertson 2016), this chapter attempted to make a strong statement on the challenges of the world religions category—in part because, after reading the pre-publication book MS, in preparation for writing the afterword, it struck me that the volume itself rather nicely exemplified the main debate in the field. As I see it, that debate entails whether the category needs simply to be expanded, to include more (and thus its problem concerns how limited and thus dated its usual membership is), or, instead, should it be studied itself as a modern socio-political management tool (first developed in the mid- to late nineteenth century and which still proves useful to a variety of social actors this day). While not openly criticizing any essays in the volume, all of which are well written and strongly argued, I nonetheless attempted to take a stand concerning where I (and, apparently, some of the other authors in the volume) see the need for future work in our field.

2 See www.iau.org/news/pressreleases/detail/iau0603/ for the press release (accessed April 11, 2015). I also appreciate conversation with Raymond White, former chair of the Department of Physics and Astronomy at the University of Alabama, and member of the IAU, for helpful conversations on this topic (over Indian food lunches).

3 Pluto is now also seen as the prototype for this new designation, as well as it also being an example of the class of what they now termed trans-Neptunian objects, i.e., a planet-like object that orbits the sun but at a greater distance than Neptune, the planet whose trajectory now sets the solar system's limit.

4 See www.iau.org/administration/membership/individual/ for the organization's own self-reported membership number.

5 By the way, April fool articles appeared online, on April 1, 2017, saying Pluto was once again a planet.

6 Come to think of it, the course of modern liberal democratic nations is determined by casting a ballot, sometimes with a surprisingly low voter turn-out, and always with profound implications ("Should we go to war?")—making the consequences of the IAU's vote seem commonplace by comparison.

7 As stated in the paper's abstract, "This resulted in the proposal that some species previously included in well-known genera like *Apatosaurus* and *Diplodocus* are generically distinct. Of particular note is that the famous genus *Brontosaurus* is considered valid by our quantitative approach." See Tschopp et al. (2015).

8 Greek: (*asteres*) *planetai*, meaning "wandering (stars)," from *planasthai* meaning "to wander." It is thought to betray the distinction of nearby celestial objects moving more quickly across the night sky as opposed to the far slower arcs of more distant stars.

9 *Nix. v. Hedden* 149 U.S. 304 (1893).

10 For example, see *Spiritual Outreach Society v. Commissioner of the Internal Revenue*, No. 90-1501. United States Court of Appeals, Eighth Circuit (Submitted Nov. 15, 1990. Decided Feb. 27, 1991) for a particularly good example of the IRS's use of a 14 point definition of church which it used to determine that, for purposes of taxation, the SOS did not constitute a church.

11 See *MTSR* 28/3 (2016) for review essays, taking the latter approach, by my three of my colleagues at Alabama—Michael Altman, Nathan Loewen, and K. Merinda Simmons—on the *North Anthology of World Religions*.

12 The selections included in the volume in which an earlier version of this chapter originally appeared as an afterword nicely exemplify this tension in the field; see Cotter and Robertson 2016.

13 McCutcheon (2003), notably the final chapter, "Religion and the Governable Self," explored this very topic in greater detail.

14 Epicycle is the term for hypothetical and necessarily unseen orbital deviations that early astronomers speculated celestial objects performed so as to account for how far their own geocentric-based predictions were from the observations they made of planets' movements.

References

Altman, Michael (2016). "Where Did This Box of Books Come From?" *Method and Theory in the Study of Religion* 28/3: 287–296. https://doi.org/10.1163/15700682-12341371

Baldrick-Morrone, Tara, Michael Graziano and Brad Stoddard (2016). "Not a Task for Amateurs: Graduate Instructors and Critical Theory in the World Religions Classroom," in Christopher R. Cotter and David G. Robertson (eds.), *After World Religions: Reconstructing Religious Studies*, 37–47. New York: Routledge.

Burnett, D. Graham (2007). *Trying Leviathan: The Nineteenth-Century New York Court Case That Put the Whale on Trial and Challenged the Order of Nature*. Princeton, NJ: Princeton University Press.

Chidester, David (1996). *Savage Systems: Colonialism and Comparative Religion in Southern Africa*. Charlottesville, VA: University Press of Virginia.

Cotter, Christopher R. and David G. Robertson (eds.) (2016). *After World Religions: Reconstructing Religious Studies*. New York: Routledge.

Fisher, Mary Pat (2014). *Living Religions*, 9th ed. New York: Pearson.

Loewen, Nathan R. B. (2016). "Teaching By Production Rather than Products," *Method and Theory in the Study of Religion* 28/3: 307–315. https://doi.org/10.1163/15700682-12341378

Masuzawa, Tonoko (2005). *The Invention of World Religions, Or, How European Universalism Was Preserved in the Language of Pluralism*. Chicago, IL: The University of Chicago Press. https://doi.org/10.7208/chicago/9780226922621.001.0001

McCutcheon, Russell T. (1997). *Manufacturing Religion: The Discourse on Sui Generis Religion and the Politics of Nostalgia*. New York: Oxford University Press.

—— (2003). *The Discipline of Religion: Structure, Meaning, Rhetoric*. New York: Routledge. https://doi.org/10.4324/9780203451793

Miles, Jack (ed.) (2015). *The Norton Anthology of World Religions*. 2 vols. New York: W. W. Norton.

Simmons, K. Merinda (2016). "Canon Fodder," *Method and Theory in the Study of Religion* 28/3: 297–306. https://doi.org/10.1163/15700682-12341379

Smith, Jonathan Z. (1998). "Religion, Religions, Religious," in Mark C. Taylor (ed.), *Critical Terms for Religious Studies*, 269–284. Chicago, IL: University of Chicago Press.

—— (2007). "The Necessary Lie" Duplicity in the Disciplines," in Russell T. McCutcheon, *Studying Religion: An Introduction*, 73–80. New York: Routledge.

Taira, Teemu (2016). "Doing Things with 'Religion': A Discursive Approach in Rethinking the World Religions Paradigm," in Christopher R. Cotter and David G. Robertson (eds.), *After World Religions: Reconstructing Religious Studies*, 75–91. New York: Routledge.

Tschopp, Emanual, Octávio Mateus, and Roger B. J. Benson (2015). "A Specimen-level Phylogenetic Analysis and Taxonomic Revision of Diplodocidae (Dinosauria, Sauropoda)," *PeerJ* 3:e857 (April 7, 2015. Retrieved from https://peerj.com/articles/857 (accessed April 11, 2015).

Chapter 3

The Sociology of Religion or Social Theory of Religion?[1]

Keeping in mind the divide in the field, at least as outlined in the previous chapter (between those who wish to debate how best to classify religions as opposed to those interested in the implications of the classification religion, or world religions, itself), consider two different starting points for the subfield that we today call the sociology of religion: both took place in the early twentieth century and both involve the so-called founding fathers of this academic discipline: the publication in France of Émile Durkheim's (1858–1917) *The Elementary Forms of Religious Life* (1912) and ten years later, in nearby Germany, the publication of Max Weber's (1864–1920) *The Sociology of Religion* (1922). Both remain in print and are easily acquired in English translation—a new translation of Durkheim's book came out in 1995, but the 1956 English edition of Weber's, with the introduction by the equally famous U.S. sociologist, Talcott Parsons (1902–1979), is still authoritative. Both books' influence has been significant, so comparing them might be a good way to frame a chapter on issues of consequence in this modern field— issues that, depending the stand you take, will lead to different futures: one concerned with studying the public expressions and social dimension of something variously called religion, the sacred, belief, faith, experience, etc., and the other with becoming a theorist who examines the prior, practical, structural conditions that lead people to organize themselves by calling something in their world "religious." While the former school of thought can be traced to writers such as Weber, the latter, though he also was interested in studying things he called religious, owes a debt to the work of Durkheim.

To begin, it is worth taking a step back and noting that, although we take it for granted today, sociology has not been an academic discipline for that long; in fact, as may be well known, the commonsense disciplinary distinctions in the modern research university are generally products of the late nineteenth and early twentieth century, when divisions of intellectual labor and forms of specialization that we're now familiar with were first being developed. (The professionalization of the university, with the admission of such specialties as engineering, nursing, education, and business—specialties once taught in distinct colleges devoted to each topic—is a far more recent development yet one with equally significant and far-reaching consequences for higher education.[2]) It is also around that time when writers were rethinking what it meant to be an individual by entertaining that the groups we live within may exert more influence than first imagined. So, although the intellectual tradition from which modern sociology develops can certainly be traced further back than this, it's thanks to scholars like Durkheim and Weber (regardless their differences) that this field was first established as a separate and academically legitimate domain within that broader area we might today call the human sciences.

For thinking back over the past century makes clear that controversies over whether individuals ought to be solely accountable for their actions or whether people are, if they know it or not, largely the products of their environments are debates that are not all that old. Prior to that—and still for many today, of course—the lone individual was taken as the pre-existent building block upon which the subsequent thing called society was based; the model that, for many, was largely accepted was the starting point for an influential piece of eighteenth-century French political philosophy that is read in classes to this day: Jean-Jacques Rousseau's *The Social Contract* (1762). "Man is born free; and everywhere he is in chains" (Book I, Section I; Rousseau 1982: 49) is likely among the most cited lines from this early study; it presupposes that what we know as society (the chains of which the quote speaks, that is, social expectations, conventions, and regulations) is the result of a series of informal and formal agreements, or contracts, between individuals. For instance, we might imagine two neighbors saying: "If you do not step here and cross this line in the grass then I won't step there," and, voila, we see (or so writers who maintain this position would argue) the invention of that collectivity we call society, by means of a newly devised social contract between two separate parties, from which they both benefit, thereby creating what they each call "my yard." Thus, one could argue, the notion of privacy was born, even private property.

This individualist model, as dated as one might claim it to be, still constitutes widespread commonsense today; most recently, and with the U.S. in mind, I think of responses to a speech by the politician Elizabeth Warren, from August of 2011, during a time when she was contemplating a run for U.S. Senate (she was eventually elected and continues to be an outspoken Democrat). Warren's often-quoted line concerned no one inventing themselves from the ground up or, as we once might have said, from out of whole cloth:

> There is nobody in this country who got rich on his own. Nobody. You built a factory out there—good for you. But I want to be clear. You moved your goods to market on roads the rest of us paid for. You hired workers the rest of us paid to educate ... Now look: you built a factory and it turned into something terrific or a great idea—God bless! Keep a big hunk of it. But part of the underlying social contract is you take a hunk of that and pay forward for the next kid who comes along.

Predictably, perhaps (especially once President Obama's 2012 re-election campaign began using the line), the other side's response was to take offense at the suggestion that their own hard work didn't result in the rewards from which they now benefit. So "We built it" soon became a chorus in reply from the Republicans, with their Presidential candidate, Mitt Romney, firing back (at a campaign stop in Irwin, PA, on July 17, 2012):

> The idea ... to say that Steve Jobs didn't build Apple, that Henry Ford didn't build Ford Motors, that Papa John didn't build Papa John pizza, that Ray Kroc didn't

build McDonald's, that Bill Gates didn't build Microsoft ... To say something like that is not just foolishness, it's insulting to every entrepreneur, every innovator in America and it's wrong.

So here the two sides of this still ongoing debate are obviously evident: on the one hand we have lone, rugged individuals carving a place for themselves and exclusively retaining the benefits of their own hard work, while on the other we're told that large collections of nameless others, paying their taxes and doing their work as part of what we might call a network, have, in a sometimes unseen manner, provided the conditions in which each of us engages in what only seems to be our isolated, individual activities. While the two neighbors in the earlier example, making their consensual agreement, provide an example of the former position, the fact that they can even speak to each other, or see each other as worth talking to, is evidence of the other; for neither just happens to have invented or stumbled upon the same language on their own; instead, their very language was created and provided to them by others (who didn't invent it either, by the way—in this model there is no chicken or egg decision to be made since it is presumes from the outset that there was always some prior group into which a person is born), such as those well-meaning parents who leaned in toward them as babies saying such things as "ba ba ba ba baaaaaa" while, perhaps, tickling their baby feet or rubbing their baby tummies. And, in this thoroughly social, institutionalized manner (people take birthing and parenting classes, don't they?), language was acquired and, eventually, a sense of self and thus a sense individual identity—all of which, like those paved roads of which Warren spoke, was made for us by others.

The point?

This latter position, that the individual is a social product, through and through, is not only a recently devised option but, more importantly perhaps, still remains a rather controversial position to adopt, all depending to whom you're speaking and in which situation. (If you're trying to win the business community's vote in an election, well, it is pretty obvious which position you'll favor.) But the fact that seeing groups as existing before individuals is even an option is thanks to those early sociologists who made it possible to imagine turning Rousseau's argument on its head so as to see the individual—much like language or highways—as a product of sometimes faceless, prior groups that were composed of people who were themselves the product of prior collectivities of which they were likely not aware either.

To illustrate this switch and how recently it was made (and before getting to Durkheim and Weber's thoughts on religion), consider an earlier, still classic book by Durkheim: his study simply entitled *Suicide* (1897). According to the commonsense of his day—which, by the way, makes plain that a commonsense view of the world can be an object of study for scholarship rather than merely being its foundation or its own starting point—suicide was attributed either to characteristics peculiar to the lone individual or to the natural environment in which a person lives. (People who live in warmer climates are more hot tempered perhaps?) Or, as Durkheim describes this position to open chapter one:

> In the individual constitution ... it is possible that there might exist an inclination, varying in intensity from country to country, which directly leads man to suicide; on the other hand, the action of climate, temperature, etc., on the organism, might indirectly have the same effects. (Durkheim 1979: 57)

To argue against this popular position he used detailed statistical analysis, drawing on data from all over Europe, studying the countries, regions, months, and even time of day when it occurred, taking into account the gender, age, mental health, and heredity—even the religion—of those who committed suicide. Predating today's interest in so-called "big data" (that is, the way amazon.com determines what you're next wanting to read as well as the way the National Security Agency [NSA] in the U.S. pores over massive amounts of communications data in search of terrorists), he arrived at a series of very specific and, at least for his day, surprising conclusions. For, contrary to those who thought suicide resulted from the lone individual's choices or a person's very nature or constitution, Durkheim concluded that there was (to borrow one of his later chapter titles) a "social element of suicide" because he could find no "regular and indisputable relation" between what he termed individual psychopathic states and suicide rates. As he went on to conclude, using suitably dated language: "Admittedly, under similar circumstances, the degenerate is more apt to commit suicide than the well man; but he does not necessarily do so because of his condition" (Durkheim 1979: 81). Neither could he find a correlation between such environmental factors as weather or temperature; looking again at data form across Europe he concluded:

> If voluntary deaths increase from January to July, it is not because heat disturbs the organism but because social life is more intense. To be sure, this greater intensity derives from the greater ease of development of social life in the Summer than in the Winter. (Durkheim 1979: 121–122)

Here we see the first hint at the cause Durkheim turns toward for the rest of his book, for the demographic data suggested a rather different set of factors—social factors that surely struck his contemporaries (maybe even some today as well) as counter-intuitive—that could account for suicide rates across a variety of populations; and so, despite its seemingly personal nature, he understands suicide as, in his words, a collective phenomenon. Durkheim therefore concludes that the greater the emphasis on the individual within any given group *then the more likely its members were to commit suicide.* Or, to rephrase, he discovered that European Jews of his time—a group to which Durkheim himself belonged, and people who were, in many ways, isolated from what might be considered to wider, mainstream social life (as a result of what Durkheim calls "the reproach to which the Jews have for so long been exposed by Christianity"; Durkheim 1979: 159)—had a far lower suicide rate than Catholics, who in turn had a lower rate that Protestants. After eliminating a variety of reasons why this could be the case, he settles on one explanation:

> We thus reach our first conclusion, that the proclivity of Protestants for suicide must relate to the spirit of free inquiry that animates this religion ... [T]he

superiority of Protestantism with respect to suicide results from its being a less strongly integrated church than the Catholic church. (Durkheim 1979: 158–159)

As for the even lower rate among European Jews at that time:

[E]ach [Jewish] community became a small, compact and coherent society with a strong feeling of self-consciousness and unity. Everyone thought and lived alike; individual divergences were made almost impossible by the community of exist-ence and the close and constant surveillance of all over each. The Jewish church has thus been more strongly united than any other, from its dependence on itself because of being the object of intolerance. (Durkheim 1979: 160)

So, it is not because Catholics have higher morals than Protestants, or Jews even higher still, or because their theologies differ in some regard, or because each of their members are more or less psychologically balanced; instead, it is because being in a minority position "obliges them to live in greater union."

And so, we were able to see that suicide—an act that seems to be so intimate and thus so private and personal—was a social phenomenon inasmuch as ones social membership (or, better put, lack of integrated membership) determined the conditions in which it was or was not likely to happen.

Although Durkheim's study goes on from here, to distinguish other types of sui-cide (all equally grounded in social life), for our purposes we can stop to consider the advances that, though possibly radical in 1897, are now taken for granted.

First off, contrary to many scholars at the time, Durkheim wasn't all that inter-ested in origins; especially important at the time in that field that we later come to call anthropology was the application of early evolutionary theory to study-ing groups of people—applying that once widely used as a framework to make sense of others, especially those in other parts of the world about whom, due to exploration and colonialism, Europeans were then first becoming aware. Though modern evolutionary theory is hardly understood in this manner today, it wasn't difficult for some then to think of evolution as a common, irresistible path down (i.e., unilineal evolution) which different species moved, at different rates, with some even getting stalled and, like a prehistoric insect, metaphorically frozen in amber, such that some groups could be seen as being further ahead than others (also known as "more advanced" or "more civilized"). The self-interested temp-tation of these so-called late-nineteenth century Social Darwinists to understand themselves as the reference point and thus the standard by which to judge all others (that is, what we would today term ethnocentrism) was, in many cases, irresistible, and thus we arrive at early notions of civilized versus primitive, of course applied to us versus them, respectively, with the local and the familiar never occupying the inferior position in these paired relationships. In its early years, the field known as sociology therefore became the study of us (that is, what many would have represented as civilized, Western, developed countries and their peoples) whereas anthropology was initially devoted to studying them (that is, so-called primitives who were considered to be underdeveloped, uncivilized, evolutionarily under-developed, and even child-like). But as we'll see, this was not Durkheim's approach.

Assuming the world was divided between primitives and moderns, an intellectual habit developed whereby people tried to understand the contemporary in light of its presumed origin (an approach that is still common today); for instance, we could make sense of why people still throw salt over their shoulder if we just understood, say, long lost beliefs about the devil being poised behind you, ready to tempt you. (What was once called a survival was the name earlier scholars gave to some behavior that, though still practiced, had somehow outlived the context in which they assumed it once made sense.) But instead of studying the present as a progressive, inevitable development (or, sometimes, a decline) from a once golden age, scholars like Durkheim studied contemporary, and thus observable, situations, thereby being among the first whom we would today call functionalists. Today we see this as a crucial move, of course, for among the marks of that form of investigation that we call science is a focus on objects that are empirical and tangible (that is, can be observed and over which we can disagree when speaking about them). For this new generation of functionalists, forming hypotheses as to why, for example, people originally threw rice at newlyweds (an ancient sign of fertility, perhaps?) required a form of unfounded historical speculation (since none of us can time travel to confirm the originary account someone might today offer) making such scholarship rather fanciful storytelling (i.e., for how could one test claims of origins?); instead, a new generation of scholars in the early twentieth century wished to study things in terms of the purpose or role they served in the present: their *function*, and not their *origin*, therefore explained their *cause*—something evident in Durkheim's approach to the reasons for killing oneself.

Second, this move toward a rigorous, empirically based science of observation followed by generalization (evident in Durkheim's use of demographic statistics) meant that we see an early example of what we might today mean by the word theory: a set of propositions that not only accounts for the cause and thus existence of something (for example, like proposing a theory of religion), but which have predictive power and can be tested. Watching a weather forecast comes to mind as an example: we would today call meteorology a science because we can all test the claims made on the television news with our own eyes tomorrow (and the times its wrong certainly stand out for us, such as when we are stuck in the rain without an umbrella, having anticipated a sunny day). Many therefore distinguish a scientific discourse from other forms of speech inasmuch as we would expect only the former to generate testable predictions about future states of affairs. Or, to rephrase it, making a claim about something (for instance, "God loves me") for which we cannot devise a controlled experimental setting in which we could test that claim means that, whether or not we think it is right, it fails to meet the rule that scientific statements are empirically testable.

Third, as mentioned above, we see a classic use of the inductive method, whereby one arrives at general conclusions by first studying discrete situations. The confidence one has in these conclusions is, most certainly, increased in direct proportion to the number of cases one has studied—as the old example goes, the conclusion "All dogs have spots" is rather shaky if one has only looked at a couple of canines. But if one has examined one hundred of them, or one thousand or, better yet, one million (and now we're back to the interest today in so-called big data), and not found an unspotted dog in the bunch, then the probability of this conclusion being true starts to increase. And this is how we arrive at the notion of a scientific law; for even though each time we drop a set of car keys form one hand into another is a whole new scenario, we've seen the regular behavior of objects of mass so many times in the past that we're pretty confident in the prediction that the keys will drop. Situations such as this, in which we are so convinced as to the outcome are sometimes termed a law of nature, such as the law of gravity. Important to note, however, is that it's to our own peril that we overlook that each new situation might introduce unforeseen variables that could affect the outcome; people all the time walk into glass doors, failing to realize that the space through which they had just successfully passed now has thick but transparent substance blocking it.

And so, with these important advances in mind, one sees why Durkheim's 1897 study provides an example of what scholarship can accomplish when it makes commonsense an object of study. For who would have thought that seeming unseen social effects could be linked to suicide rates? Such scholarship therefore invites us to look at the world in a novel manner. (Maybe religion too is, as Durkheim argues in the book to which we'll eventually turn our attention, "an eminently collective thing"; Durkheim 1995: 44.) For an interest *not* in prehistoric origins and supposedly exotic others but, instead, in examining our own contemporary and seemingly ordinary situations (and thus *we* are the exotic no less than "them"), and doing so by means of a focus on observable data and the more or less probable conclusions that result from the use of the inductive method, produced new knowledge that went entirely against the grain.

Although we wouldn't want to assume that research from over one hundred years ago was still cutting edge (after all, the postmodern turn, from a few decades ago, has rather complicated the tale of self-evidently empirical or tangible situations), what is curious is just how durable Durkheim's conclusions have proved. For while research on religion has progressed since his time (making his broad generalizations about seemingly homogeneous groups known as Protestants, Catholics, and Jews rather troublesome today) and while many still probably put suicide down to individual psychological factors, others now see it rather differently. For instance, consider the case of suicide on college campuses—it's a problem that universities have long been addressing. Case in point: Emory University reported that, in the U.S., there are approximately one thousand suicides on college campuses annually and one out of every 10 college students has made a plan for suicide, whether they act on it or not.[3] As for Emory itself, they report (on their Emory Cares 4 U site) that "approximately 0.9 percent of Emory students have made a suicide attempt in the last 12 months" and "approximately 5.2 percent of Emory students have seriously considered suicide within the last 12 months." So how can we address this problem? Thinking back to Durkheim, who ends *Suicide: A Study in Sociology* with a chapter entitled "Practical Consequences," he advises multiplying "the centers of communal life without weakening national unity," with each such decentralized site being "the focus of a special, limited activity" such that "they would be inseparable from one another and the individual could thus form attachments there without becoming less solidary with the whole. Social life can be divided, while retaining its unity, only if each of these divisions represents a function" (Durkheim 1979: 390). This would not just allow an individual to be integrated into groups in different places but also creates a variety of sites so that differing people could form attachments at sites that better suited them. Returning to our example of universities, in their efforts to address suicide on their campuses they follow Durkheim surprisingly closely; for they institute a wide array of programs to ensure that all of their students get involved in some way—notably the incoming first year students for whom "going away" to university can sometimes be quite traumatic.

Why? Well, citing again from the Emory site, going to college means that one enters a brand new (that is, alien, unknown) environment, resulting in the loss of already well-established social networks, which can lead to isolation and experiences of alienation—which are themselves seen as high risk factors for suicide. What's more, given research by the subsequent generations of sociologists, we could go so far as to say that our very identity is at stake in all this—the person we take our selves to be and assume that we always are (such as looking at a childhood picture and saying "that's me"); for it can be understood as a work in progress, the sum result of the many managed relationships into which we are each routinely placed (a point central to Louis Althusser's important work on the social constitution of identity; see Althusser 2001); this means that "going away to find oneself" takes on new meaning, for alienation and estrangement result in people reconstituting themselves due to the new networks into which they are placed. (There's good reason, then, that coming home for the first visit from college sometimes results in family and friends not quite recognizing returning students, who may now dress differently, wear their hair differently, talk or act or even think in new ways. It also makes sense why many cite international travel as a transformative experience.) So, while organizing campus sports or building a rock wall in the student rec center, along with hosting after-hours seminars and public events, or forming a bunch of new student clubs or study groups will not necessarily lessen suicide rates on their own, they're part of a decentralized but still coordinated effort to help a diverse array of students who are far from home avoid feeling marginalized and alone by integrating them, at a variety of more or less overlapping sites, into new social networks—and thus transitioning them into new identities.

But before returning to examine those two early books as a way to find a new way forward in the sociology of religion, we see a great irony that such research has helped us to identify: for although we all seem to value, or see as a role model, the rugged, lone individual—think of all those Hollywood action films where the lone, mysterious hero saves the day or, if that's too much of a pop culture reference, what about all the polling data where reports of individual belief are assumed to be the cause of such actions as political affiliations—it is the socially integrated member of the group who stands a far better chance. In fact, we could now go so far as to argue that the individual, let alone the beliefs they claim to possess, is *always* a social phenomenon, whether existing in a so-called pre-modern, low division of labor setting (where, in our idealized model, each person pretty much carries out all the same daily tasks, creating a feeling of shared affinity for them inasmuch as they all mirror each other's roles) or in a contemporary, so-called modern, highly diversified setting (in which individuals seem to differ to a great degree, inasmuch as they each take on unique, specialized roles—i.e., the labor is divided and so very few of us, if any, keep a cow on hand to get milk for our morning cereal; instead, we buy it from a store that in turn bought it from a dairy that in turn ..., etc., etc.—but where those roles are deeply interconnected, producing group members whose sense of affinity derives from being mutually reliant upon one another—what Durkheim, as early as 1896, distinguished as *mechanical* versus *organic* forms of solidarity; see Durkheim 1964: ch. 2–3). Thus, the truly lone, self-sufficient social actor, regardless your social setting, is a myth (in the popular sense of that term) that obscures the many networks that not only surround but also form and support the social actor (regardless the social groups in which they live their lives). For, even despite the appearance of the modern individual, alone within his or her seemingly specialized role, each of us is alive due to a prior social relationship over which we exerted no control (that is, biological parents meeting, dating and mating, all according to a series of social rules and expectations neither of them created either). But, more than this: the individual self that we now take ourselves to be can be seen as a cumulative result of countless past interactions with innumerable other social actors, against whom we defined ourselves or were defined by others (what Althusser called interpellation)—giving a whole new meaning to the old adage, "You made me what I am."

For instance, to say, "I'm the baby of the family" (as I indeed am) is as much a statement about self as it is a statement about everyone else's birth position in my social orbit (and thus their role, authority and influence) in the family. So not only is any attribute that we ascribe to ourselves or that others associate with us a social marker that identifies us *in relation to others* (such as hardworking, honest, stingy, generous, moody, untrustworthy) but that very biological person whose attributes we describe has been formed and continually shaped by forces not of his or her making (suggesting that what Durkheim identified in *Suicide*, using now outdated language, as "social man" versus "physical man" may, in fact, be one in the same thing, for our biological selves are no less a social product, for both our physical bodies and any social attribute instantiated by them are products of prior, situated social actors' behaviors and decisions—and so on, and so on ...); so, taking the social nature of the individual seriously means being mindful of the tremendous number of non-agential, structural factors (systems beyond the control of the individual, such as the rules of grammar or the features of the economic system in which we work) that establish the operating conditions in which we live and interact with each other (much as the non-agential birth order of my family created a specific sort of me, "the baby of the family"). For, thinking back to Rousseau's or even Romney's model of the bold individual: despite feeling like we are each in control of our own destiny, none of us devised the way to be masculine or feminine (does one even recall being taught, perhaps by a mother, "to stand up straight" or to "sit with your knees together"?) and even those who now identify themselves outside that paired system do so in ways that conform with yet others who feel equally alienated from what we now term the dominant gender models to which so many of us subscribe (correction, are *taught* to subscribe, just as young girls are taught how to sit in a skirt, "like a lady": discretely and demurely, with knees held tightly together)[4]—for not only is conformity a social phenomenon but even dissent takes socially accepted forms; deviate too greatly from the norm and society has a host of techniques at its disposal to ensure and enforce conformity, from mildly disapproving glances from passersby to the far more extreme interventions of police forces, courts, prisons, and, in some places, the death penalty.

Returning a little more explicitly to the topic at hand: for some, as evidenced early on with Durkheim's focus on the social impact on comparative suicide rates, there is a special interest in the role religious beliefs, behaviors, and institutions play as one such structural force that predates our arrival as individuals, seeing it too as a site that helps to constitute a certain sort of self or, as we might also call it, a certain sort of subject (signifying both the notion of subjectivity that we each feel that we possess but also, and with a more critical edge, to name our position within a dominant system of power, whereby we are subjected to conditions not of our making—such as, to name an example that is seemingly benign but significant nonetheless, the publisher's style guide, not to mention the rules of English syntax, that governed the writing of this very chapter). And while there's a tremendous literature that has grown in the sociology of religion, there are now those who see the very fact that a subset of social life is identified *as* distinctly religious, as if this domain is somehow set apart and distinguishable from other aspects of daily life, as the curious thing that deserves our attention. Although we're getting the cart ahead of the horse by identifying this distinction now, suffice it to say that while studying the social influence of religion on subjects is a thriving academic field, over the past decade or two a rather different focus of research has developed, examining the social influence on, and effects of, those who classify various things *as* religion, and who thereby treat objects, actions, institutions, or other people them *as* holy or sacred. But to get to this point in the development of the field, and to formulate some thoughts on where the discipline might be going, we need to go back to those two early twentieth century books, one by Durkheim and the other by Weber, to begin to identify some of the longstanding differences that have today resulted in a group of scholars who study religion and yet others who study the very category "religion" itself.

So, as mentioned above, among the things that, to my way of thinking, set Durkheim apart from his predecessors was his interest in the contemporary, not as the triumphant culmination of all that came before it but, instead, as a social site no less curious than any other. For, if one no longer takes society for granted, as if it is a naturally occurring, collaborative element of individual lives and, rather, becomes interested in how groups are made and reproduced, how collectivities make the individual and vice versa (we do each tweak the rules in which we move, after all), how they sometimes fail and disintegrate, and the many competing and subgroups and social components that constitute them—not to mention how differing groups constitute different limits on what counts as a legitimate and thus allowable form of individuality—then, unlike a late-nineteenth century scholar being curious about the so-called primitives on the other side of the world, one might become fascinated by seemingly mundane things that are right in our own backyard. For example, consider a family, that intimate unit with which some might be able to identify and that, in many cases (though, of course, not all), is composed of a mother and father and a variety of children—or, better yet, consider the so-called extended family, in which there are more variables inasmuch as there are also uncles and aunts and cousins and grandparents. While the existence and make-up of this social group has a self-evidency and thus necessity, even inevitability to it, at least from the point of view of its youngest members (those who were born into its pre-existent structure), from the viewpoint of its senior members, those who easily recall a time before this or that marriage, prior to the death of some of its members, the departures of yet others by divorce, and long before the birth of yet others, it is easy to imagine the group as anything but eternal and inevitable. What becomes fascinating, then, is how a structure that is itself an historical phenomenon (that is, it changes over time) can be experienced by some of its members as timeless and unchanging and, as a result, as authoritative or natural. For just looking around either the kitchen or the dining table at a typical family gathering, whether an informal or formal occasion, and paying attention to who did the cooking and who just sat once the food was on the table, who asks questions and who answers and who sits silently, can result in enough data for several book length studies. And it is this turn to the formerly unseen, exotic nature of the everyday that sociology helped to make possible. Moreover, given how easily we tend to displace those things that we call religious, as if they are members of a distinct or privileged class, it was the sociology of religion that helped move a number of scholars toward talking about religion in a fashion rather different than the devotees themselves (though, like the people we study, many scholars persist in defining religion as a pre-social, inner feeling or personal experience that only secondarily gets expressed publicly in language and social settings, but more on this below and in the next chapter); for, not too different from the above example of how interesting a commonplace family can become if looked at in the right fashion, for the sociologist the self-evidently sacred nature of an institution can, if also examined in the right way, become but one more familiar site where basic social principles are exemplified and played out.

So, to work back to this current distinction within the field—between studying the way social forces merely *shape* the expression or interpretation of what we often call religious experience, on the one hand, and studying the way those same forces allow us to see something *as* religious or private in the first place—we must return to those two foundational studies in the sociology of religion, published in 1912 and 1922 respectively.

Although the later of these two early works, we'll begin with Weber's posthumously published *The Sociology of Religion* (originally not a separate book but part of a much larger published work) because, although first published nearly one hundred years ago, it is surprisingly representative of where much of the field still stands today. Although we'll turn to Durkheim's famous 1912 definition of religion in a moment (a forerunner of which was found in his 1897 study of suicide; Durkheim 1979: 170), there's likely no better place to begin to examine Weber's book, and its place in the modern field, than with the definition of religion that guides his own research (or, better put, lack of a definition). For in the first sentence on page one of his three hundred page study he famously writes:

> To define "religion," to say what it is, is not possible at the start of a presentation such as this. Definition can be attempted, if at all, on at the conclusion of the study. The essence of religion is not even our concern, as we make it our task to study the conditions and effects of a particular type of social behavior. (Weber 1993: 1)

From just these three sentences we can tell much about all that is to follow—both in the book as well as the academic tradition that today traces itself from Weber's work. First, when studying religion it is often possible to proceed with one's work even though one has not defined what, of all the things within the historical and cultural domain, will count as religion. This is remarkable, if one thinks about it for a moment: a study that refuses to identify its topic and how one knew it to be worth studying. (Curiously, we see the same line repeated, with regard to defining "the spirit of capitalism," in his earlier and even more famous book: Weber 1996: 47.) Second, Weber also employs the inductive method, presuming, it would seem, that only once all of the different cases of religion have been thoroughly described can one arrive at a definition that unifies them all as members of the same family or class of objects. Equating a definition with the "essence" of religion, he concludes his opening paragraph by making plain the philosophically idealist assumptions that drive his work (assumptions that were quite influential in German scholarship at the time); that is, Weber brackets out making claims about its inner *sine qua non*, the necessary but non-empirical element to religion, and limits himself merely to discussing the undefined cause's "conditions and effects." This is reinforced in the opening line to the second paragraph, which reads: "The external courses of religious behavior are so diverse ..." The moral of the story, then, is that, for Weber, the study of religion can either be about the *exterior* forms that it takes and the effects that is has or (insofar as the concept "external" makes no sense without its paired opposite) its essential inner or private dimension. As a sociologist Weber is limited to the former, of course, inasmuch as he's interested in studying social behaviors, yet it is evident that these empirically observable actions to which he is drawn are presumed merely to be the subsequent *expressions* (not an insignificant word to use, inasmuch as it means to press something outward from an inner source) of some internal, undefinable force—what he immediately goes on to describe as "the subjective experiences, ideas, and purposes of the individuals concerned" (Weber 1993: 1).

Within just the first two paragraphs of his book, comprising only the opening four sentences, it is evident that Weber's approach reproduces a set of assumptions common to the people whom we, as scholars, generally understand as being religious and whom we therefore study: religion itself is conceived as an indescribable inner feeling or sentiment that is then projected outward into the world. It makes sense, then, as his second paragraph concludes, that religion must therefore be studied "from the viewpoint of the religious believer's 'meaning'"— and "meaning" here translates the German word *Sinn*, which roughly overlaps also with such other English words as consciousness, sense, mind, feeling, idea, or way of thinking. So, as mentioned already, Weber's approach constitutes a classic example of a philosophically idealist way of studying religion that focuses on individuals (the site of this meaning-making and meaning-perception) and therefore requires the scholar to carefully, empathetically, understand this inner meaning for him or herself; thus, the world of matter, of objects, of actions and institutions, and more importantly wider social structures, is all assumed to be a derivative world, a projection from out of the prior, inner world of mind, belief, experience, and meaning. In fact, Rousseau might have recognized some of himself in Weber's interest in seeing social groups of all sorts as reducible to, and thus properly understood in terms of the "particular acts of individual persons" (Weber 1947: 101–104). So, given that researchers cannot access the individual's private world except by inferring its outlines from carefully studying the observable actions of individual whom we refer to as "believers" or, as many today prefer, "people of faith," a Weberian sociology of religion becomes an effort to document that inner, undefinable essence's "external course," as Weber himself phrased it; in this version, it is a field that has no theory of the mundane sources of the thing called religion but, instead, is concerned mainly with chronicling the—as Weber's third paragraph begins—"most elementary forms of behavior motivated by religious or magical factors ..." It is precisely this interest that we see in his even better known 1904–1905 book, *The Protestant Ethic and the Spirit of Capitalism* (1996), in which the existence and growth of a modern economic system is explained by appealing to an *attitude* that results from Protestant *ideas* (for example, as he argues, predestination and the frugality and industriousness that develops to compensate for the anxiety that it produces in the individual). This presumption about the causal force of religious ideas is still widely evident today—for example, as mentioned above, recall the polling questions, come every election, that try to determine the likelihood of one supporting some social policy depending on one's religious *beliefs*.

Apart from how a book that proclaims in its opening lines that it cannot define what it seeks to study could be received by its readers as anything but a fundamentally flawed project (for in what other field of intellectual pursuit could one open a book in that fashion?), what is perhaps most fascinating (or to be expected?) is that Weber nonetheless proceeds to study this undefinable thing, for he somehow knows that one needs to break it down into a variety of specific component parts. These parts sort themselves (or are sorted by Weber? Now *that's* the question!) into such chapter headings as "Gods, Magicians, and Priests" (chapter 1), "The Prophet" (chapter 4), "Theodicy, Salvation, and Rebirth" (chapter 9), and "Judaism, Christianity, and the Socio-Economic Order" (chapter 15), to name but four of the sixteen. So not only does Weber seem to have privileged knowledge, inasmuch as he somehow already knows the contours of this undefinable thing and where to find it, but he also already knows that Judaism and Christianity, along with such other things as Hinduism, Islam, Jainism, and Buddhism are types of religion (thereby utilizing what was, at his time, the fairly recently devised, Dutch and German notion of the family of world religions). That the chapter following chapter 15, which is itself devoted exclusively to Judaism and Christianity, is significantly entitled "The Attitude of the Other World Religions to the Social and Economic Order" also tells us much about what counted to scholars then as authoritative or normative and what, in turn, was relegated to the status of miscellaneous Other, occupying the periphery.

Yet despite such clear problems with this book, its emphasis on reproducing how people see themselves has, one could argue, likely helped to make it a favorite of scholars who also see themselves in this way and thus who wish not to theorize religion's cause but, instead, desire only to interpret its meaning and describe its effects—a desire indicative of those who confirm (by conforming to) the participant's own way of talking about the things scholars study. And so, to be clear, the problem, here, is that such scholarship uncritically reproduces the assumptions of the people under study, taking for granted their way of talking about the world and their place in it, and, in doing so, further legitimizes that viewpoint inasmuch as it is now seen as inevitable and natural. For instead of asking about the practical conditions and the implications of this idealist viewpoint—in a word, instead of seeing it as historical and thus situated—such scholarship merely reproduces a folk or commonsense view and, in the process, takes something that could have been understood as a curious problem worth examining and, instead, sees it as a fact that merely needs repeating. That people the world over claim to have active, inner lives, and that they then say that they are "expressing" their private ideas, as if they're being pushed out into the world, with private meanings riding on the back of public language is not in question; for, indeed, this is a common claim—but that it is common does not make it correct. Why people who claim to be individuals, each with an inner, authentic nature, all make the *same* claim is, however, the thing that ought to attract the sociologist's attention (as also argued in the following chapter). Why, despite the obvious uniformity of this way of talking, do those who engage in it seem to feel as if their way of talking is somehow original and distinct? What sort of shift in approach might we be required to entertain making if we wished to do something other than repeat and reinforce such claims?

And this is where Durkheim's slightly older book, as well as the tradition that develops from it, enters. For despite both being by European writers, from roughly the same era, each of whom played a significant role in helping to establish what we today known as the sociology of religion, *The Elementary Forms of Religious Life* couldn't be more different from *The Sociology of Religion*. This is apparent from comparing their opening lines, for while Weber's state his resistance to defining his object of study Durkheim's read as follows: "I propose in this book to study the simplest and most primitive religion that is known at present, to discover its principles and attempt an explanation of it" (Durkheim 1995: 1). Making allowances for the obviously problematic nature of this term primitive and the set of assumptions that once drove its use, Durkheim is here stating a basic and now common scientific principle: one must control the variables as much as possible in order to focus in upon, and thereby isolate, the element that attracts ones curiosity. And the thing that attracts his attention in this book ("the problem I wish to treat" as he phrases it himself; ibid.: 3) is not those whom we would now call the indigenous people of Australia (the so-called aborigines, from the Latin *ab origine*, meaning: from the beginning), among the groups he sets out to study, but, instead, is, as he phrases it a little lower on his opening page, "a fundamental and permanent aspect of humanity." For Durkheim, then, the discrete examples he studies, not unlike his earlier use of demographic data in *Suicide*, allow him not to reproduce the viewpoint present in each group but, instead, to generalize his findings so as to create new knowledge about the larger family of which each example is, from the comparativist's vantage point, seen as but a subtype. Running counter to the commonsense of his day once again, which would likely have quickly distinguished higher, and thus more civilized and rational, religions from the so-called lower and more primitive religions, Durkheim opts to ground his work in examples drawn from societies with a lower division of labor (that is, societies that are not as complex or as diversified as our own), not because he seeks the evolutionary origin of religion but, rather, to more easily identify general social principles *that, he will argue, are applicable to our own world.* And it is this boldness, to undermine commonsense of one's own time, that immediately sets his book apart; for, to many readers of his day, comparing the so-called "crude cults of Australian tribes" to, say, Christianity, would have been no less shocking than to suggest that suicide was a social phenomenon. But, if we grant his once controversial premise—that all human communities exemplify the same general set of social principles—then it is unavoidable that the long-assumed superiority of European culture would come to be seen as an unhelpful assumption. "These religions are to be respected no less than others. They fulfill the same needs, play the same role, and proceed from the same causes; therefore they can serve just as well to elucidate the nature of religious life," as he phrases it (ibid.: 2–3).

In just his book's first few pages it should therefore be evident just how different these two scholarly works are; if not, then consider that much of Durkheim's first chapter, is concerned with arriving at a precise definition for what he will study over the following four hundred and fifty pages. Or, as he writes in its first sentence: "In order to identify the simplest and most primitive religion that observation can make known to us, we must first define what is properly understood as a religion" (Durkheim 1995: 21). In just as systematic a fashion as was seen in *Suicide*, where he devoted six pages of his introduction to defining that key term, Durkheim ensures that his readers understand precisely what it is that he is studying when he employs the word religion—and why he thinks it worth examining. After all, recalling the second sentence in *Suicide*'s introduction: "the words of everyday language, like the concepts they express, are always susceptible of more than one meaning, and the scholar employing them in their accepted use without further definition would risk serious misunderstanding" (Durkheim

1979: 41). Following common usage, then, as did Weber, is hardly the path for a scholar in Durkheim's tradition, especially one seeking not just to *describe* the contours of what the person under study thinks about the world but, rather, to *theorize why* she even thinks or acts that way in the first place. So, the first task is to fashion a technical definition, driven by the scholar's own technical interests, a stipulative definition that seeks not to describe the item being examined or to identify its essence—as was Weber's inductive approach—but which states from the outset what, given the researcher's own interests, will count as something work examining. And, in twenty or so opening pages, Durkheim does just that; guided by his interest to study not the social *effects* of faith or the venues in which private meaning is *expressed* publicly but, instead, to generate a theory of the crucial social *function* religion plays (a function that thereby accounts for religion's existence), he arrives at a technical definition that sets the table for the rest of the book:

> *A religion is a unified system of beliefs and practices relative to sacred things, that is to say, things set apart and forbidden—beliefs and practices which unit into one single moral community called a Church, all those who adhere to them* ... In showing the idea of religion is inseparable from the idea of a Church, it conveys the notion that religion must be an eminently collective thing. (Durkheim 1995: 44; emphasis in the original)

There is much to comment on in this already much-repeated definition, but the fact that it is offered at the outset of the book should make plain the divide that lies between this and *The Sociology of Religion*. More specifically, what distinguishes Durkheim's approach is:

- First, for the scholar, religion is not to be assumed to be what it might seem to be for the devotee or participant. Instead, and anticipating today's emphasis on identity studies, Durkheim makes plain that what we call religion is a social identity like any other—or, better put, the thing we call religion is a technique for establishing social identities.

- Second, this identity is not eternal and neither is it an essential feature of the human condition but, rather, it is the result of people's common or shared beliefs and practices (the conjunction "and" is crucial here, naming a conjoined complex of mind and body). While one could spend much time on this part of his social theory, suffice it simply to say that Durkheim argues that our impressions of personal and collective identity are formed and continually reformed in discrete situations, inasmuch as people reproduce shared assumptions and common behaviors, periodically (and necessarily) doing so within eyesight of each other. Thinking back to the example of the family, we now can theorize why families reunite periodically, for example during holidays or, more poignantly, to mark births or funerals. For, as he argues, the group to which the members belong is nothing but a shared sense that they each have of it, concerning who gets to, for instance, carve the turkey or who tells which story on which occasion and how one ought to react despite having heard it on various past occasions (for example, see Lincoln 1996). But given its nonempirical existence, he argues that members benefit from periodically seeing and hearing their peers act out their shared membership, in the flesh, much like fans participating in the ritual of the wave at a game; at such an occasion their assumed shared identity motivates their participation *while at the same time* their common participation further creates that very impression of sharing an identity with the thousands of other strangers in that stadium. Or, as he writes in his conclusion, "The cult [or ritual system] is not merely a system of signs by which the faith is outwardly expressed; it is the sum total of means by which that faith is created and recreated periodically" (Durkheim 1995: 420). Thanks to Durkheim, then, we began to see groups as highly dynamic, changeable affairs that involve bodies as much as minds; they can now be seen not as the expression of primordial identities (a term borrowed from Bayart 2005) but as historical phenomena that are not only subject to change and reinvention but which create the conditions in which different sorts of social actors can come into being.

• And third, Durkheim uses in his definition what, for many, is a significant term: sacred. Though often employed as a technical term, denoting an inner quality (not unlike Weber's notion of an essence or meaning) that scholars often try to grasp in their studies, Durkheim humanizes and thereby historicizes this term, for now the quality of sacredness or holiness is no longer an inherent possessions of objects or people but, instead, is theorized and seen to result from the simple condition of something being "set apart and forbidden"; it is therefore not insignificant that, in using this term to define religion, he immediately goes on to define the term sacred as well, ensuring that this quality is also seen as a result of human beings who create, employ, and police rule systems (this goes here, not there; I can touch this but you cannot; you're allowed over there while I am not ...). For now, rule systems are seen as the means by which group identity is made and continually remade, inasmuch as instituting such rules and then following them creates a seeming aura around (what is quite possibly arbitrary) items, thereby providing a focus for collective attention and action. But, to repeat, that focus is not a naturally occurring event, for it is now understood by scholars as the result of human actors, drawing lines, making choices, and working within prior authorized structures. For despite what the participants themselves might claim, the altar—when sold in an antiques shop after the church has closed or been renovated—can just as easily become a desk or a dining table, all based on the changeable interrelated beliefs and practices that make something worth paying attention to in this rather than that way.

A fourth distinguishing mark might be the fact that, closing with a long conclusion that makes explicit the general sociological principles proposed in his book—principles that apply far beyond just those beliefs and practices that are relative to so-called sacred things—Durkheim's contributions to the sociology of religion therefore go well beyond the study of religion, for he offered a theory of religion which was, in fact, a theory of society inasmuch as the thing that we commonly call religion (the making of, and practices associated with, sacred things) was but a component of how members of groups create their shared sense of collective identity. And this is what is so important in his work and which, today, opens the way for studying the sociology of religion in a fashion far beyond simply examining how social conditions do or do not influence the *expression* of religious experiences. For from Durkheim's focus on how we—it's no one but ourselves doing it—create the distinction between sacred and profane things we get, a generation or two later, Mary Douglas's interest in how classification systems, and the human interests that drive them, make it possible for us to arrange our impression of the world in a fashion that allows it to make sense to us, thereby taking the same brute stuff of existence and enabling us to see some of it as, in her example, soil and other of it as dirt (after all, dirt is simply "matter out of place," as she famously wrote in her 1966 book, *Purity and Danger*; see Douglas 1992: 35); linking Durkheim's work with that of his predecessor, Karl Marx (1818–1883)—against whose work some of Weber's writings were directed—and thereby adding to our interest in classification an attention to power relations and ownership, brings us to the social theory work of a contemporary scholar like Bruce Lincoln (2014). Or, if we instead mix Durkheim with Swiss linguistics scholar, Ferdinand de la Saussure (1857–1913), whose interest was (again, unlike Weber's) in not interpreting meaning correctly but, rather, studying how meaning or, better put, significance was created in the first place (leading to the field known as Semiotics), we arrive at conditions helpful in producing such later twentieth century developments as postmodernism—an ironic approach that sought to make plain the constructed and thus ad hoc nature of all meaning and culture. And so, although certainly not directly or irresistibly causal of later developments, that initial foray made by Durkheim into understanding the wider ramifications of setting something apart and forbidding others from approaching it helped to influence generations of writers whose interests stretched far beyond seeing religion as all about being religious. Instead, the claims and actions known as religion came to be seen to be about something else, entirely.

While I would argue that many in the modern field have followed Weber, inasmuch as there are few interested in offering a redescriptive theory of religion since, instead, they seek either to interpret the meaning of religious beliefs and actions (for example, the noted U.S. anthropologist of religion, Clifford Geertz; e.g. Geertz 1973) or to develop a theory of religious change or expression (such as the late American sociologist of religion, Robert Bellah, and his work on religious evolution; e.g. Bellah 2011), it is the opportunity created by pursuing a line of thought indebted to Durkheim that seems to me to be more promising for the future of the study of religion—so long as it is seem as a pursuit more involved than mere repetition of commonsense or insider self-understandings. For unlike rational choice theory (a once popular brand of sociology, found especially in the U.S., which sought to study religion as the result of lone rational actors making choices that struck them as being in their best interest, such as Stark's study of the origins of Christianity which, rather than being a theory of why it exists was, instead, a theory of why its membership expanded which left untheorized why it came into being in the first place; see Stark 1996) and unlike today's preoccupation with studying so-called material or embodied religion (a now popular subfield that, though seemingly focused on material artifacts, nonetheless reproduces a conservative, idealist approach by studying them as the tangible sites where an intangible, inner meaning is projected outward into the world; see Morgan 2005), the work carried out by social theorists in the study of religion use what they call religion—as did Durkheim—as but one example of wider social principles, in an effort not to study religion but to study social life itself, seeing what we stipulate as (that is, what we set apart as) religion as but one subset of a far larger family of mundane, historical acts and organizations. It is for this reason that, though retaining the disciplinary identity of the academic study of religion, a number of scholars of religion today find themselves attracted to the wider field of identity or culture studies, seeing much to be gained from applying the work of such contemporary social theorists as the above-mentioned Jean-François Bayart (2005) or Rogers Brubaker (2000), along with Michel Foucault (1979), Benedict Anderson (1991), Michel de Certeau (1988), and Judith Butler (1999), to only name a few who, despite differences among them, can all be placed in a post-Durkheimian tradition of social theory that sees groups and identities as historic creations, prone to change, all depending on not only *what* is set apart but, more importantly, *who* is authorized to do the choosing and to police the decisions and the boundaries we ourselves create.

So, despite how eager scholars sometimes appear to be to have their presumptions about the world confirmed for them—presumptions such as their view that inner faith somehow transmutes into, and thereby motivated and grounds, outer action—it is the tradition that develops from Durkheim, I maintain, that holds most promise for what we might as well just call a science of religion (a disciplinary term for the field once preferred by our intellectual predecessors and still widely used in French). For a science is, if anything, a method that enables us to see the world in a counter-intuitive light—for instance, the world does not seem to us to be round but disciplined observation nonetheless confirms that it is. And so the danger in the academic study of religion is, as Durkheim warned, our failure to turn popular, folk categories that we, in the English language and in European/North American culture, each use in our daily lives (to talk about the world and ourselves in an effort to make a space that's habitable and selves that are identifiable) into technical terms that have analytic utility, that allow us to pose and answer questions that strike us as curious, doing so in a fashion other than how the people we may study already talk about the world for themselves. As much as we have gained from Weber's tradition—and much in the modern sociology of religion owes a debt to his work—it is a tradition that failed to theorize its main technical term—religion—and therefore seems to offer little that the self-identified religious people, when queried by us, are not already saying about themselves and their world; whereas it is the Durkheimian tradition, those who wish not only to theorize religion's cause but who are willing to see that term itself dissolved into broader examinations of what makes social life itself possible along with its interplay with personal identity, that seems largely unexplored in our field today—and these are the queries that will likely lead to the creation of new, unexpected, and provocative knowledge.

Acknowledgments

My thanks go to Aaron Hughes, Craig Martin, and Vaia Touna for feedback on an earlier draft of this chapter, as well as to William Parsons for his very helpful comments.

Notes

1 First appearing as an invited chapter to a reference resource intended for senior high school students or undergraduate readers, this chapter nonetheless attempted to make a contribution to the current field by arguing, in what was hoped to be an accessible form, that the usual shape taken by scholarship in the sociology of religion exemplifies some of the recurring problems in the modern field; for, despite the appearance of an empirical basis (e.g., polls and questionnaires) the field could still be argued to exemplify the same philosophical idealism that some have repeatedly argued against. While flattered to be included among the authors in the volume, the aim was to argue for an approach that might differ from some of the other chapters in the volume—an alternate termed here social theory, in distinction from what we usually come to know as the sociology of religion.

2 Case in point: after completing high school, my own two older sisters, born in 1946 and 1947 respectively, did not attend university but, instead, enrolled in what was then simply called nursing college and teacher's college.

3 At time of original writing, this was posted at www.emorycaresforyou.emory.edu/resources/suicidestatistics.html (accessed May 13, 2015).

4 For example, see my own chapter, "Who Am I? I'm a Leg Crosser," in McCutcheon (forthcoming), where I use styles of sitting as a way into discussing the social conditions of gender roles.

References

Althusser, Louis (2001) [1971]. "Ideology and Ideological State Apparatuses: Notes Towards an Investigation," in his *Lenin and Philosophy and Other Essays*, 85–126. New York: The Monthly Review Press.

Anderson, Benedict (1991) [1983] *Imagined Communities: Reflections on the Origins and Spread of Nationalism*. London: Verso Books.

Bayart, Jean-François (2005). *The Illusion of Cultural Identity.* Chicago, IL: University of Chicago Press.

Bellah, Robert N. (2011). *Religion in Human Evolution: From the Paleolithic to the Axial Age.* Cambridge, MA: Belknap Press of Harvard University Press. https://doi.org/10.4159/harvard.9780674063099

Brubaker, Rogers and Frederick Cooper (2000). "Beyond 'Identity'," *Theory and Society* 29: 1–47. https://doi.org/10.1023/A:1007068714468

Butler, Judith (1999) [1990]. *Gender Trouble: Feminism and the Subversion of Identity.* New York: Routledge.

Certeau, Michel de (1988) [1980]. *The Practice of Everyday Life.* Steven Rendall (trans.). Berkeley, CA: University of California Press.

Douglas, Mary (1992) [1966]. *Purity and Danger: An Analysis of the Concepts of Pollution and Taboo.* London: Routledge.

Durkheim, Émile (1964) [1896]. *The Division of Labor in Society,* trans. George Simpson. Glencoe, IL: Free Press, 1964.

—— (1979) [1897]. *Suicide: A Study in Sociology.* London: Routledge & Kegan Paul.

—— (1995) [1912]. *The Elementary Forms of Religious Life,* trans. Karen Fields. New York: Free Press.

Foucault, Michel (1979) [1975]. *Discipline and Punish: The Birth of the Prison,* trans. Alan Sheridan. New York: Vintage Books.

Geertz, Clifford (1973). *The Interpretation of Cultures.* New York: Basic Books.

Lincoln, Bruce (2014) [1989]. *Discourse and the Construction of Society: Comparative Studies of Myth, Ritual, and Classification,* 2nd ed. New York: Oxford University Press. https://doi.org/10.1093/acprof:oso/9780199372362.001.0001

—— (2014) [1989]. *Discourse and the Construction of Society: Comparative Studies of Myth, Ritual, and Classification,* 2nd ed. New York: Oxford University Press.

McCutcheon, Russell T. (ed.) (2017). *Fabricating Identities.* Sheffield: Equinox Publishers.

Morgan, David (2005). *The Sacred Gaze: Religious Visual Culture in Theory and Practice.* Berkeley, CA: University of California Press.

Rousseau, Jean-Jacques (1982) [1762]. *Of The Social Contract, Or Principles of Political Right,* trans. Maurice Cranston. New York: Penguin Books.

Stark, Rodney (1996). *The Rise of Christianity: A Sociologist Reconsiders History.* Princeton, NJ: Princeton University Press.

Weber, Max (1993) [1922]. *The Sociology of Religion,* trans. Ephraim Fischoff, intro. by Talcott Parsons. Boston, MA: Beacon Press.

—— (1947). *The Theory of Social and Economic Organization,* trans. A. M. Henderson and Talcott Parsons. New York: Free Press.

—— (1996) [1904–1905]. *The Protestant Ethic and the Spirit of Capitalism,* trans. Talcott Parsons, intro. by Randall Collins. Los Angeles, CA: Roxbury Publishing Co.

Chapter 4

Redescribing Spirituality: The Strategic Use of the Solitary Identifier[1]

> We're no longer squabbling about what it means to be the church. There is a new mood. You know when you walk into the place it's now an inclusive church, open and ministering to people of all kinds and lifestyles. It's alive spiritually. It's been a great turnaround from the old place it used to be. (Sarah Caughman, in conversation with Wade Clark Roof; Roof 1999: 27)

In 1536 the French writer Jean Calvin (1509-1564—his birth name was Jean Cauvin) published (in Latin) his *Institutio Christianae religionis*, an exhaustive representation of what we would today call a Protestant theological belief system—a two-volume set of books that has sat on my office shelf, unopened and gathering dust, for well over two decades. It was published in his native French in 1541, and is widely known to English readers as *Institutes of the Christian Religion* (first published in 1845), a document studied to this day—as I myself once studied it in a graduate class—as a prime example of Reformation-era theology that aimed to correct errors in Roman Catholic understandings. That we today still talk of "Calvinism"—sometimes also known as the Reformed tradition, now a large collection of varying denominations that, at its beginning, differed from its Protestant rival, Lutheranism (also named after an influential reformer, of course)—should tell us all we need to know about the success of Calvin's particular way of refashioning Christianity.

While the finer details of how Calvinists differed from, say, their Lutheran counterparts is not the focus of this chapter—though it is not insignificant to observe that the very term "Calvinist" dates to anti-Calvinist rhetorics, nicely illustrating that names, and thus identities, are often given to us by others and can therefore be evidence of a prior dispute[2]—it's the manner in which so-called reformers (or what a social theorist might term members of an emergent, oppositional social formation), such as Calvin himself, attempted to differentiate themselves from those with whom they had mounting disagreements (i.e., those representing the interests of a dominant social formation, such as the Roman Catholic Church of his day), that does occupy our attention. For there may be something to be learned from reconsidering how we read this nearly five hundred year old text—a reconsideration that has prompted me to get those mildewed volumes down off my shelf—something, I further argue, that can be applied to the study of those who, as we see in the epigraph to this chapter, now commonly claim that spirituality has supplanted religion, such as those who see themselves as being "spiritual but not religions" (or SBNR, as some now abbreviate it). For, much as how we might re-read *Institutes of the Christian Religion*, seeing it not as being about theology (as most readers of course do) but, instead, as using a specific sort of language (which includes words like sin, grace, or salvation), relevant within specific settings and institutions, to accomplish all too ordinary social effects (such as negotiating place and privilege), we might also come to hear claims about this seemingly ethereal thing, spirituality, as being just as deeply invested in no less practical work.

That there's a productive comparison to be made between "spiritual but not religious" claims today and a Protestant reformer's rhetoric nearly five hundred years ago is, I hope, evidence enough as to why we can term this way of talking a cliché; for after all, how else do we define the term cliché but as something overused, trite, unoriginal, and thus commonplace.[3] For using rhetoric to make oneself and those with whom one feels some affinity stand out as unique because you are somehow pure, authentic, original, unrivaled, one of a kind, and thus uninfluenced by circumstance and surrounding is not an unfamiliar technique in the social actor's tool box. The irony, however, is that within the claim that one is unique, and thus asocial (inasmuch as being distinct means one is incomparable to all others, in a category of one's own) there lies an all too social implication inasmuch as the privilege that is assumed to attend this status is just that—*a status.* After all, the spirituality and inclusivity now supposedly exhibited in Sarah Caughman's church (as per the epigraph to this chapter) is a mark she uses to distinguish it not just from the past (how "it used to be") but also to set it apart from all others—it is a difference that is clearly linked to place and rank. So inasmuch as "they" are not like those of "us" who are spiritual we see the fundamental, yet still curious, contradiction at the heart of such claims: despite the universal claims of such actors there are limits to this inclusion—if everyone was included then there'd be no one from whom to distinguish ourselves—and so, as suggested, status implies relations of rank and thus power (whether you're on the top or the bottom of the classificatory scheme), all of which suggests that there may indeed be something to be gained when scholars rethink how they hear everyday claims about the inward thing, spirituality, being somehow different from the supposedly routine, humdrum, and unthinkingly outward daily habits of religion. For, at least to the social theorist, assuming the existence of authentic inner cores as well as classifying and ranking our own and other people's actions and associations are simply common ways that people manage each other and the worlds in which they live.

It would therefore probably be an error to hear "I'm spiritual but not religious" as most do, as if it was a substantive, descriptive, and disinterested claim about some actual thing or disposition in the world; because, much like any attempt to distinguish a this from a that, it can instead be understood as a way to make sense of the world by ordering it, and thereby prioritizing some over others.

Before briefly looking at Calvin, and then applying those lessons to how many today self-identify as spiritual, it's worth anticipating where we're going with this argument. For the approach advocated here understands claims concerning not just spirituality but also such related words as faith, experience, and belief (all things generally assumed to be secretly interior to the lone human subject yet somehow universally shared as part of this thing known as human nature) to be common social rhetorics (i.e., ways of doing practical and thus public things with language) that people use in situations of contest (e.g., when one is seeking to identify oneself in distinction from others—such as the case of Calvin's *Institutes* commonly being termed an *apologia*, classically understood as a rigorous defense or justification of a position one holds); this chapter, picking up on themes already identified in previous chapters, therefore examines the irony of how widely shared and common habits and forms of social organization are presented as individualized claims about a supposedly unique and deeply personal dimension of the human. The chapter argues that if this now popular, yet hardly unique, rhetoric is indeed a way to create a privileged but fictive social space (where agents who otherwise conform to pretty much the same practices, language, and norms as others can still claim to possess what seems to be a uniquely set-apart identity), then that very experience of having a solitary identity can itself be redescribed as the result/effect of a social management technique whereby people signify themselves (whether to marginalize or centralize) and thereby regulate themselves—figuratively standing in orderly, well-groomed lines. For despite how social actors themselves understand how they talk about the world, to the scholar the rhetorics of belief, faith, experience, and spirituality can be understood anew as the way that we represent collective (i.e., social, political, economic, etc.) aspirations as if they were idiosyncratic, ad hoc, and ahistorical choices of the lone individual—as if they were authoritative inasmuch as they are free of the taint of historical influence and happenstance.[4] And so the individualization and thus privilege that seems to come with claiming oneself to be spiritual and not religious (i.e., as not bogged down in and thus hindered by the doctrines, rituals, and institutions of some orthodox group, such as a church or synagogue) ironically represents and, if left untheorized, also promotes a new but no less particular way of organizing and identifying human beings *en masse*. Simply put, there is a long tradition of people claiming not to be part of any tradition.

Now, the project I attempt to model here derives, in part, from my own interest to redescribe, as a social theorist of religion influenced by the work of the late Jonathan Z. Smith might phrase it, sites related to the academic study of religion—topics that, in my estimation, still betray all the markings of how religious insiders may already talk about them, such as my earlier suggestion of a way for scholars of religion to theorize discourses on evil rather than just assuming evil too exist and then setting out to explain its existence (e.g., as I did in McCutcheon 2003: ch. 7). In turn, this refocusing has something to do with a comment made by Smith: in a brief paper entitled "Are Theological and Religious Studies Compatible?" (1997), after succinctly answering his title's question—"From the perspective of the academic study of religion, theology is a datum, the theologian is a native informant"—Smith comments as follows:

> We need to be far more attentive to the exegetical labors of religious folk, to their systematic projects of articulation and understanding. In the same spirit in which I welcome the study of the totalizing mythic endeavors, the *univers imaginaires*, of an Ogotemmêli ... or an Antonio Guzmàn ... I would hope, some day, to read a consonant treatment of the analogous enterprise of Karl Barth's *Church Dogmatics*.[5] (Smith 1997: 60)

For many readers, this is surely an overly provocative juxtaposition (though for some it should be an alluring dissertation topic!), inasmuch as it improperly takes Karl Barth (1886–1968)—the famous Swiss Reform theologian and author of the mammoth, multi-volume exercise in systematic theology, cited by Smith—as comparable to just a mythmaker from any other culture. Yet the comparison is intellectually useful inasmuch as it challenges readers familiar with such terms as the above mentioned "sin," "grace," and "salvation"—that is, readers who, like Barth himself, may use such terms in their daily lives, as part of a vocabulary and thus system of signification that helps them to manage those daily lives (as part of their cosmology, if you will)—to read them not as representative of actual things in the world but, rather, as metaphors that have various social effects when used in this or that way, by this or that speaker or writer, and in this or that setting. For many of us would no doubt feel that we had somehow misread, say, the ancient Greek epic, *Odyssey*, or the ancient Sanskrit one, *Mahabharata*, if we saw these texts to be accurately representing actual events in the past; instead, many today see them as important mythic texts perhaps indicative of a long past view of the universe and a people's widely shared thoughts on their and others' places in it.[6] So too, Smith advises disengaging our reading of those works that are familiar to us as if our claims, and ours alone, uniquely correspond to real things or situations in the world; for if claims about Odysseus's wanderings or Pāṇḍu's heroic exploits on the battlefield function on the level of myth then so too may Barth's claims about this thing he (and others, to be sure) terms "the Grace of God in Jesus Christ."

Our question, then, is: "If we are able to make this shift then how will we hear Sarah Caughman's claims in the epigraph to this chapter?"

For example, when we no longer assume that such texts are talking about actual things in the world, but instead see them as crafting a picture of the world in which humans (and sometimes specific sorts of humans, such as only the men or only the members of a particular race or class) are claimed to play a certain part, what do we make of Barth's following text:

> The atonement is the source of all life and knowledge. It is a sovereign act of God's grace. Reconciliation is God's crossing the frontier to man. The abyss is crossed by God alone. Man is accused, humbled, judged; and received, reclaimed, hidden, sustained. We have peace with God, by the Word of God, in Jesus Christ, by faith in Him, by the Holy Spirit who awakens faith; all of which is to say by the grace of God. (Barth 1936–1977: vol. IV, 1.79)

Smith's challenge to us, then, is to re-read rhetorics that are familiar to us (and thus work for us)—a familiarity that goes beyond whether we agree with them or not—as using language not just *to represent* the world but *to craft* a world conducive to those who share our interests, a palatable world that may even persuade others to join us. Read in this way, the above passage tells us much not about Barth's *theology*, as some assume when they read such writers, but, rather his *anthropology*, inasmuch as it presents a view of human beings as radically alienated and limited—yet somehow fulfilled should they adopt his self-authenticating viewpoint. In precisely this way, then, the question before us is: "What might be gained by coming to a work such as Calvin's *Institutes* and its effort to distinguish itself from the dominant social world of its time (what we might as well just call Roman Catholicism), with a fresh set of eyes?" My hope is that the gain can then be applied to the analogous moment when you meet someone who, in reply to some query, answers: "I'm spiritual but not religious."

But prior to beginning this exercise let me be clear concerning its difficulty. For while I've admitted that Calvin's books sit unused on my shelf, but I once also owned the entire massive set of Barth's *Church Dogmatics*, almost 30 years ago, long before coming across the work of Jonathan Z, Smith; then, near the completion of my Ph.D. and just as I was reinventing myself as a scholar of religion (as opposed to a theology student, having previously earned a Master of Divinity degree and a Master of Theology degree at Queen's University, in Canada), I sold the complete set, along with a fairly large collection of other theology and philosophy books (the work of the British philosopher Alfred North Whitehead prominent among them, though I kept my heavily annotated copy of his *Process and Reality* as a taste of a world in which I once worked) to a used bookstore in Toronto. It was my act of distinction, I now think—a ritual act of separation; I had no use for them any longer since—or so I thought at the time—they were engaged in an entirely different discourse, one with which I then disagreed and was therefore intent on leaving far behind. So the books stayed in Toronto and I moved to Tennessee to begin work in a department of religious studies—thereby putting about 750 miles between me and my past. But had I then been able to rethink those works, in the manner akin to Smith's above advice, then it might have occurred to me that, not unlike a lucky anthropologist discovering that she already possessed a transcription of a people's elaborate view of the universe, I already owned a complete, majestic epic deserving careful study, comparable to any of the epics studied by others; selling it, then, was hardly the reasonable thing to do (though it was understandable, I guess, given how close I then was to that prior world and how preoccupied I likely was with distinguishing my new scholarly self from it); for that sale and distancing exemplified a misreading or, to rephrase, a lack of scholarly imagination, inasmuch as it was evidence that I was incapable of reading such work in any way other than how those who use the text apparently read it themselves. So, instead of seeing the ostensibly theological text as a datum in need of historicization I now see that I could only understand it, back then, as a series of propositions and arguments with which I disagreed—thereby failing to appreciate that agreement or disagreement with such texts had entirely missed the point of studying how they *function* in groups.

So, as an exercise in such re-reading, and in order to rethink how we hear claims like "I'm spiritual but not religious"—claims analogous to classic sixteenth-century Protestant reformers' attempts to contest and thereby dele-gitimize the well-established authority of what they portrayed as the Catholic Church's "mere popery" and "empty rituals" in favor of their picture of an indi-vidual believer's "faith"—begin by considering that Calvin's text is addressed to "His most Christian Majesty, The Most Mighty and Illustrious Monarch, Francis, King of the French." Recalling that the Europe of this time was hardly the place we understand it to be today (i.e., that those social units we call nation-states were not to develop for several centuries, that what we today refer to as the Roman Catholic Church was then hardly a church, as we understand it today, but can be better described as a pan-social institution that was intertwined with virtually every level of governance—from rural village affairs to governance of entire king-doms, and, most importantly perhaps, that the modern distinction that we take for granted today between, say, religion and politics had yet to fully develop), may assist us to understand the intimate relationship then between an exercise in what we'd term systematic theology (i.e., producing an organized statement concerning a total and consistent theological system) and the seemingly mun-dane exercise of ruling and administering power.[7] Important also to recall, when rethinking how we read such documents, is the violence that attended the social and political revolution that often gets idealized, as if it was all about some private thing called belief, and which therefore goes by the name of the Reformation. The very fact that Calvin wrote in Basel, Switzerland, despite being born in Noyon, in northern France, and then later living in Paris, may be evidence enough; for the then twenty five year old Calvin had left France for Switzerland—after already having spent a year in hiding—in October of 1534, due to the violent backlash that followed a friend's pro-reform (i.e., anti-Catholic) address, delivered on November 1, 1533, at the Collège Royal (in Paris). So the fact that Calvin penned the "Prefatory Address" to the *Institutes* on August 1, 1536, in Basel should not go unnoticed.

He opens there by writing the following:

> But when I perceived that the fury of certain bad men had risen to such a height in your realm, that there was no place in it for sound doctrine, I thought it might be of service if I were in the same work both to give instruction to my countrymen, and also lay before your Majesty a Confession, from which you may learn what the doctrine is that so inflames the rage of those madmen who are this day, with fire and sword, troubling your kingdom ... (Calvin 2015: 3)

This should not be read as simply being an idle foreword to the text. For while it may seem unfair to liken such a supposedly theological treatise to, say, what we would now term Niccolò Machiavelli's openly political treatise, *The Prince* (1532),[8] it may be anachronistic to think that such neat and tidy modern distinc-tions can so easily be read backward in time. That both works are dedicated to powerful rulers—Machiavelli's "To the Magnificent Lorenzo Di Piero De' Medici" (1449–1519; the ruler of Florence from 1513–1519)—suggests that we might be mistaken to assume too easily that, because the linguistic conventions of each text is different, they are therefore representatives of entirely different genres of text. For a totalized system of thought, practice, and organization, addressed to a monarch, concerning how the universe works and the place of humans within it (i.e., Calvin's so-called systematic theology) may productively be redescribed as a political treatise like any other.

Should we entertain such a redescription of his book, then its arguments take on new significance. To name but one example, consider book 1, chapter 7, entitled: The Testimony of the Sprit Necessary to Give Full Authority to Scripture: The Impiety of Pretending that the Credibility of Scripture Depends on the Judgement of the Church. Should we be willing no longer to be concerned with answering the normative question about what the scripture "really means" and, instead, see this as Calvin's attempt to unseat a long dominant model of interpretation, and thus meaning-making, then this portion of the text becomes interesting for a whole new set of reasons. Adopting a strategy common to the so-called reformers of his day, Calvin argues, in the opening to book 1, chapter 3, that the authority of the church and its teachings are undercut by what he portrays as a natural propensity in all humans (what later European writers will call natural religion, as opposed to revealed religion):

> That there exists in the human minds and indeed by natural instinct, some sense of Deity, we hold to be beyond dispute, since God himself, to prevent any man from pretending ignorance, has endued all men with some idea of his Godhead, the memory of which he constantly renews and occasionally enlarges, that all to a man being aware that there is a God, and that he is their Maker, may be condemned by their own conscience when they neither worship him nor consecrate their lives to his service. (Calvin 2015: 43)

Making the switch in reading strategy advocated earlier, we can now hear this argument not as being about knowledge of God, whatever that may signify, but, instead, as being an attack on a certain mode by which authority was established and exercised within his society; for now the role of the Church as an unrivaled institution in many day-to-day matters is challenged by what we today might term commonsense, thereby effectively moving power from an administrative body controlled by elites to each person him- or herself.[9] This is something that the title of book 1 chapter 7, noted above, makes abundantly clear: Calvin, adopting yet another prominent reformer's position, argues that it is impious to hold that individuals cannot interpret the scriptures for themselves. Removing once again the role of the Church as an authorized and necessary intermediary body, his argument is not so much about scripture but a general claim about the irrelevant role of the previously unrivaled institution. "A most pernicious error has very generally prevailed," he argues in section 1, "—viz. that Scripture is of importance only in so far as conceded to it by the suffrage of the Church; as if the eternal and inviolable truth of God could depend on the will of men." Failing to see this as being about what qualifies as a legitimate form of institutional authority in his time, and thinking it is instead all about scripture or accurate understandings of powerful invisible beings, reproduces the error discussed above, whereby I sold my set of *Church Dogmatics* because I did not agree with its author's argument.

Instead, "conscience," "Holy Spirit," "conviction," "belief," etc., are now all rede-scribed as rhetorical terms, doing practical social work, thereby functioning to create the impression of an alternative, oppositional, and thus supremely legiti-mate source of authority which, in turn, helps to create a discursive position from which social actors, such as Calvin himself, could challenge his society's current monopoly on knowledge/power (to nod toward Michel Foucault's well-known and, in this case, rather apt, term).

As he goes on to argue in section 5:

> Let it therefore be held as fixed, that those who are inwardly taught by the Holy Spirit acquiesce implicitly in Scripture; that Scripture, carrying its own evidence along with it, deigns not to submit to proofs and arguments, but owes the full con-viction with which we ought to receive it to the testimony of the Spirit. Enlightened by him, we no longer believe, either on our own Judgment or that of others, that the Scriptures are from God; but, in a way superior to human Judgment, feel per-fectly assured—as much so as if we beheld the divine image visibly impressed on it—that it came to us, by the instrumentality of men, from the very mouth of God. We ask not for proofs or probabilities on which to rest our Judgment, but we sub-ject our intellect and Judgment to it as too transcendent for us to estimate. (Calvin 2015: 72)

I would argue that, when read in this new light—as a contest over social authority, waged in a specific discursive and institutional domain, by means of a specialized vocabulary, and one that creates a space in which actors could ask such new ques-tions as: How should we read a text? Which ancient texts have modern applica-bility? Who constitutes the authorized class of interpreters? In what domains are their interpretations relevant?—it is difficult to understand the above quotation as anything but an artful way to evade the means by which legitimacy was then commonly negotiated and established (i.e., logical proofs and rational argumen-tation) so as to constitute a new, alternative position (one that was, somewhat ironically, established, in the case of Calvin's book, by means of over 1,200 pages of rational argumentation, by the way) from which to credibly speak, act, and organize—a position which was proclaimed to be unassailable and thus ultimately authorized, since it resides in people's hearts. We thus see the tremendous utility to the rhetoric of conscience—the presumption of a timelessly authentic, private realm, intuitively connected to the very rhythms of the universe, and thereby unsullied by the interpretive and behavioral ambiguities of the historical, social, political, economic, etc., world.

And it is at this point that I return to this now common (or, with Calvin's clichéd notion of a conscience and a faith that is free of institutional constraint, should I say *still* common?) reply "I'm spiritual but not religious"; for it seems that we find here the same socio-rhetorical move, inasmuch as the speaker presumes to exist a pre-social, ahistorical interior realm, unpolluted by the inevitable intermixings and ambiguities of daily life, from which they can make unimpeachable judg-ments on others. For "spiritual not religious" names not an innocent difference but, much as a reformer's thoughts on faith vs. tradition, a ranked distinction—as was all too apparent in Sarah Caughman's opening quotation; participating in a modern discourse on the subject (i.e., the individual, the citizen, be true to yourself, etc.), judgments of authenticity are now thought to be anchored in the lone actor's very personhood—despite the fact that personhood, and thus one's status and place, pretty clearly being the result of circumstances over which they exert little, if any, control (think here, for a moment, of earlier generations of African Americans being judged as only three-fifths of a person).[10] And this is the irony, as suggested from the outset: the individualist rhetorics that drive such claims are not just social tools used by actors in situations of contest but are social effects of the worlds they inhabit, allowing us to predict who might use these rhetorics and on what occasions.[11] Much like vast numbers of people who have never met each other but nonetheless all agree on how to look and act like an individual (something that differs based on class, race, gender, generation, etc.) so too claims of being spiritual but not religious comprise a chorus sung by people who are all alienated from a once dominant mode of organization and who, despite claiming to be free of tradition, collaboratively invent and then inhabit but new traditions that work in opposition.

As exemplified in the previous chapter, the key to this re-reading, then, is to assume from the outset that human life is social through and through; that none of us invented how to tie shoelaces or recite the alphabet is the key to understanding the collective situation in which we exist. While this hardly means that we are determined (since we each inhabit innumerably different and sometimes competing, even contradictory, sub-groups, making possible a variety of roles that may or may complement each other, leading to slippage, happenstance, disagreement, unanticipated outcomes, etc.—thus I am not arguing for a form of determinism), it does mean that being lulled into thinking that claims about being uniquely set apart are factually true is the sign of a rather poor social theorist.

And so now when we see an ad, as I recently did online, for a "spiritual but not religious Shabbat dinner," in Pittsburgh, billed as "a hyper-inclusive vegetarian Shabbat dinner surrounding ideas of faith, God, and meaning" for those who "cringe" at the word religion and wish to "find meaning by crafting our own spirituality,"[12] we may pause for a moment, recognizing that ardent meat-eaters have just been excluded from this supposedly hyper-inclusive gathering—let alone anyone who wishes not to celebrate Friday night dinner in a traditionally Jewish manner—and thereby be all the more curious about how groups draw lines, how they prioritize just theirs, the effects of being on this as opposed to that side of them, and what we do with the boundaries that others are equally busy limiting and protecting. For the notion of a center, an essence, or a still quiet place that transcends the mundane will start to sound more and more to us like a competitive edge that some players use to get ahead in the social game of identity formation.

If so, then hearing someone say, as did Karen Potter (when speaking with the sociologist of religion, Wade Clark Roof, during research for his book on those claims of spirituality that we now hear so often)—

I had to give up the notion that the only place you could find spirit was here [at church]. It was like I thought spirit is at the church. Then I'd go and I wouldn't feel it. I love some of the people. And miss them. But I just don't feel like being a part of it now ... and don't want to have somebody telling me that it is right for me right now ... I feel my connectedness with other people. When I feel the feeling, it's very much feeling like I'm okay. And I am the source of the spirit. It's coming from within, not without, and that's what it feels like. And I feel that. I have that now with the women. We get together and we sit in a circle and we meditate and we share and spirit is there with me. (Roof 1999: 21)

—we may come to hear not claims about some more authentic mode of being but, instead, just as we did with Calvin's writings, we may discover the trace of a newly asserted, emergent identity trying to establish a place for itself in a hectic social economy.

Notes

1   My attempt in this previously unpublished chapter is to redescribe "spiritual but not religious" rhetorics in a fashion comparable to an earlier effort to make plain the socio-rhetorical work being carried out in discourses on evil (see McCutcheon 2003: chapter 7). Too often, it seems to me, we take the signifiers of the people we study—notably those with whom we have some degree of overlap or affinity—as being in a an unmediated relationship with actual items in the real world, as if, for instance, things called evil are, well, actually and uncontestably evil. So, instead of assuming that spirituality names a state distinguishable from that of being religious, the chapter argues that both terms are rhetorical techniques by which social actors do things in their world (as the previous article argued in the case of calling something evil). Moreover, in both cases it should be clear—but readers who regularly seem to characterize my work as offering nothing but a negative critique may not catch this—that the critique of chapter is interwoven with a model for how scholarship at such discursive sites could instead be carried out.

2   As phrased by McGrath: "The term appears to have been introduced around 1552 by the Lutheran polemicist Joachim Westphal to refer to the theological, and particularly the sacramental, views of the Swiss reformers in general, and of John Calvin in particular. Once introduced, the term rapidly passed into general use in the Lutheran church. In an increasingly nationalist region of Europe, it conveniently emphasized that this religious movement was foreign—unlike Lutheranism, which possessed impeccably German pedigree" (McGrath 2007: 98).

3   If we take Ecclesiastes 1:9 seriously—"there is nothing new under the sun"—or at least adopt the social theory position that assumes form the outset that all human action takes places within prior structures, then perhaps culture is itself a cliché inasmuch as nothing is original and, instead, is but a variation on a handed-down derivation.

4   I am here paraphrasing the conclusion reached by Arnal (2000) in his analysis of how the modern category religion, defined primarily as faith or belief, functions socially and politically.

5   Ogotemmêli was the name of an elder of the Dogon people, in western Africa, and the subject of Griaule's 1947 anthropological study concerned with a series of 33 interviews on the topic of his people's esoteric cosmology (Griaule 1965), while Guzmàn was a Desana Indian, in South America, and the lone informant for Reichel-Dolmatoff's

anthropological work on Amazonian cosmology (Reichel-Dolmatoff 1971). As for Barth, he will be discussed below.

6 It should be clear that I am not using the term myth in the common manner of a lie or a falsehood.

7 It is for this reason that I refrained from terming Calvin a theologian in my opening line (as he is usually classed), for now we can come to understand him as not just a writer on supposedly religious topics but also as a political theorist, rhetoritician, or even propagandist, inasmuch as his arguments concerned determining the proper place of humans in a cosmic, and thus authorized, order.

8 The first published edition of what was then entitled *De Principatibus* (*Of Principalities*) appeared a few years after Machiavelli's death, though it appears that earlier versions of the text had already been in circulation.

9 Since gender equity was hardly a fact of life in the sixteenth century, it may be more historically accurate to use male pronouns in such cases. And since Calvin himself was keenly interested in developing the interpretive rules by which scripture *ought* to be read, we should perhaps fine tune his text's seemingly egalitarian spirit to read more as his attempt to put himself, and those with whom he agreed, in the authorized position once occupied by the Church.

10 I refer, of course, to the so-called Three-Fifths Compromise which was reached in the U.S. in 1787, whereby southern and norther states determined a way to count citizens for such purposes of taxation and representation in the government.

11 For a further elaboration on this analysis, see Alexander and McCutcheon (2017).

12 See www.pajc.net/events/spiritual-but-not-religious-shabbat-dinner (accessed February 13, 2016).

References

Alexander, Andie and Russell T. McCutcheon (2017). "I'm Spiritual but not Religious," in Brad Stoddard and Craig Martin (eds.), *Stereotyping Religion: Critiquing Clichés*, 97–112. London: Bloomsbury.

Arnal, William (2000). "Definition," in Willi Braun and Russell T. McCutcheon (eds.), *Guide to the Study of Religion*, 21–34. London: Continuum.

Barth, Karl (1936–1977). *Church Dogmatics*, trans. G. T. Thomson. Edinburgh: T. & T. Clark.

Calvin, John (2015) [1845]. *Institutes of the Christian Religion*, trans. Henry Beveridge. 2 vols. Grand Rapids, MI: W. B. Eerdmans Publishing Co.

Griaule, Marcel (1965) [1947]. *Conversations with Ogotemmêli*. Oxford: Oxford University Press.

McCutcheon, Russell T. (2003). *The Discipline of Religion: Structure, Meaning, Rhetoric*. New York: Routledge. https://doi.org/10.4324/9780203451793

McGrath, Alister (2007). *Christianity's Dangerous Idea: The Protestant Revolution; A History from the Sixteenth Century to the Twenty First*. New York: HarperCollins.

Reichel-Dolmatoff, Gerardo (1971). *Amazonian Cosmos*. Chicago, IL: University of Chicago Press.

Roof, Wade Clark (1999). *Spiritual Marketplace: Baby Boomers and the Remaking of American Religion*. Princeton, NJ: Princeton University Press.

Smith, Jonathan Z. (1997). "Are Theological and Religious Studies Compatible?" *Bulletin of the Council of Societies for the Study of Religion* 26/3: 60–61.

Part II

In Practice

For our task, in the long run, is not to introduce or teach our field for its own sake, but to use our field in the service of the broader and more fundamental enterprise of liberal learning.

Jonathan Z. Smith, in *Teaching the Introductory Course in Religious Studies* (Scholars Press, 1991)

Chapter 5

Making Experts Curious about Their Expertise in the Introductory Course[1]

Judging by how those new world religions textbooks keep pouring onto the market (and yet more editions of the older textbooks), the standard in many departments, I'd say, is still the world religions course—whether taught as a traditional survey (i.e., two weeks on Buddhism, two weeks on Islam, etc.) or a thematic course (i.e., covering myths, rituals, traditions, etc.), but one that still draws on world religions information (i.e., Hindus believe this or Jews do that, and Sikhs commemorate that event while Christians celebrate something else). There's certainly some intro courses that, instead, talk about the history of the field and its scholars, or their approaches—the sort of courses that, thirty years or so ago, didn't really much exist and which today likely use Daniel Pals's book (2014); in the early 1990s, as a grad student, I surveyed North American programs, for the late Bruce Alton (then a Professor at the University of Toronto), and had trouble finding many courses like that, but even if such an alternative intro course does exist today there's probably a good likelihood that it's reserved for majors, since the sorts of courses that we assume satisfy the interests of the first year students who find our classes—speaking from my setting here in the U.S, at a public state university—are more than likely not about theory but, instead, all about data.

Given my view of the field, the risk of such classes, taught in a traditional manner (that is, descriptive, maybe even comparative) is that they normalize what, to my way of thinking, ought to be our object of study—for it takes as settled that the world is already divided into a discrete number of things called religions, and then sets out to make the student competent in using this taxonomy to carve up all of human history (what some refer to as religious literacy). Instead, as I've argued on prior occasions concerning our scholarship, I think we ought to be inviting students to be curious about the persistence of this late-nineteenth century taxonomy itself—after all, many other ways of talking about the world that date from that era are hardly used today—asking why it first came into existence (i.e., what were those Dutch and German scholars up to when they were distinguishing world religions from what they termed ethnic religions and why were they so concerned to find out who, like their assumed norm, Christianity, had had a global effect?) and what it still accomplishes for those who use it today; for we now seem to have perfected it, since, over the past 100 years or so, we've taken what were originally just a couple so-called world, or world-class religions (versus all those local or national religions that supposedly hadn't moved much beyond their original kin group or region) and so expanded the tent that you can now easily find world religion maps that assign a meaningful color to every single inch of the globe. In fact, even people who disavow having a religion are treated by scholars of religion as fair game (e.g., all the excitement, over the past couple years, among scholars of religion about studying the so-called Nones). And that, as I've argued in the past, is the problem with the category religion in general or world religions in particular: they're totalized categories (as the late Gary Lease would have phrased it), presumed by their users to encompass all possible variations and situations. Case in point: should we recognize that ancient people didn't have anything near to the modern category religion we nonetheless proceed as if they were at least religious. Or, we just add on qualifiers and create subtypes, like primitive religions (which was eventually retooled as tribal or primal and then low scale society and today indigenous), which functions as a miscellaneous category that helps to make the world religions taxonomy work as a universal type, for now, voila, you have what I understand as a thoroughly modern way of talking not just about all present human beings, but, more than that, a way of naming what's presumed to be an essential feature of this thing called the human, the human condition, or human nature.

But it strikes me as more interesting to study how modernity has been made possible by, among other interconnected tropes, such notions as religion and world religions—operationalized in such things as a census or a legal system.

The limitation of our field, then, is in assuming that our job, as college professors, is to hone our students' use of such categories, and to recreate the sort of social world that their use helps to make possible, instead of using this way of talking about the world as an example of how people (including us!) create identities through their use of (and sometimes resistance to) such classification systems, thereby using these notions of religion or world religions as our way into a much larger topic that cuts across academic disciplines. It seems to me that the latter effort is the one that has long term value for a student, especially one who comes across our courses as part of a core curriculum or general education program (meaning that they'll likely never take another course with us);[2] for whether or not they continue to draw on the specific information about religions that we may have taught them (such as knowing the difference between Hinayana and Mahayana, for example, remembering the name of the river to which people in India sometimes make pilgrimage, or recalling the differences between John and the other three gospels) they'll hopefully recall something about some of the basic techniques people (themselves included) use to identity self and other— something they'll surely witness a fair bit throughout the rest of their life. So, in approaching how I teach the introductory course, I try to imagine that future when a student hears someone on the news start talking about authentic Islam, or maybe distinguish true from false patriotism, or maybe even an older relative spin a yarn about how hard they had it when they were kids; hopefully, that onetime student will be able to see the work taking place in each claim, thereby seeing them all as having something in common, and not just a series of uncontestable, factual statements.

Since there were no resources out there that helped me accomplish such a goal in this class, like a lot of others before me I decided to create my own. So although I wrote my intro book (*Studying Religion: An Introduction*—published first with Equinox but now published by Routledge) in the mid-2000s, publishing it in 2007, I had long had a one-page handout that I wrote, about what the study of religion—at least as I understood it and approached it—was and wasn't, that I used to start off my own intro course (which I usually taught every semester, sometimes more than once), and it lived as a PDF on the web, which a surprising number of other people seemed to find useful too (at least judging by the emails I'd get asking to borrow it—to this day, in fact).[3] That interest from others, coupled with my own need in my classes, was the motivation to write the book. So that means that I first reconceived my own class, over a number of years and many iterations of the course (each paring down the topics covered, realizing the "coverage" wasn't the aim I wanted to achieve), and, eventually, wrote the book that I needed for what I ended up doing.

And what I've ended up doing in that class (as already hinted at above) is moving from its earlier world religions version to using the course as an opportunity to focus on what I consider to be broad-based skills that I hope anyone going to university ought to think about a little.[4] It's a gen ed course, as are many of these courses (thereby bringing in the credit hours that many departments need to justify their existence in today's university), so I take seriously—as many of us in our department have as well—that it's about *the acquisition of skills* rather than being aimed at merely conveying descriptive, historical, or ethnographic information. Since you've got to use a tool somewhere, doing something by means of it with some e.g.s, the students get plenty of the descriptive information, of course, much of it contemporary and often taken from the current news. For example, I might play a radio news story for them, or pass around a newspaper article, so as to ask: What do you make of a town council denying a so-called pagan group the right to erect a monument next to the Ten Commandments monument that's already sat in a local city park for decades? My hope is that they always come to see not just that the tools we use help us to work with the material in different ways, thereby learning different things, but, more importantly, also recognize that different things stand out as relevant or interesting (perhaps even newsworthy) all depending on which tools we decide to pick up—which, in turn, may tell us much about how important it is to be able to examine the interests and assumptions that people employ when they talk about the world (and yes, ourselves included).

So the main goal of my both my intro course (which I teach now at least once a year and often once a semester, usually with between 100 and 150 students, sometimes with a graduate teaching assistant to help with grading assignments) as well as my intro book, are not about acquiring *data* but about acquiring *skills*;[5] for, as suggested above, over the years I've taken Jonathan Z. Smith's (1991) advice that "less is better" quite seriously—moving from a onetime interest (for example, see the description of a possible introductory course in McCutcheon 2001: ch. 13) in moving an intro student from considering how to define to describing, comparing, and finally explaining (equally influenced by reading Smith, by the way) to now biting off far less and focusing only on the skill of defining something as worth talking about (though the other cognitive operations also come in, all throughout the course, to be sure).

The fact that my intro book is focused only on the topic of definition means that the instructor who might adopt it is asked to step up and provide all the e.g.s (i.e., the historic and ethnographic case studies as well as further examples of the various approaches examined in the book). I'm not a fan of textbooks—I certainly used them early on in my own career but stopped soon after, preferring PDF readings that I selected and posted on a course webpage (something I still do, in fact). For the textbook strikes me as but an earlier, hardbound version of today's digital learning management system—I'm not really sure what instructors' roles are in a course when a ready-made class, complete with assignments and testing instruments, is dropped in their lap (especially evident when early career people are sometimes just given the required book or even syllabus by their chair). Now is likely not the time to go into this in detail but there are larger, structural issues in higher education that, I think, can be identified and discussed in the case of professors being asked to adopt, or voluntarily opting for, course content that was set by another. Given that we work in a field that (at least to date) lacks a national credentialing association we should, I think, revel in that freedom—which also means taking responsibility for what we each decide to put in front of our students in our classes. So textbooks strike me as reflecting the interests of the textbook writer (and publisher) far too much, leaving far too little room for the novelty introduced by each instructor, who comes to the class with different expertise, background, and curiosities. So what I tried to do was not write a textbook but, instead, to provide a way to set the table for a course, providing a structure by making decisions of my own, of course, as its writer (or better, as someone already teaching a course and needing a resource for it), but then leaving the door wide open for where an instructor would go with it. After all, 60 percent of the book is supporting material (glossary and further discussions of the authors mentioned in the eight brief chapters), so it really is a short little book with easily read chapters that hardly constitute a full course—not unless an instructor brings an awful lot of supporting material of their own to it.

For example, not long ago a young scholar in Europe wrote asking about the book—she was interested in using it but was having trouble thinking what she would do with it, short little chapters an all. So I emailed back the following:

> It all depends what you're trying to accomplish in this course. For me, the goal is to persuade them [students] that not only different definitions but also different types of definitions allow us to do different things—so the goal is to persuade them that we can profitably distinguish an essentialist from a functionalist from a family resemblance [definition], and the backdrop [for all this] are the needs of the publicly funded science of religion, so which [type of definition] suits our purposes and why. And then, in the process, to introduce them to a wide array of writers who are each used either to exemplify the type we're looking at (Marx qua functionalist, for example) or to illustrate it (or critique it) once we have the types up and running in our minds.

So, you have a reading that allows you to identify a Marxist def'n—sure, discuss the work, the definition, etc. But then you'll need to illustrate how one might use that definition, what one might now say about the world if you come armed with that definition, so you'll need some practical example, you'll need to describe the historical or ethnographic example enough so that the student understands it sufficiently to then be able to use the definition on it, but then a follow-up reading from a contemporary (in this case, Marxist) scholar, further illustrating what is to be gained (or not) would be quite nice. All depending how much time you have to devote to this one item, you've now come up with 3 or 4 classes devoted to this one item, which constitutes but one example of a functionalist approach—Marx's is a highly normative approach, to be sure, so how well does it allow a scholar to avoid making normative judgments about the object of study (are we here to say it is illusory?)? Thus a critique of the definition is likely called for, ensuring the students start seeing definitions as tools that have inevitable limits and prices that comes with their gains ...

So my goal is to get them acquainted enough with each [definition] that they can try it on, like someone else's coat, and wear it around a bit and use it and see what they can now see going on in the world, which is made possible by seeing it through this or that definition of religion ...

What I hope characterizes the book is therefore that it asks a lot of the one who has decides to use it—and I think that's good for the long term health of our profession, what with the shrinking governance faculty in some universities now seem to have over their own syllabi and courses. If I was teaching 4 different courses a semester, or moving between more than one school as a part-time teacher, then I could see those work conditions as a rationale to *not* opt for a book such as this—a textbook might make a lot of sense in such a situation—but I'd hope that person could profitably use it as well, seeing the introductory course(s) they're teaching as an opportunity to incorporate much of the data with which their specialty makes them particularly comfortable and knowledgeable.

Important to recognize when approaching teaching such classes, I think, is that given that our primary taxon, religion, is a word of common English usage, students come to this class with specific assumptions and interests—often at odds with where I hope to take them in the course. For if you take into account the widespread understanding of religion as an interior sentiment that everyone apparently just has—something most of my students take entirely for granted, and which I've already addressed in earlier chapters—then you arrive at a room filled with experts *on the first day of class!* For they not only come to class assuming it is a world religions course—even when the catalog's course description made it quite clear what the course was and wasn't about—but also that either their prior parochial school training or their own experience has already prepared them for what we're going to study. I don't think there's any other field that has to deal with quite this problem—even an American history class likely doesn't have to deal with the presumed expertise of the students just because they're American themselves. For though they may have taken plenty of such history courses in high school they nonetheless likely assume a degree of depth in the university course to which they've not yet been exposed. But in the study of religion it often takes some doing to put some of our students into a more epistemologically humble (and thus pedagogically open) position, so as to make them a little more curious about that expertise that they once thought they possessed.

So I find that a key move, early in the course, is to gently or ironically defamiliarize what they take for granted, and thereby to open just a little space for eventually asking some unanticipated questions. So the way I sometimes have done this was to get them to go with a partner to the library and to come back with 5 or 10 different definitions of religion—not from the web but, instead, from books whose pages they have to turn and through whose indexes they have to browse. The goal is to make sure that they look through what they consider to be scholarly sources, thereby introducing the first wedge in the course, *to distinguish popular from technical usage of terminology*. Then, armed with all those submitted lists of definitions, cited properly of course (another goal of the assignment: *there are details and a structure specific to what we do, as scholars*), it allows me to start to go through them as data, right in front of the class, and I think that they get a little curious to see, once I point it out, how many times words like belief and faith and feeling and experience come up, in these randomly collected definitions that they've put in my hands, instead of words like behavior, practice, and institution. We don't spend more than a class doing this, but it establishes a beachhead, as they say, or a reference point, that I can return to later in the course, when we give this all a name (i.e., philosophical idealism) and can start to compare this commonsense way of talking about religion to the things from other times or cultures that we routinely translate by the English word religion but which may have carried none of those idealist overtones to the people who, say, talked about *pietas* in ancient Rome, for example. (The lesson there? *Translation bridges gaps, yes, but the gaps remain despite the artful bridges.*)

From there I often move on to talk about some items in the news, like the one about the monument that I referred to above,[6] and someday soon after (as mentioned in a previous chapter) I'll try to get the class talking about whether a whale is a mammal or a fish, and so on—the goal is to get students to the point of seeing not religion as the object of study but our presumption that there are such things *as* religions and I try to do this by keeping their eyes on all sorts of other classificatory disputes (analogies and examples—the means by which we exhibit the unanticipated similarities or differences that prompt new thoughts—are our best friends not just in research but also in teaching), looking at the effects of such systems and the interests that might drive their use, always with the punchline being something about how what we've learned over there does or does not shed some light over here (such as our habit of calling something in the world sacred versus secular). And within a week or two I think most students start to understand the shift we're making; for we're studying people (like us) who talk about religion and not studying religion itself, whatever that may or may not be; it really interests some, yet others who came in a little defensive, assuming the course was going to criticize things they thought were important, seem to be freed up by the course's approach and more easily come to think about themselves as their own object of study. For the shift I try to make recognizes that they are the experts since they're all completely versed in how to talk about religion, what to call a religion (and what not), etc. But through a well-placed e.g. that cuts against their commonsense the course invites them to examine that very expertise—making, as the old saying goes, their familiar just a little stranger, and hopefully more curious, for them.

Also, as noted earlier, important to bear in mind is that students are in this course for a wide variety of reasons—from finding the material, or at least the course title, interesting (and thus potentially a future major) to students from across the university forced to choose something to satisfy a core/gen ed requirement. But despite the initial appearance that these two sorts of students are radically different—and the common assumption that satisfying one risks alienating the other—I tend to think that these two ideal types of students are, in fact, one in the same, since so few incoming first year students have ever heard about what we do—high schools generally don't have an equivalent, after all. So while serving the needs of the core curriculum (making this a so-called service course), it's also from these very courses that we recruit many of our future majors. And in many cases, at least in our experience at the University of Alabama, they're students who have eventually become dissatisfied with whatever it was that they declared as their major when they first applied to university. Whether they eventually switch to the study of religion (in, say, their junior year) or declare it as a second major or a minor, they're often people who, for whatever reason, were particularly engaged in some intro course that they took in our department. So I think it is an error to assume that instructors need to address two possibly incommensurable constituencies in such courses for, often, there's not a major in the bunch; instead, the way to approach such courses is that you're trying to create more articular students (who will either get interested enough to declare the major or simply become better at what they're already majoring in) by showing them *how to be curious about the taken-for-granted*—which, come to think of it, is a general skill that anyone going to university ought to acquire, suggesting why that's a profitable approach to take in any sort of core or gen ed class. Whether or not they'll declare a major eventually, who knows, but even if they don't you've done your job of initiating a group into asking some provocative questions that they'd never thought of asking before. And now they also know that answering them is how we create new knowledge.

With the unanticipated effects of a core course in mind, I recall a student who had recently completed my intro course and who once stopped me in the cafeteria, wanting to thank me for how the course had helped in her own major by getting her to think more carefully about how a test works and, thus, how to prepare for it and manage her time and focus while taking it. Although I give out plenty of free advice during class, knowing that few students give much thought to approaching a test strategically, the few who come by for office hours often benefit from more practical advice on test-taking—such as the student who wanted me to know how much her performance in other classes had also improved. When I went up to Chicago a couple years ago, to give a talk on teaching the introductory course (to which I'll return in the next chapter), there was a question that cut to the heart of the theme of my talk (on the tough choices we likely need to make when teaching such courses; it concerned the fact that, yes, I use multiple choice tests in this intro course.[7] For when I teach it—again, with between 100 and 150 students in the class—I admit that I use multiple choices tests that focus both on lectures as well as content in the book. By the way, the book I mentioned earlier contains bolded technical terms (i.e., the first time a term that's defined in the glossary is used in each chapter it is bolded) and also bolded scholars' names (they too are discussed in greater detail in the back of the book, with a few quotes from each that illustrate their approach to defining and studying religion); one of the reasons why the chapters are all so short is because each chapter, somewhat like clicking links on the web, opens onto both a variety of interconnected paragraph-length discussions of terminology later in the book as well as several two to three page discussions of the scholars that are mentioned. This format then paves the way for the tests which, along with lecture content, emphasize technical terminology as well as information about the scholars that we've mentioned in each unit. So, in the midst of entertaining the rethinking I'm inviting them to do, concerning how classification makes cognitively habitable social spaces, I also ask the students to learn at least four or five things about every new term we discuss and also to be able to talk about each scholar mentioned in at least three ways: roughly when did they live (don't memorize birth and death dates but know if they're a late-nineteenth-century writer or a contemporary one); what part (aka academic discipline or department) of the university they worked in (or might today work in); and why they were relevant for us in our course.

But back to that question: why multiple choice tests? Don't they cut against some of the critical thinking that I'm trying to accomplish in such a course? After all ... multiple choice tests are ... well, let's just be honest: they're multiple choice tests.

When I was a teaching assistant during my own Ph.D. at the University of Toronto, I was a teaching assistant for a couple years for the late Will Oxtoby and the late Joe O'Connell's co-taught world religions survey course. (You likely know the two volume textbook, edited by Oxtoby, that, to a large extent, resulted from that class.) There was a whole team of us (5 or 6 doctoral students) for a class that likely wasn't larger than 200 students, and, as I recall, we all ran a couple of required tutorials each (i.e., discussion or recitation sections), one before and one after the main lecture, so that students had the opportunity to participant in a small (20 students or so?) discussion, thereby not getting entirely lost in the large lecture. Bill Arnal and I did the same for Michel Desjardin's night course intro to the New Testament one year as well—leading small discussion sections before and after the large, main lecture. The first large lecture class that I taught on my own was when I first started working fulltime, back in Tennessee in 1993, and I've been doing them ever since, but, unlike those classes I worked for in Toronto, I've never had the luxury of a team of TAs able to staff multiple discussion sections; instead, like most people around the country, I've mostly done it on my own—though, several years ago we were lucky enough to get our first TA lines in our Department, allowing us to assign a grad student to the course for approximately

10 or sometimes 20 hours per week (but that's hardly enough personnel to offer smaller discussion sections for 100 or 150 students). That means that our TAs help with grading, keep the grade book, offer office hours, etc.—for just attending the class exhausts three of those 10 weekly hours, leaving not a lot of time for preparation, grading, and running multiple discussion sections.

So, given this practical setting, writing assignments are likely not plausible in this course—I'm a department chair and, besides a 100-level intro course, and sometimes an upper-level seminar or independent studies, there's lots of other things competing for my attention each day and I can only imagine what life would be like if, like earlier in my career, this were one of several classes I was teaching each Fall or Spring—whether different preps or not, we all know that all that grading adds up, especially when you're also trying to do your research and write. Which brings me back to those tough choices I mentioned speaking on up north: in those early days of my career, when I was finishing my dissertation and involved in a variety of other projects, I developed some group assignments and a style of multiple choice tests that I was willing to live with in this intro course—it was hardly ideal, given my own pedagogical hopes and dreams, but, given the practical circumstances of my labor, it seemed to be a compromise I could live with. And I've happily lived with it since then.

After all, I couldn't help 150 students develop and write original research papers, much less read rough drafts, comment on them, and then grade them all. So the question became what *could* I do and what ends that I valued could these assignments help me to achieve. And that's how I settled on some small group work (mentioned earlier) to start the class—on the most rudimentary level it's a good way for students in a large class to meet someone, to learn where the library is, to have a taste, at the 100-level, of a required format for citing a source, and also a great way to discuss what it means to quote a source properly and what counts as plagiarism. So, as I said earlier, for the second class of the semester, I sometimes send them all to the library to find those different definitions of religion. They have to hunt and peck and flip through the table of contents and index of a bunch of books—which is a pretty good introduction to what it often means to do research, by the way; for we usually don't know what we're looking for when we start looking. Once they turn it in, and apart from debriefing on it in class, in search of the easily found idealist assumptions in most definitions, I keep ahold of that assignment and give it back to them at the end of the semester, when they now have to make data of those five definitions for their second group assignment. (Which definition is functionalist? Which might a scholar in a public university opt for—and, more importantly, why?)

It's an assignment that allows us to apply things from the class, yes, or gain material to focus on at a later date, but it also accomplishes so much more that, more than likely, the students don't even realize. For one, it got them into the library. (That the library staff has sometimes not appreciated 150 students all descending on the BL section of the stacks at the same time deserves mention; there are better and worse ways to go about this assignment and I've learned that alerting the library in advance as to when the students will be arriving is never a bad idea.) But what about the multiple choice tests? Well, like that definition assignment, its more about form than it is about content—sure, you've got to know something about Freud and something about the notion of etic, but excelling on test on which these two items may appear is more about how students prepare and how they come to learn new information, over the course of the semester. (It's also about just attending class regularly and paying attention.) For the key is building relationship between discrete items, about being able to link one seemingly distinct piece of information to another and then to another, and maybe another as well, making semantic chains or webs, if you will, so that when my test comes along and throws a little curve at them by introducing a new ball into what they're already juggling they'll be able to accommodate the new information by linking it to something that they already know, which in turn they'll link to yet something else and, like solving for X in a quadratic equation, they'll then look among the various choices I've offered for the correct answer. For, come to think about it, that's what the course is all about: studying how we create knowledge, make spaces sensible and habitable, by establishing and then managing a host of relationships of similarity and difference—our field's been known as Comparative Religion, after all, no? So the multiple test exemplifies the method at the heart of our discipline: comparison.

But it doesn't just test this, for I tend to write rather long questions, making it a test of reading comprehension as well. (Who among them will write the GRE or the LSAT someday ...?) Often, students perform unsatisfactorily though they say that they know the information—their difficulty, it often turns out, is often linked to reading, to being able to simplify the sentence, to find what it is actually asking, in distinction from the background info it's also giving to them. Did they see the word "not" in the question, to then realize that I was asking the exact opposite of what they at first might have thought? So, instead of asking how Karl Marx defined religion I'll instead start off the question by writing two or three lines, beginning with something like: "A nineteenth-century political economist whose functionalist definition was concerned with distinguishing ..."; it's a confusing approach for some students, for they get lost in the verbiage, but, for others, they come to see that I've just given them all sorts of hints and prompts, inviting them to make certain sorts of connections—especially helpful if, as is more than likely the case, Marx is the only political economist, let alone one from the nineteenth century, whom we've studied that semester. (That's only apparent to those who did the reading and attended classes regularly, of course.) But the goal—which I let students in on should they take the trouble to make an appointment to talk over the problems they seem to be having in the course—is, again, to exemplify how knowledge itself works: by making links while then continuously extending and moderating that series of like/unlike relationships. And those who come to office hours start to "get" this by the time they leave and, as with that student who stopped me in the cafeteria that day, they start to stick around a little longer during the tests (why do they all race through them?), going over questions and using the questions themselves as assistance in answering other parts of the test; and so, their grades inevitably improve. And since it strikes me that the course is actually about learning how to learn, late in the semester I often offer all the students a chance to reweight their tests, to minimize on poor early performances by maximizing on their newfound skills.

And for many it pays off. Sometimes dramatically.

It's not ideal, of course—who wouldn't rather be teaching 10 students in a small seminar room *à la* Mr. Keating in *Dead Poets Society*, where you can look each student in the eye to figure out whether they understand the material or not, having them each do weekly writing assignments on which you can comment at length, to see them incorporate your feedback and continually improve across the semester. But that's not where many of us work—and, in the modern university, those conditions are getting further and further away from many of us. So, whether or not one can change the fate of higher ed in North America, it at least seems to me that one is challenged to figure out what's important to you, as an instructor, and then to devise assignments that take your time commitments into account but which also strategically address those pedagogical values and goals that you have and on which you're not willing to compromise. Being placed into a setting such as that, where the teaching situation might be far from ideal, is what I think makes good teachers for it prompts us to be deliberate and mindful about what we're doing and how we're going doing it.

So yes, I use multiple choice tests in my 100-level intro course, but because of some of the choices I've made, I think they're doing a lot more than meets the eye. So, in the case of our department, when some of our own more experienced majors find themselves in the course, I think they find that they too are challenged by the form (if not by the content); but, more often than not, they usually take it so early in their own degree that they do not normally come with much more technical knowledge (i.e., content) about the field than do all the other people enrolled in it, so, as already suggested, the possible conflict between the more specialized student and the gen ed student doesn't really materialize in such cases either. (Lacking pre-requisites in our upper-level seminars—where such obstacles would lessen the students enrolled in each course, thereby jeopardizing the number of students taught by the department—means that we'll probably see the conflict or the gap there instead, since our own senior majors often have no choice but to enroll with more novice students. The challenge of moderating the gap in those important courses is therefore very real.) So the one approach I've adopted for the content and assessments seems to work well for the two audiences since, for all intents and purposes, they're just one and the same audience, i.e., experienced folk users of a local classification system that makes use of the word religion in a variety of identification acts. Their shared challenge, then, is to focus on the requirement to define an area of study, in keeping with First Amendment issues (in the case of working in a public university in the U.S., as I do), that requires us to do something other than use the term in our accustomed ways. So, really, much like any good introductory course at college, the class is an exercise in alienation, from a taken-for-granted way of talking about the world, as much as it is in initiation into a scholarly discourse (as once pointed out by Smith, an introduction in the most technical of senses; on this technical sense of "introduction," see Braun and McCutcheon 2008: xv–xvi). Whether such an approach counts as what others call deconstructive and whether it results in the student being left with a depressing mush—to borrow from the way Jeff Kripal's own recent textbook represents approaches different from his own—I certainly leave to others to decide.

With Kripal's own textbook, *Comparing Religions* (2014), I recall him talking to me, early on in conceptualizing it, about the book that he wanted to write and it's turned out quite nicely (though rather different from my own approach—a difference worth considering, I think). I was president of the (now defunct) Council of Societies for the Study of Religion (CSSR) at the time, which had recently moved its headquarters to Rice University, where he was Department Chair, so I'd make periodic trips down to Houston for CSSR meetings and we'd sometimes end up going to a lunch or having coffee, to chat about work and the field. What interested me was his idea to focus on comparison in an intro book—as evidenced above, I tend to think it's important to emphasize skills over content. Given the nature of the 100-level course and the students who enroll in it, it's the skills that will likely come in more handy, down the road, than remembering the name of this ritual or that doctrine. Because of that, and before writing my own intro book, back when I was interested in the interrelated skills of definition, description, comparison, and explanation, I'd thought of either a single book or a series that would exemplify all of these interrelated skills—e.g., having described all that falls within a defined domain, can you look for the similarities and differences among the items and then account for why (i.e., explanation) this unanticipated similarity or that difference exists?—but that idea eventually transformed into a book, *Studying Religion*, just on defining religion. So, for a while, I'd been jotting down some notes for what a comparative book might look like.

So, while in agreement on emphasizing the skill, it's the data that I think Kripal and I may differ on, making our two books useful e.g.s to put alongside each other; for by design some of the items that I was thinking of using, had I tackled an intro book on comparison, didn't necessarily have anything to do with religion. Or, to be a little more precise, if we see the things we call religions as but examples of cultural projects that human actors create in their efforts to mark territory and fabricate identities, doing so in a busy economy of other possible places and things to be (or, better put, things to be seen by others as being), then it seemed to me that learning to compare religions to so-called nonreligious things was an important skill, to elucidate that the items that we name as religion are no more or less special than any other item of culture (i.e., we see the same general social principles happening there as we do here).

Given my interest in critiquing approaches to the study of religion that presuppose our objects of study to be unique, set apart cases, it seemed strategic always to ensure that you would destabilize something's seemingly set apart nature by comparing it to what may at first seem to be a counterintuitive class of objects, in order to illustrate that, despite the way we treat the supposedly religious item, it shared some possibly surprising trait with some other mundane element of culture. Could one see, for example, Dorothy Gale's "There's no place like home," speech from end of *The Wizard of Oz* as a species of discourse that functions similarly to, say, virtually any origins tale that routinely makes its way into the world religions classroom? For if so, then we've made a significant step toward humanizing and historicizing the stories formerly known as sacred, for now we see in both instances an example of situated social actors conjuring into existence a nostalgic focus, bearing all the traces of their current circumstance and present interests, but which is portrayed by them as a destination somehow removed in time and place (and, thereby authorized).[8] So in the midst of learning about the two objects of study that were put into a structured relationship by means of this comparative exercise (over which we, the comparativists, exert control) the student would, implicitly, be entertaining a specific theory of religion—for now the items formerly known as religion are but a subspecies of wider cultural practices. Our comparative efforts have therefore been designed not to find something out about religion (say, by looking at more than one example of sacred ritual) but, instead, to figure out something about how people do or don't work with each other on common, socially formative projects.

So it's the examples in Kripal's book that my attention is drawn toward. There are a number of pop culture references but they seem mostly to set the table for the religious material that, sooner or later, are the main illustrations that are chosen. Though certainly supportive of his focus on comparison, my inclination is pretty much the opposite of his—his being, as his introduction puts it: "*privileg[ing] the extraordinary and the uncanny over the ordinary and the common.*" In fact, I'd say what we need to do is (by inviting students to become curious about their taken for granted expertise) to consider just how exotic the ordinary actually is— taking account of the sorts of intellectual and social operations that (tipping my hat again to Roland Barthes) are required to make something seem natural, mundane, commonplace, etc. For, anyone who is just a little outside the status quo knows that commonsense isn't all that common; so the trick, for me, is to make that very pairing—extraordinary/ordinary, much like sacred/profane or private/ public and experience/expression, to name only a few—*the object of scrutiny.* So, as you might guess, unlike Kripal, I don't find myself talking about the sacred or deep patterns or ultimate or meaning or the anomalous; for, placing myself in a tradition indebted to writers like Émile Durkheim and Mary Douglas, I'd prefer to talk about the situated social actors who are creating structures (and working within structures created by past actors, and so on, and so on, all the way down), and then, in light of this situation, deciding what constitutes a norm and thus what ends up being anomalous—and always being careful to add, *for them!* For I'd say that the egg-laying, semi-aquatic platypus, for example, just is what it is and only *becomes* anomalous when *we* arrive on the scene with a specific definition of mammal, one that is of our making, that we're using to sort the world in this rather than that way. (That's why I like to use the example of the whale in class, since, for most of human history, it was just a really big fish to everyone and saying it was a mammal counted as the weird claim.) And I also don't talk about or aim to draw conclusions about this thing called human nature or the future of the planet, for the course is an introduction to being a member of a specific academic field, which can get going only once we get curious, pose questions and choose tools to come up with some answers—which, to my way of thinking, makes arriving at such transcendental conclusions overly ambitious, since it seems to erase the situated nature of the questions we're posing, i.e., the situations of the people posing them. After all, I'd wager that the irreducible plurality of the world that Kripal's conclusion seems to celebrate, also includes a lot of things he and I are likely not willing to live with in any way, shape, or form; so getting students, even at the 100-level, to examine how we invariably eliminate certain options from consideration by, whether we admit it or not, reducing the complexity to just those that exist within what we consider a tolerably diverse range, seems ambitious enough.

So I try to excite students no less than Kripal, of course, but it's not by trying to get more things into the big tent of religion (such as the so-called mystical or fantastical dimensions that he feels the standard world religions textbook opts not to include—and I don't disagree with him concerning the choices that animate more traditional and thus implicitly comparative world religions text-books); instead, I try to make students curious about why they even need to make the decision about what's more or less anomalous or weird by simply putting a picture of a tomato on the big screen, at the front of class, and asking whether it's a fruit or a vegetable, in hopes that making them curious about the rules of the taken-for-granted that we collectively invent and which they largely accept and then put into practice each day (i.e., we all know how to find a tomato in the grocery store, right?) empowers rather than diminishes them, so that they start to see everything around them to be far more fascinating that they at first might have thought—including themselves. And, in my experience, things start to get going around the time they find out there was actually an 1893 U.S. Supreme Court case on that tomato's identity.

Notes

1 Asked to produce a document, to be posted on a university blog as part of a larger discussion, elaborating on how my introductory book (McCutcheon 2007) and course are related/organized, along with the goals that they each try to attain, I wrote a shorter draft of the following in the spring of 2015. For whatever reason, that project never came to fruition and it was never posted or published; so, given the structure/internal division of this volume, I've decided that this essay was worth including since it may be of practical use for others who are thinking through how they wish to organize their own introductory-level courses. Though written after the chapter that follows, it also establishes the larger setting from out of which Chapter 6's "tough choices" arise.

2 Perhaps it should here be made explicit that, unlike in many European universities (where what we in North America term undergraduate students would take their entire degree in their specialty), students in the U.S. and Canada generally take a broad array of classes as part of a Bachelor's degree (ensuring that, regardless their degree's specialty, they all share in the same general education). Such students therefore only spend approximately one quarter of their time on courses in their major area of study. Thus, much like the math or physics departments helping engineering students to

fulfill their requirements, departments of religious studies often function as "service departments," inasmuch as they are said to serve the needs of the so-called core curriculum by offering general education courses to students who, enrolled in other majors, will likely never again take another course in the academic study of religion.

3 Following a paper on the contributions of the late Huston Smith that I delivered at the 2017 annual meeting of the American Academy of Religion, held that year in Boston (and which is published in McCutcheon 2018), a member of the audience introduced herself to me so as to remark on the important role this handout continues to play in her own classes.

4 The course I was required to teach, much earlier in my career, was to be a world religions course but, while still offering a course that met the needs of such a rubric (thereby satisfying the expectations of my department's leadership whenever they scrutinized my syllabi), I was able to begin changing it, incrementally, such that the data presented was increasingly in the service of a broader theoretical point. My hunch is that this is how all good courses are devised, over time.

5 Perhaps I should here add that by skills I do not mean the sort of transferable skills that we sometimes hear discussed when the relevance of the humanities is in debate, i.e., as if undergraduate degrees in the Humanities are, or ought to be, reducible to a series of practical tools useful in succeeding in other careers. While such success may be the result of the skills that I have in mind, I think here far more broadly about the sort of so-called critical thinking skills that any university student likely needs to acquire and be accomplished in using—such as the cognitive skills just mentioned: definition, description, interpretation, comparison, explanation.

6 I have in mind the summer 2014 judgment, against the city of Bloomfield in the state of New Mexico, that a Ten Commandments monument (though originally erected with private funds) had to be removed from city property; it was based on a law suit, first brought in 2012 by the American Civil Liberties Union (ACLU), representing two local self-identified pagans. The city appealed the judgment that the monument be removed and two years later, the 10th Circuit Court of Appeals sided with the lower court, ordering its removal. For background see www.santafenewmexican.com/news/local_news/battle-over-bloomfield-monument-pits-beliefs-against-rights/article_5a97c39e-30d8-560c-a16a-f7b31868fb0d.html (accessed June 25, 2017).

7 The following discussion of multiple choice testing is based on what originally appeared as a blog post at http://practicumreligionblog.blogspot.com/2015/05/multiple-choices.html (accessed June 25, 2017).

8 Although some scholars might go in the opposite direction, of course, and take the apparent similarity as evidence that nonreligious things were implicitly religious, as some might term it (following the late British scholar, Edward Bailey, the longtime advocate for this approach). This tradition—not unlike those who once used the term secular religion or those, following Robert Bellah, who still discuss civil religion—strikes me as, whether they recognize this or not, normalizing a problematic notion of *sui generis* religion inasmuch as its adherents seem to resist reducing things identified as religious to any other aspect of human society. It is noteworthy that the journal Bailey founded, *Implicit Religion*, has now undergone a change and, as it now describes itself, "offers a platform for scholarship that challenges the traditional boundary between religion and non-religion and the tacit assumptions underlying this distinction" (see the journal's website: https://journals.equinoxpub.com/index.php/IR/index, accessed July 1, 2017).

References

Braun, Willi and Russell T. McCutcheon (2008). *Introducing Religion: Essays in Honor of Jonathan Z. Smith*. New York: Routledge.

Kripal, Jeffrey (2014). *Comparing Religions*, with Andrea Jain, Erin Prophet, and Ata Anzali. Hoboken, NJ: Wiley-Blackwell.

McCutcheon, Russell T. (2001). *Critics Not Caretakers: Redescribing the Public Study of Religion*. Albany, NY: State University of New York Press.

—— (2007). *Studying Religion: An Introduction*. New York: Routledge.

—— (2018). *Fabricating Religion: Fanfare for the Common e.g.* Berlin: Walter de Gruyter.

Pals, Daniel (2014). *Nine Theories of Religion*, 3rd ed. New York: Oxford University Press.

Smith, Jonathan Z. (1991). "The Introductory Course: Less is Better," in Mark Juergensmeyer (ed), *Teaching the Introductory Course in Religious Studies: A Sourcebook*, 185–192. Atlanta, GA: Scholars Press.

Chapter 6

A Baker's Dozen of Tough Choices[1]

Preamble

Taking seriously Jonathan Z. Smith's line from his contribution to Mark Juergesmeyer's unfortunately out-of-print *Teaching the Introductory Course in Religious Studies: A Sourcebook*, that "there is nothing that must be taught, there is nothing that cannot be left out" (Smith 1991: 187; reprinted in Smith 2013: 11–19)—a conclusion he draws from the practical constraints of any class, for, as he writes there, "no course can do everything, no course can be complete"—I've decided to consider here some of the difficult choices that, in my experience in the classroom, the instructor of an introductory course likely has to make. More specifically, I have in mind people early in their careers: from ABDs teaching their own course for the first time to newly hired assistant professors confronting a full teaching load along with research and service expectations—e.g., the person who, in hindsight, I imagine myself to have been when I now look over those syllabi, which I still have on my office hard drive, for my own World Religions in History (Religious Studies 101) and Comparative Religion: An Introduction (Religious Studies 102), courses that I regularly taught, from 1993 to 1996, as an Instructor at the University of Tennessee, where my own full-time teaching career began. Moreover, with where I started my own career in mind (not to mention the other two universities where I have worked in the U.S., one in Missouri and the other in Alabama), I also direct these comments toward those teaching in the public university—the place where, I'd wager, many end up working, at least at some point in their careers (if, that is, one is lucky enough to earn one's living by means of the skills and content we acquire in doctoral programs).

What strikes me now about those two old syllabi is how overly ambitious they were, or, maybe I should say, dropping the passive language, how overly ambitious *I* was in designing them; when hired (which was about 18 months before defending my dissertation at the University of Toronto—my full-time job likely extended the time needed to complete the dissertation by a year or so) I was told I must use Huston Smith's *The World's Religions*, the still-in-print and lightly revised version of his Cold War-era textbook, *The Religions of Man*,[2] but I added to the list Ninian Smart and Richard Hecht's significantly subtitled primary source anthology, *Sacred Texts of the World: A Universal Anthology* as well as John Hinnells's *A Dictionary of Religions* (a book that I added to many of my textbook orders in those early years, inasmuch as I then made learning world religions vocabulary a key element of my courses—what's the difference between *śhruti* and *smriti*?). As for teaching what was then UT's other, more thematic but no less encyclopedic, introduction to the field—and in which I had an entirely free hand in setting the book order—I opted, that first year, for no less than five books, including works by Plato, Freud, and Jung, along with Bill Paden's then popular, thematic intro book *Religious Worlds* (whose chapters are on such topics as myth, ritual, gods, and purity), and John Lyden's edited anthology, *Enduring Issues in Religion* (a book of excerpts on a series of debates largely organized around the world religions model). But whether the material was divided in terms of the world's religions or arranged thematically, my goal in both courses was *to fit it all in*—for all I knew, my possible reappointment as an Instructor hung in the balance and so I seem to recall feeling that a demonstration of universal competence was directly linked to my job security as well as my sense of professional legitimacy (in both the eyes of my students, who I wasn't all that much older than, not to mention my new colleagues—scholars who, to me at least, seemed infinitely more knowledgeable, credible, and thus authoritative, than I).

Today, about twenty five years after first developing these courses, I no longer teach a world religions survey—I stopped doing that about seventeen years ago, when I became chair of a department which, for some inexplicably good reason, wasn't even offering such a course when I first arrived in 2001 (though my colleague Steven Ramey now regularly teaches it, but as a way to invite students to consider problematizing that very way of naming and grouping people)—and when I do teach the introductory course (which, as mentioned earlier, as a large enrollment lecture, with between 100 and 150 students, that I offer at least once and sometimes twice a year), I require students to purchase just one little book (though students also use a short online dialogue by Plato devoted to the problem of definition [the *Euthyphro*], available for free via a classics cite at MIT[3]). As discussed in the prior chapter, the book I use is my own (McCutcheon 2007);[4] if pressed, I'd say that it is not a textbook at all but a resource, useful in almost any class, that merely sets the table for an instructor who then needs to bring a considerable number of dishes to the meal. The book, which includes as an afterword a short but, in my opinion, important essay of Smith's on teaching (2007), arose from years of developing and teaching the course; and so, despite my efforts to continually revise the class and to ensure it incorporates new examples drawn from current events that my students might recognize (who, teaching such a course a couple years ago, could resist making reference to what was then going on first with Indiana's and then Arkansas's religious freedom legislation when discussing the political utility to naming something *as* religion?),[5] if it sometimes seems to students that I'm "teaching to the text" I'd like to think that's because the text is mimicking me, and not the other way 'round. And so, as you might guess, long ago I stopped reading lectures verbatim, as I certainly did in those early years in Knoxville, especially when, right off the bat, I was teaching a course in an area that was entirely new to me, entitled Myth, Symbol, Ritual, which my new Chair (the late Charles Reynolds) had asked me whether I could teach, in a phone call not long after I was hired for the year but prior to my departure from southern Ontario for east Tennessee. They'd had a retirement (the now late Stan

Lusby), so his popular upper-level class (popular = produced credit hours for the department and had a student following) needed an instructor. "Of course I can," I recall answering and then scrambled to begin writing out full lectures—relying on, among other sources, Brian Morris's still important book, *Anthropological Studies of Religion: An Introductory Text* (1988) and William Lessa and Evon Vogt's onetime standard (though still in print) anthology (1979). Luckily, the days of writing out four or six full lectures each week, not even being just one class ahead of students, and standing in front of them at a podium, wedded to a text, are long over.

So, when I compare what I do now to what I did then, what immediately catches my eye is that nothing I do today has a grandiose, or totalized intent, making my current classes much less ambitious than they once were. But, come to think of it, I don't think "unambitious" is the correct word, for I don't think (or at least do not wish to think) that I've become a stereotypically entitled full Professor who spends a surprising amount of time gardening; instead, I've learned to make some of those choices that Smith talked about when drawing his readers' attention to the fact that one university course, at least as taught at my own school, amounts to just 40 hours of instruction per semester (and that's not counting the days off for testing and the inevitable snow days that even we now seem to have in Alabama). For unlike that "universal" anthology of sacred texts that I once used (which included chapters on not just ten of the expected world religions but also on ancient religions, small-scale traditional religions, new religions, and, predictably, at least for anything Smart was involved in, so-called secular worldviews), over the years my focus has narrowed considerably, making my current introductory course, the one for which I wrote that book, seem incredibly *specialized*—after all, as noted in an earlier chapter, it is concerned solely with the problem of defining religion. But, again, I'd avoid that term, "specialization," for, to my way of thinking, it is actually incredibly *general*—since, whether students start out knowing it or no, by the end they may come to realize that the course is not on religion at all, though we talk about religion all the time; instead, we use the example of various attempts to identify something *as* religious, and the implications of lending or withholding that designation from some act, group, or occasion, as opportunities to examine how we, as scholars, signify and compare things—two skills that, I would argue, are applicable to any activity that we undertake as human beings. And, to my way of thinking, that's what makes it a successful core curriculum course.

Since I'm on the topic of specialization, and because I presume I'm addressing at least some readers who either are or soon will be on the job market, let me digress just a little, to reinforce a frustration that I have also addressed elsewhere—speaking, now, as a department chair who has seen his fair share of CVs and cover letters—with how poorly we train many of our graduate students for full time employment as professors whose jobs will require them to work in a department with others as colleagues. (Come to think of it, I'm probably addressing not early career people here so much as their supervisors, since it's the latter who may be able to effect some change ...) Case in point: a few years ago we searched for a position in what we termed Religion, Global Conflict, and Law. The ad's main text read as follows:

> Proficient in critical and social theory, the ideal candidate will analyze the roles played by legal and religious systems in cross-cultural conflicts (whether physical, economic, racial, ethnic, or social). While the research specialty, region, and historical area are open, they should complement without reproducing the expertise of current faculty in the department.

I've written a little about the experience of this search in the Afterword to a recent essay collection (McCutcheon 2014) so suffice it to say here that I tend to think that because we did not use any of the accepted keywords in our field—you know, words like Buddhism or Judaism or religion and politics, or religion in America or myth and ritual, etc.—our ad was probably passed over by people whose expertise might have been directly relevant. We only received around 40 applications (whereas we usually get closer to 100, or more—in fact, for a more recent search we had over 150), and we met some wonderfully gifted young scholars in the process (who, I hope, find a place and have a career in the field—as has already happened to several whom we met and with who I have remained in touch), but only a small group of applicants took seriously that we were looking not for a world religions content specialist, or someone working on so-called peacebuilding, but for someone who could conceive of their work as being focused on a problematic, one applicable to any number of other situations, concerning how a variety of disputes and formal behavioral codes intersected with whatever it is that we mean by this designator "religion." The words "critical and social theory," were, after all, the first things one read in the ad. Sure, we hoped that they would be able to study this in detail at a specific site, ideally one that—as also stated in the ad—brought something new to what was then our mid- to larger-sized B.A.-granting department that only covers so much of the world and its history (though, recalling Smith, we'll never cover it all), but that they'd also recognize that that the place where they do their work is but an instance of a wider thing that can also be seen elsewhere. For, in my experience, it is that ability that is at the heart of a departmental identity—i.e., the ability of faculty members to see themselves as not just happening to have an office next door to someone but as being in a common conversation with colleagues despite our widely divergent specialties and even if we don't always agree on the issues. While some may have the luxury of finding jobs in large departments with highly specialized faculty positions, many will instead more than likely be interviewing in places where no one works on what they do, no one knows much about what they study, and therefore it will fall to them to try to make connections with other people, to communicate the wider questions their work investigates and to suggest its possible significance for the things others already know something about. (Come to think of it, perhaps this was not a digression after all, for isn't this precisely the situation we're all in with those introductory students?) And when it's phrased in this way, when the content which you've no doubt worked so hard to master is seen as but one among many examples of things that we, as humans, cross-culturally do or produce, then I tend to think that our ad was likely the most general one out there that hiring season; for I can think of very few people who could *not* have somehow creatively demonstrated their relevance for such a position. But because we did not phrase it in terms of how graduate programs, encyclopedias, professional societies, and publishers routinely divide up and thereby signify the content that often defines our field, but instead framed our needs in terms of skills we share and teach within our department, our ad probably stumped many who read it, perhaps prompting some to see it, or dismiss it, as far too specialized (i.e., "I don't do religion and law" they might have responded, after reading it)—which is really quite lamentable, given how highly competitive the academic job market is. Thus my frustration for the specialized silos into which we're all slotted in graduate school and how, because of that, we often fail to understand that the long term well-being of a field of study, let alone that unit we call a department (which in many of us presumably hope to earn our daily bread), is directly related to the problems that we (plural pronoun intended) think worth tackling, is related to questions of method and theory, and not so much to the many different places where we do or do not each happen to tackle them. That so many early career people, understandably focused on their dissertation's suitably narrow topic (though, how is this any different from many mid-career and senior people in the field?), fail to think about the field-wide issues that their work exemplifies and are therefore unprepared to discuss how this one specialty might not only intersect with the work of their potential colleagues but also contribute to the larger life and curricular needs of a department, is a problem that many graduate programs (rather than their graduate students themselves) need to consider addressing head-on if they wish their students to continue to be competitive and successful in joining the ranks of our profession.

But, to return to the topic at hand (though, as you can guess, I don't think we've ever left it, making my digression merely a move to an analogous situation where I think the same problems are apparent), I'd like to offer a few of the interconnected choices, in no particular order (though, I hope it's evident that it is all directly related to what I've been discussing so far), that I think faculty need to consider making in order to be effective in the introductory class. As is already evident, I can't resist the temptation to elaborate, so I'll deviate somewhat from Bruce Lincoln's enviable success with the genre of bold, pithy thesis statements (Lincoln 2012; Lincoln and Grottanelli 2012).[6]

Choices

And so, with that long, but hopefully relevant set-up behind us, I'll present thirteen situations in which I think early career instructors will need to make a choice—whether a stark or modulated choice I leave to others to decide. But each choice concerns a particular classroom problem that, in my experience, the instructor of a successful lower-level undergraduate course somehow has to negotiate.

1   Will your course be about gaining command over *content* or will it be
     about the acquisition of *skills* that your students will find relevant in
     other courses, at other times? This I term *the problem of applicability.*
     For while knowing the name of the river crossed by whomever
     on such and such an occasion may come in handy in some future
     situation (e.g., should they go on to earn graduate degrees or simply
     join a trivia night team at the local bar), being able to understand
     that "similar" does not necessitate that things are "the same" might
     have surprising relevance for all of your students.

2   If your course is primarily about command over content, then
     you are more than likely deferring to others to determine what
     your students ought to know—i.e., how can a survey of Hinduism
     avoid talking about its Indus River Valley origins? For these details
     are all part of a well-known story on which you'll presumably be
     testing your students, much as others might quiz them on their
     grasp of tribal lore so as to determine the legitimacy of their
     membership. This I term *the problem of orthodoxy.* For, despite the now
     almost unheard of freedom the comes with not having a national
     credentialing organization that sets standards, compels course
     content, and assesses student performance,[7] a surprising number
     of our field's classes nonetheless conform to a very specific model,
     covering standardized and curiously self-policed content. But if,
     instead, you opt to emphasize skills in your classes, making your
     course about, for example, description and comparison, then at what
     practical sites will students give these methods a spin? This I term *the
     problem of the unorthodox e.g.*; for there are times when, because the
     example you choose is alien to the student, so much of your time will
     be spent sufficiently describing the e.g. that you have no energy or
     time left to demonstrate how it serves as an instance of some wider
     issue you're trying to bring to their attention. Courses, like academic
     papers, can sometimes get lost in the details, prompting us to forget
     of what the e.g.s are an instance, leading us to sometimes seeing the
     objects we study as so self-contained and self-authenticating that
     they exhibit nothing but their own brilliance.

3   Will your class have a thesis? Is there something at stake, of which
     you're trying to persuade your students or is the information that
     you convey each class, each unit, merely items in a list that you've
     got to get through just so that you can have the satisfaction of
     completion or, maybe, get to reuse last year's test? Or will there
     instead be an argumentative point that, day by day, steadily develops
     throughout the course, just as each paragraph of an essay has a place
     within the overall structure? If so, then what will we do with those
     absent students who later come up and ask what they missed—for
     now it's as if they were reading an article with a page or two missing

(which happens to be each conference presenters nightmare). I think here of some of the early career people I've worked with who report that they have teaching experience but who, it turns out, have never before taught (or taken?) a course where the goal was to persuade students of something and thus the difficulties such instructors have when given an opportunity to lecture in a way that moves away from a model of conveying discrete pieces of memorizable information and, instead, toward stringing together information into an argument that stretches over a semester. This I term *the problem of persuasion.*

4 To return to the topic of e.g.s, will you approach your object of study as a precious item, unlike all else in nature, whose study is a specialty unto itself, or will you invite students to see it as but one among many *arts de faire*, as Michel de Certeau phrased it, and thus something that is comparable to different, yes, but now unexpectedly similar items from the all but limitless archive of human doings? In other words, will all the things that they study, read, or examine in your class be obviously religious or, perhaps, will they find themselves reading an 1883 U.S. Supreme Court decision on whether a tomato is a fruit or a vegetable (i.e., *Nix v. Hedden* 149 U.S. 304) to help persuade them that disputes over definition and identity— no matter how ethereal they may at first seem—have practical motivations and effects. This I term *the problem of analogies.*

5 Because few undergrad students in North America will enroll in their first year's classes with any knowledge of what the academic study of religion is the vast majority of students therefore first take our courses simply to satisfy their university's core curriculum or general education requirements—however, the irony is that it is from these very students that possible majors (the life blood of departments such as my own[8]) will eventually be recruited. Such classes are therefore both service courses to other departments, thereby generating credit hour production for your own, *as well as* the place where your department reproduces itself by creating potential majors and thus graduates.[9] So will you aim the books that you select, the topics that you examine, and the tone of your lectures toward those students who will more than likely never again return to one of our classes or to the (sometimes painfully small) minority of budding specialists who may one day graduate from your department? Or is such a binary choice misleading; instead, as you plan and teach this class, will you have in mind those non-majors who, when many of them are disillusioned with whatever their high school selves, their parents, or their onetime guidance counsellors thought they ought to become, are reminded, a year maybe two later, of that interesting and unexpected material they covered in your class, and of how it made

them think about, I don't know, why they still set the table with the knife over there and the fork over here, and the cup to the top right of the plate, *even when they eat alone*—i.e., those students (perhaps like each of us, so many years ago) who stop by a professor's office to chat long after the class is over and who then enroll in a second course in your department, and maybe a third … So to whom are you speaking as you plan a course and teach it? I term this *the problem of audience*.

6   And with that audience in mind, will you see your students as conversation partners, prompting them to read the cutting edge work that so excites you now, as scholars who are yourselves immersed knee-deep in dissertation writing or first book revisions (or your second, or third, or …), or will you see in them yourself, many years ago, long before you knew what the words "dialectical," "diacritical," and "dialogical" meant or whether "phenomenological" was yet another one of those dirty F-words. This I term *the problem of imagination*: put simply, as an undergraduate teacher can you imagine yourself as 19 years old, long before knowing what you now take for granted or have you so naturalized (i.e., dehistoricized) your current state that you've forgotten the more than likely bumpy and crooked road you traversed in order to get here? As a graduate supervisor, can you do much the same—either recalling your enthusiastic self on the verge of specialization, more than likely armed with big ideas though not yet knowing how narrowing one's gaze is crucial to tackling any thesis or dissertation research (since any topic will probably quickly balloon out of control) or your failure, at that early stage of your career, to see producing a dissertation as a credentialing exercise and not a magnum opus that would change the field? The interesting thing is that I think it takes great confidence to just say something simply and to return to first principles with either undergraduate or graduate students—the pedagogical technique from which many of us benefited in our own earlier training.

7   With that last choice in mind, will you be the sort of lecturer who teaches students what you have already come to know, thereby turning classes into monologues by which you transmit information by radiating it outward from its source behind the podium, or, instead, will you start from where the students themselves currently are, moving with them—even physically among them, as you teach, being brave enough to venture out from behind the protection of the lectern—going with them step by step, toward a position by the end of the semester when they will have acquired the information that, perhaps unbeknownst to them, you knew all along. This I term *the problem of proclamation*—for there is a difference, I'd argue, between proclaiming what you know and teaching someone else how to know it as well. It's the old story of giving someone a fish versus a fishing rod.[10]

8 With yet another nod to Smith's own efforts to tease out their
   distinction (2005: 9), I suppose I should finally ask: whether you'll
   teach a *survey* or an *introduction*? For whereas the first is a broad
   overview and summary of a content domain (think here of the
   unsolicited promotional copies of the *Norton Anthology of World
   Religions* that many of us were receiving in the mail just a few years
   ago) the latter is, in its technical sense, a movement of something
   from outside in, or the entry of something foreign—think here
   of how a scientist "introduces" some species of critter into a new
   environment or how a "letter of introduction," not unlike today's
   more professionalized "letter of recommendation," once might have
   been your ticket to the best *soirées* and salons of the nineteenth
   century. For if a survey, then you must decide which mountain tops
   will you touch upon as you skip across them—and which will you will
   just completely skip altogether—in your mere 40 hours of contact
   time to teach the history of the world. But if an introduction, then
   your goal is not coverage but to devise ways to help novices acquire
   enough expertise to use the tools of our trade (an expertise that
   they may hone in subsequent classes where such skills as defining,
   describing, comparing, interpreting, and explaining are relevant).
   This I term *the problem of initiation*.

9 Given the state of higher education today—in which state
   legislatures are annually cutting budgets, in which for-profit
   corporations tell us the future lies outside of the bricks and mortar
   of the traditional university campus (perhaps in the MOOCs they
   own and hope to sell to universities, possibly replacing you[11]),
   and in which publishers, in collaboration with some enterprising
   colleagues, aim to development and deliver self-contained and
   cloud-based "courseware" that seems to require an administrator
   rather than a professor—will you build your course around any
   one of the many prefab textbooks/course readers that are now
   on the market (useful for an orthodox course based on "covering
   the material," perhaps) or will you develop resources of your own,
   such as finding and making PDF readings, in order to accomplish
   goals that are specific to you, your sense of the field, and thus your
   syllabus and class? This I term *the problem of governance*.

10 As a slight variation on the last: Given the state of higher ed today—
   in which teaching loads are getting higher (case in point: North
   Carolina's state senate debated the "Act to Improve the Quality of
   Instruction at Constituent Institutions of the University of North
   Carolina (SB 593, March 26, 2015), which would have required a
   minimum 4/4 teaching load of professors; the bill was dropped a
   month later), when class sizes are getting larger and larger,[12] when
   not only contingent but even tenure track or tenured faculty are

sometimes asked to teach a surprisingly large number of different courses each semester (i.e., each being a different "prep"), and when recurring, fulltime non-tenure track lines are being invented in some schools, confirming the impression of a two-tiered faculty where some teach and some carry out research—as I say, given these conditions, will you opt to build your class around any one of the convenient prefabricated textbooks/course readers that are now on the market (thereby saving you considerable effort conceptualizing and organizing your own course—after all, why reinvent the wheel?) or will you be able to find and develop resources of your own, that achieve a point unique to your class? This I term *the problem of time*.

11 Unless you have the luxury of being hired into the same sort of elite program that may have trained you as a doctoral student, given the number of (different) classes you may be teaching each semester, will your survey or introductory class provide students with an opportunity to write and rewrite papers in light of your comments or will you rely upon optically scanned bubbled-in score sheets for multiple choice tests? And if the latter, how can a multiple choice test assess more than just memorization (can it also address reading comprehension or analytic skills?) and will you be able to devise other inventive ways to engage and then evaluate students who find themselves one among many others in your 100-level course's lecture hall? This problem I term *the double-edged sword of engagement and assessment*.

12 Should you decide all of the above in a manner that does not adequately complement the way your department's senior gatekeepers have made *their* decisions, then how will you either identify and then rethink those choices that are negotiable or, perhaps, strategically represent to your colleagues the results of your nonnegotiable decisions, doing so in a way that, ideally, helps you to acquire a secure, long term space in which to carry out the work that you desire to do despite the (perhaps inevitable) differences of opinion that can sometimes (dare I say often or perhaps usually?) characterize life in an academic unit? (As an aside, I should say that we're an odd breed, university professors: for while likely seeing ourselves as freelance or self-employed, we work within massive institutions that, in many cases, are supported by taxpayers and which constitute but one wing of the modern nation-state— making us more like ultra-privileged versions of employees at the DMV than many of us would like to think.) This issue of negotiation and representation I simply term *the problem of politics*.

13 And, finally, will the class constitute a group of curious observers intent on studying the alien and the exotic (separated from us

whether in time or geography) or will you continually remind your students that, as human beings themselves, whatever it is that we find curious about others ought to be no less applicable to ourselves—whether we're scholars or not—thereby ensuring that the overall point of the course is to initiate a group of people who *come* to the class as already skilled users and navigators of a commonsense folk system (for instance, they are all expert enough participants within a culture to be able to decipher both Gilbert Ryle's and Clifford Geertz's "wink" without giving it too much thought; Ryle 2009; Geertz 1973) but who will hopefully *leave* as a different sort of expert, one able to make the transition to seeing their own mundane as no less interesting than, say, the things some rural Appalachian Pentecostals do with rattle snakes that seems impossible for us not to find so curious. (Come to think of it, it's no less curious that we all hurdle down interstate highways without a care in the world despite the National Safety Council's estimate of 35,200 people killed in U.S. traffic accidents in 2013 alone, no?) This I term *the problem of identification.*

Postscript

I'm sure that there are many other choices an instructor needs to make (see the following chapter for some others); but these are at least a few of the issues and decisions that I know I and others had to navigate—correction, *continue* to navigate, making these choices hardly isolated to early career scholars as I might have suggested above. And so I put them before you here—applicability, orthodoxy, e.g.s, persuasion, analogies, audience, imagination, proclamation, initiation, governance, time management, engagement, assessment, politics and identification—to invite readers, novices and experienced "full bulls" (as some once called tenured, senior faculty members) to begin thinking a little more about their situation as a teacher in a university and thus the costs and benefits to what they choose to tackle or ignore in those few hours that they have each semester with their students.

Notes

1   Thanks to my colleagues Steven Ramey and Vaia Touna for comments on an earlier draft of this paper and also to Brandon Cline and Aaron Hollander for arranging my visit to Chicago as well as Dean Margaret Mitchell for her kind invitation to come speak at the Divinity School—where an earlier version of this chapter was presented to graduate students (and then published in *Teaching Theology and Religion* with four of their solicited responses/commentaries). Because this paper was written for and delivered at Chicago's Craft of Teaching workshop (on April 6, 2015), I feel I should add here that, as it makes evident (implicitly throughout and, at times, explicitly), my classroom habits are deeply indebted to the late Jonathan Z. Smith's many

thoughtful writings on teaching. Thus, although I was never a student of his in a university classroom, I consider myself to have been a student of his in his writing and in conversations over the years; it should therefore be said that I see his pedagogical contributions rather differently from what I read in parts of Lofton (2014).

2 If memory serves, that's how references to what I soon realized was a rather troublesome book later made their way into my dissertation and, eventually, into my first book (McCutcheon 1997)—being just one example of the intimate relationship teaching and research have had in my own career.

3 See http://classics.mit.edu/Plato/euthyfro.html (accessed June 25, 2017).

4 This requires me to make an annual transparency disclosure to the university, and thus the state of Alabama, concerning what I do with those royalties (assuming students buy new copies of the book, that is). However, we have no way to determine how many students actually purchase the book let alone whose copy is used.

5 Opponents of such "conscience protection laws" argue that they are merely a way to protect what would otherwise be prosecuted as discriminatory actions by shrouding them in the protections afforded the discourse on faith and belief.

6 See the opening few minutes of Brad Stoddard's interview with Lincoln for the back story to his "Theses on Method" at www.religiousstudiesproject.com/podcast/the-critical-study-of-religion/ (accessed June 23, 2017).

7 It should be noted that our main U.S. professional society, the American Academy of Religion, has periodically produced such guidelines and standards, though they have no enforcement power. See, for example, those for K-12 teachers (find the April 2010 report at www.aarweb.org/sites/default/files/pdfs/Publications/epublications/AARK-12CurriculumGuidelines.pdf, accessed February 24, 2018), as well as its current working group devoted to developing goals for college courses and undergraduate majors on religion (both within and outside of departments of religious studies), whose first public presentation of an early draft of their recommendations took place at the 2016 annual meeting, at a session entitled Seminar on Promoting Religious Literacy College-Wide. Learn more about this current initiative at www.aarweb.org/about/religiou-literacy-guidelines-for-college-students (accessed June 26, 2017).

8 While overall credit hour production, publications, and external grants are certainly among other measures of a unit's productivity (especially relevant to deans and vice presidents for academic affairs/provosts), in my state the number of graduates (and thus majors, not minors) is the coin of the realm from the point of view of the state credentialing body, the Alabama Commission on Higher Education.

9 Aside: I was hired in 2001, as an outside chair, to help revive the University of Alabama's department since it was then graduating so few students that it had been judged "nonviable" by the state credentialing board (the above-mentioned Alabama Commission on Higher Education) and, because of that, it risked losing its major (i.e., being demoted to a service department, and thus offering 100-level core courses only, or, an even worse possibility, closed entirely); I'm happy to say that our reinvention (led also by Ted Trost, who chaired the unit for 4 of the years since then), has been quite successful. We have more than quadrupled the number of students taught annually, gone from 4.25 faculty in the Fall of 2001 to 8.5 tenure-track or tenured in the Fall of 2015 and, beginning the Fall 2017 semester, started a new M.A. program. For more details on this reinvention see McCutcheon (2015).

10 A brief word of advice: carry a mug of coffee or a water bottle as you roam the class; it's far smaller than a podium, yes, but you can still hide behind just enough, when necessary, and you can nurse a long sip to buy yourself a little time to think about

the curve you were just thrown when students inevitably ask you an unanticipated question.

11 For those unacquainted with the acronym, massively open online courses (MOOC), developed initially as a way to reach large numbers (i.e., massive) of students with free (i.e., open) online university courses; eventually, though, the idea was linked to the profit motive, whether through fees associated with private providers or tuition with universities. Today, the promise once thought to be offered by MOOCs—such as in the early to mod-2000s—has lost considerable ground when it was realized that their students' rather poor completion rates were not nearly as strong as traditional university courses. See www.newyorker.com/science/maria-konnikova/moocs-failure-solutions for a critical assessment of MOOCs (accessed July 1, 2017).

12 Among the courses we teach—if the course is thought to be attractive to larger numbers of students—every tenured and tenure-track faculty member in our department teaches one large enrollment 100-level course each semester (with up to 150 students per section), ideally but not always with TA assistance (we have only four TA lines in our department); large enrollment courses in our department were unheard of prior to 2001. Note: instructors no longer teach large enrollment courses in our department; see the next chapter for elaboration on this decision.

References

Geertz, Clifford (1973). "Thick Description: Toward an Interpretive Theory of Culture," in *The Interpretation of Cultures: Selected Essays*, 3–30. New York: Basic Books.

Hinnells, John (1984). *A Dictionary of Religions*, 1st ed. New York: Viking Penguin.

Lessa, William and Evon Vogt (eds.) (1979). *Reader in Comparative Religion: An Anthropological Approach*. New York: HarperCollins.

Lincoln, Bruce (2012). "Theses on Method," in his *Gods and Demons, Priests and Scholars: Critical Explorations in the History of Religions*, 1–4. Chicago, IL: University of Chicago Press.

Lincoln, Bruce and Critiano Grottanelli (2012). "Theses on Comparison," in Bruce Lincoln, *Gods and Demons, Priests and Scholars: Critical Explorations in the History of Religions*, 121–130. Chicago, IL: University of Chicago Press.

Lofton, Kathryn (2014). "Review essay on Jonathan Z. Smith, *On Teaching Religion.*" *Journal of the American Academy of Religion* 82/2: 531–542. https://doi.org/10.1093/jaarel/lfu027

Lyden, John (1994). *Enduring Issues in Religion*. San Diego, CA: Greenhaven Press.

McCutcheon, Russell T. (1997). *Manufacturing Religion: The Discourse on Sui Generis Religion and the Politics of Nostalgia*. New York: Oxford University Press.

—— (2007). *Studying Religion: An Introduction*. New York: Routledge.

—— (2014). *A Modest Proposal on Method: Essaying the Study of Religion*. Leiden: Brill.

—— (2015). "Afterword: The Reinvention of the Study of Religion at Alabama," in Steven Ramey (ed.), *Writing Religion: The Case for the Critical Study of Religion*, 208–222. Tuscaloosa, AL: University of Alabama Press.

Morris, Brian (1988) [1987]. *Anthropological Studies of Religion: An Introductory Text*. Cambridge: Cambridge University Press.

Paden, William E. (1994) [1988]. *Religious Worlds: The Comparative Study of Religion*. Boston, MA: Beacon Press.

Ryle, Gilbert (2009) [1968]. "The Thinking of Thoughts: What is le Penseur Doing?" in *Collected Papers, 1929-1968*, vol. 2, ch. 37. London: Routledge.

Smart, Ninian and Richard Hecht (eds.). (1982). *Sacred Texts of the World: A Universal Anthology*. New York: Crossroad. https://doi.org/10.1007/978-1-349-05927-0

Smith, Huston. 1991 [1958] *The World's Religions* [revised and updated edition of *The Religions of Man*]. New York: HarperSanFrancisco.

Smith, Jonathan Z. (1991). "The Introductory Course: Less is Better," in Mark Juergesmeyer (ed.), *Teaching the Introductory Course in Religious Studies: A Sourcebook*, 185–192. Atlanta, GA: Scholars Press.

—— (2005). "Religion in the Liberal Arts: Reflections on Teaching," in the Chicago Forum on Pedagogy and the Study of Religion, *The Place of Religious Studies in the Liberal Arts*, 6–14. Chicago, IL: Martin Marty Center at the University of Chicago.

—— (2007). "The Necessary Lie: Duplicity in the Disciplines," in Russell T. McCutcheon, *Studying Religion: An Introduction*, 73–80. New York: Routledge.

—— (2013). *On Teaching Religion: Essays by Jonathan Z. Smith*, ed. Christopher Lehrich. New York: Oxford University Press.

Chapter 7

There Are Advantages to Knowing Your Limits: On Making a Difference for Non-Tenure Track Colleagues[1]

Late one night, in episode 5 of the first season of the television reboot of *Fargo*—a series based on the plot as well as the aesthetic of the Coen brothers' quirky 1996 crime drama—a man who lives directly across the alley from the Duluth Police Deputy Gus Grimly (played by Colin Hanks) sees Gus through their windows late one night and ends up coming over to his apartment, where they commiserate about family and work. After Gus tells him, in vague detail, about a crime he's having trouble solving, and while both are drinking a warm glass of milk, in that darkened kitchen, the neighbor recounts a parable about a rich man who, despite repeatedly trying to make the world a better place (such as by first donating all of his money and then a kidney), nonetheless continues to be disillusioned by people's misery. When his doctor declines to allow him to be a liver, a heart, and a cornea donor—since this would kill him—the man goes home, stoically draws a warm bath, and commits suicide in the tub, with the words "Organ donor" written above him on the wall.

In reply to the story, Gus asks:

> And does it work? Does it stop the suffering?

To which his neighbor dryly responds:

> You live in the world. What do you think?

Adding:

> Only a fool thinks he can solve the world's problems.

To which Gus comments:

> But you've got to try, don't you?

This seems to be an apt story to open a chapter on the current labor conditions in U.S. higher ed—notably, the increasing reliance on instructors who, though in many cases well qualified, are not part of the tenure-track system—whether they be full-time employees (who are on some sort of limited term contract), part-time employees (teaching one or two courses, but possibly doing this at more than one institution each semester), or graduate students who are either teaching (sometimes multiple) courses of their own or acting as teaching assistants in large enrollment classes. Now, in using just this scene as the opening, one is forced to ask whether, when thinking about the labor problems facing universities today, one ought to identify with idealistic Gus or with what some might see as his far more realistic neighbor. But the invitation to choose between the two is part of the problem, I think, for taking both positions seriously strikes me as the most sensible way to operate within our institutions. For, sticking with the tone of the neighbor's advice, while only fools would think that a single actor's agency, whomever that actor may be, could have any effect on, say, altering a university administration's priorities, let alone changing the funding decisions made by the federal government or state legislatures (both of which establish the context in which those administrators make their decisions) and thereby solving the problem, it would be equally foolhardy, I'd maintain, to think that a lone social actor, let alone one in the middle management position of being a department chair, is powerless to effect some sort of change—the one who is positioned to at least "give it a try," in Gus's words. So, while agreeing with his neighbor's skeptical conclusion, we also ought to side with Gus—if, that is, what we're trying to do is not to change the course of U.S. higher ed but, instead, to creatively and strategically work within the structures as we find them, in our own locale, to effect whatever change we're capable of accomplishing to better the situation of the people with whom we work and, in the process, enhance the conditions in which all of our students pursue their studies. Whether we band together and try to effect change on the national level is, of course, another choice that we may make, but it seems to us a long term project that does not preclude having strategic and far more immediate effect locally.

Think globally, act locally, as the old saying goes.

Yet too often it seems as if tenure-track or perhaps especially tenured faculty members—not unlike social actors in any other setting—side with Gus's neighbor and act—or, better put, fail to act—as if they are paralyzed by the larger structural conditions in their institutions, blaming "the administration" and thereby failing to see that there are likely always a variety of situations where they (individually or collectively and thus as a department) can employ strategies to moderate and even enhance the work conditions of the non-tenure track colleagues with whom they work and from whose labor their departments (which is code for saying they themselves) benefit (something too infrequently recognized, I'd argue—have you ever added up the annual credit hour production, in your own unit, that results from the work of those not in the tenure stream?).[2] Now, this strategic and structural shortsightedness is an understandable outcome of the institution that has produced us as credentialed experts, I'd argue, inasmuch as the increasing specialization required of our studies often seems to breed scholars who perceive themselves as working in isolated silos and who therefore have little in common with others in their department and, thus (as noted elsewhere in this collection) difficulty being colleagues—by that I mean that while many faculty members are deeply concerned with their own research and teaching they often have difficulty thinking beyond those two domains to entertain both the ways that their work necessarily intersects with those around them and the fact that the units in which they do their work—from departments to college and even universities as a whole—have needs and priorities of their own. In fact, having seen this first hand on a number of occasions, I sometimes have difficulty blaming the current tendency among senior administrations and board of governors/trustees to go looking outside of academia for administrators since so few faculty seem interested (or should I say "seem capable"?) not just of talking simply about their research specialty to non-specialists (something sometimes painfully apparent in job application cover letters and interviews), but also of thinking widely and tactically about where an institution—be it a department, a college, or even the university as a whole—ought to be going and how to get it there. Simply put, what I think we need is not just more social theorists in the study of religion, but, more importantly, more social theorists capable of theorizing our own social conditions in academia—colleagues who recognize the limitations entailed by (f)actors well beyond our own pay grade but who nonetheless also go looking for the lacunae and contradictions (let's just call them opportunities) inherent in any social structure—and who then get to work at that specific site to make changes that, although hardly capable of reinventing the institution or solving its problems, nonetheless have effect and thus impact in people's lives.

So, while knowing that we cannot each singlehandedly ensure that our universities obtain sufficient state funding or private donor support to, say, double the size of the tenure-track faculty, there's nothing stopping us from more carefully and purposefully going down the road of employing part-time or full-time temporary instructors. For example, as noted earlier, when I began at the University of Alabama, in August of 2001, my task was to help revive a department that had long failed to graduate a sufficient number of majors and which therefore faced the very real possibility of losing the major, being demoted to a service department, or perhaps closing altogether. This means that the faculty (which was less half the size then that it is now), clearly understood what was at stake for them personally if our experiment failed. They were therefore cognizant of the need for speedy but successful and long lasting collective action—since their own jobs hung in the balance (Did I mention that I was the only one with tenure at the time? My colleagues' situation was therefore rather precarious, though I assume, had the department been closed, the faculty [and, ideally, staff as well] would have been moved to other units on campus—suggesting that closing the department would have saved some space but not much money.) Now, although their situation made the inevitable sand on which any social group is built profoundly apparent to them (i.e., their program was judged to be non-viable, according to the state credentialing board, and they were therefore poised to lose the major), I would suggest that the members of every department—no matter how successful or well entrenched it appears—would be wise to keep in mind that their continued existence is never a forgone conclusion and that, as a little dose of social theory tells us, collective life is always premised on persuading members continually to reinvest energy into the unit (be it a family, a department, or a nation-state), a reinvestment that, if done just sufficiently, leads merely to what we call the status quo (suggesting that new initiatives require far more investment than one might think).

You may have noticed that I've so far not specifically mentioned anything about non-tenure track labor—though I'm happy to, as part of the discussion, name a few strategies that, as chair, one can use to create as favorable work conditions for these colleagues as we think we can manage, given the (limited) agency one has in this administrative role—but as I've said, I've not talked specifically about non-tenure track labor because it seems to me that *too often we focus on this topic to the exclusion of the larger context in which such faculty work*; for the only way to address this issue, doing so within the agency that is the department's chair's or faculty members, is to ensure that it is seen by all members of the department as a department-wide issue. After all, it is the department as a whole (which includes the people to whom the university has made a long term commitment [aka the job security that comes with tenure and the hope for tenure]) that benefits from the creativity and labor of its non-tenure-track members. So while I could focus on such things as whether contingent faculty have offices and computers at their disposal, asking whether they have phones, routine access to a copier, or whether they appear on the department website and have library privileges, asking if they are part of the department's governance structure, mentored in their work, welcomed at faculty meetings (because they too have a stake in the department, no?) and...—or, better yet, while we could strategize on ways to obtain such things as office space, computers, copiers, phones, library privileges, etc.—I would argue that none of those strategies will be successful (or, perhaps, possible) if the rest of the faculty fail to understand their own investment in the conditions of this part of departmental life. So, I think it is worth considering whether the department's tenured and tenure-track faculty accurately understands the surprisingly thin line of situational happenstance (aka luck) that most often separates themselves from those who sometimes work in their midst for rather less salary and with very little (if any) job security. For, at least in our experience, only when everyone feels an investment themselves and thereby an affinity for their colleagues, will the entire faculty be united in equitably sharing the many different tasks that constitute the work of making a department exist from day to day, and doing so by strategically identifying those factors that are within their power to alter and stepping up to invest the energy needed to change them in ways that support the careers of all those with whom they work.

So although this may sound counterintuitive, I think that the only way we can try to make a difference by addressing—and you'll notice that, somewhat like Gus's neighbor, I am purposefully less ambitious than saying "solving"—the problem of contingent faculty members is to work toward ensuring that no one sees it merely as a problem of the contingent faculty themselves.

As an example of what I mean—i.e., of using what agency one has to address issues of relevance to contingent faculty but in a manner that doesn't ghettoize either them or the issue—consider the contents of the following 2012 memo of agreement that the faculty at the University of Alabama developed and which still animates much of our decision-making when it comes to such topics as teaching loads and the assignment of duties.

The occasion for generating this document, as described below, was the realization of just how many students were being taught by non-tenure track/ non-tenured faculty in the years leading up to the memo—a realization that members of the department found rather shocking, to be frank. After setting the stage by describing the situation in which its faculty saw themselves, the document—which received much discussion at the time and, then, was met with unanimous agreement—outlined a series of practical strategies that, importantly for the topic at hand, ensured that non-tenure track faculty within the department are seen as integral members of the unit, making a specific contribution, and are not seen as, to be frank, cheap labor that merely produces credit hours to subsidize the rest of the faculty. For while not controlling such things as their required teaching load, the department was able to identify a critical contribution such instructors could make to the future toward which the department was moving while at the same time establishing conditions to prevent them from teaching multiple preps, working every day of the week, and working in ever-increasing large enrollment class sizes.

The document (appearing here pretty much as it was written and distributed to the faculty back in 2012)[3] reads as follows:

Premises

1. While REL's overall undergraduate enrollment is steadily climbing, the number of REL majors (single and double) has decreased in the past 4 years (it is approx. 30 now). The goal 4 years ago of doubling majors from 48 to 100 (i.e., the premise of the Tracks proposal) is now well out of sight, and just reaching 50 would be desirable.

2. Such growth in majors is desirable because the University has doubled its enrollment since 2001, yet, when comparing 2001 to 2012, our number of majors is flat (2001 = 29). As you recall, 2001's numbers were seen by ACHE [Alabama Commission on Higher Education] and the University as sufficient cause to question the viability of our major, risking losing it and either being turned into a service Department or closed outright.

3. This stagnant level of majors has direct implications for the number of graduates (always with an eye toward ACHE's 7.5 graduates per year, judged on a rolling 3 year average, in order to remain viable) as well as for our place within the College (i.e., access to new resources, the College's continued support for our initiatives, etc.).

4. At present, a large number of our students are taught by non-tenure-track/ tenured Instructors, either in classrooms or online. That is, in 2011–12, all tenure-track/tenured faculty together taught a total of 486 students while the FTTI [full-time teaching instructor] alone taught 276 students and online Instructors together taught 221 students. Thus, more than 50% of our students are taught by non-tenure-track/tenured faculty and 29% of our students do not interact in a face-to-face venue with a full-time faculty member. These numbers directly undermine how we portray ourselves to students and the administration (i.e., a small Department with a rigorous but personal touch).

5. Online courses are not a desirable setting to recruit majors for a variety of reasons (i.e., many such students already have majors and are simply looking for 3 credit hours, Distance Learning [DL] students cannot even major in REL since the degree is not offered online, etc.). This suggests that we have over-estimated the significance of online enrollments.

6. For a variety of reasons, non-tenured track Instructors should not bear the responsibility of teaching the largest number of students in the Department.

7. The Department's effort to provide its Professors each with their most desirable teaching schedules has meant that the Department is largely absent from the MWF schedule, thereby lessening our attraction for/exposure to students.

8. The 2/2 teaching load is valuable to all REL faculty and we ought to maintain this equitable load for all tenure-track/tenured professors.

9. The Instructor's mandatory 4/4 teaching load [determined by the university] ought to be off-set, as much as possible, with few course preps, smaller class sizes when possible, etc., to make this a more beneficial professionalizing experience.

Proposal[4]

If we are to remain viable and relevant within the College of Arts & Sciences, and perhaps grow the number of tenure-track colleagues within our Department (i.e., compete successfully for resources), REL needs to formalize and then enact conversations that its faculty have been having recently concerning changes to address each item above. We need to agree on this very soon and then operationalize this in a manner that ensures that our 8 Year Review committee [part of a regular, internal review process] understands this to be a part of a long term project that we have been working on.

The following proposal follows inter-related steps that were first outlined in our recent faculty meeting:

1. In order to maintain the 2/2 teaching load for tenure-track/tenured faculty, under routine circumstances they will all teach one lower-level and one upper-level course per semester.
Rationale: All experienced faculty will address both the needs of recruitment to the major (lower-level) and degree requirements of the majors (upper-level), offering a sufficient number of upper-level courses each semester so as not to have courses compete against each other for enrollments.
Action Plan: Implement this in the Fall 2013 semester.

2. In order to avoid offering one lower-level course too often, and thereby exhausting student demand for it, all tenure-track/tenured faculty will develop a new lower-level course that, along with their current lower-level course, will be offered every second semester.
Rationale: A new lower-level that is provocative, engaging, timely, etc., will be a gateway course for each faculty member and their current 100-level course can then be seen as the more in-depth introduction to their field/the Department. Ideally, the second/"follow-up" lower-level course can be renumbered as a 200 level (though these two courses as not an actual/formal sequence), to provide students with an impression of progress through a curriculum, perhaps helping one to make the argument later that they have already begun to complete the major.
Action Plan: All REL faculty members will begin developing new lower-level courses

and a Core Curriculum [i.e., General Education] designation will be applied for in all cases, but receiving this designation is not necessary for offering the course.

3. REL should no longer classify/think of its courses as large or small enrollment; instead, we should exclusively classify them as lower or upper-level, knowing that all lower-level courses will be offered in as large a venue as the Department believes the class will enroll.

Rationale: This will shift enrollment from the Instructor to the tenure-track/tenured faculty, thereby maintaining our high overall enrollments, and place these experienced faculty in front of an increasing number of new students as a form of recruiting to the major.

Action Plan: Implement this in the Fall 2013 semester.

4. All faculty members will agree to teach on both the MWF and TR schedules.

Rationale: REL will increase its attractiveness and exposure to students by offering more courses at a variety of times, thereby limiting any impression of course conflict while scheduling most faculty only on TR.

Action Plan: Implement this in the Fall 2013 semester. Devise a plan to (i) regularly rotate this schedule among all faculty and (ii) make allowances for those teaching on MWF so that their upper-level course is offered either on the MW 75 minute schedule or provide them with priority for the M or W late afternoon 3 hour seminar times. Likely, no MWF class can meet later then 1-1:50 pm due to Friday attendance issues among students.

5. Online courses will no longer be offered that compete with the topics of lecture courses, i.e., no-online REL 100 will be offered if it is also offered in a live lecture.

Rationale: In an effort to recruit majors the Department will not create conditions to enable a student to avoid meeting its experienced faculty face-to-face

Action Plan: This has already been implemented.

6. Online courses will (i) be limited to Fall 2 and Spring 2 semesters,[5] (ii) focus exclusively on those courses not regularly taught in live lecture, and (iii) if possible, when offering the online course outside of Fall 2 and Spring 2, focus exclusively on serving the needs of DL (Distance Learning) enrollees.

Rationale: Online courses should be seen as mainly assisting the University to fulfill its enrollment mission but not be seen as undermining the Department's ability to recruit majors through face-to-face contact with our experienced faculty.

Action Plan: Implement this in the Fall 2013 semester.

7. The Tracks Proposal,[6] which we are told is currently being considered by the Office of Academic Affairs, should now be conceived as but one part of this overall proposal—the part specifically aimed at (i) upper-level courses that serve the degree requirements of the major and which (ii) will increase the likelihood of attracting second majors.

Rationale: We have far fewer second majors than we once did—this is encouraging, since we have far more single majors, but it means we are also not capitalizing on the sort of interest that once defined the majority of our majors—i.e., successfully portraying REL as a complementary degree track.

Action Plan: Implement the Tracks Proposal as soon as it is approved but do not await its approval in order to move on the other parts of this proposal; all new lower-level course proposals should anticipate which track requirements they will fulfill (with each course fulfilling a max. of two tracks).

8. If REL continues to be given an FTTI (Full Time Temporary Instructor) position each year, this person will, under routine circumstances, teach 4/4 and focus mainly on lower-enrollment Honors courses, with limited enrollments per section (possibly also upper-level Core Writing courses) with one upper-level course per semester in his/her specialty as it supports our curriculum/needs.
Rationale: The FTTI currently generates a disproportionate number of credit hours and, with this change, will thereby experience more professional development in his/her role, while also contributing to much-needed part of our service to the University.
Action Plan: Implement this in the Fall 2013 semester, if we once again have the FTTI position.

9. The third part of the proposal (Part 1: Lower-Level; Part 2: Upper-Level/Tracks) will be to develop a Thesis Option.
Rationale: This will further set apart our Department as encouraging independent research among our students and will also support the impression of implementing this overall plan in stages.
Action Plan: Implement this in the Fall 2014 semester.[7]

10. Interim and Summer I and II, though providing a valued opportunity for extra income for the faculty member who opts to teach then, cannot focus on offering courses that satisfy demand for classes that are otherwise taught in the regular semester.
Rationale: We must rethink how we use summer school since offering REL 100 too often in that venue undermines our ability to attract students to this course in the Fall or Spring. Because salary for these sessions is additional to our regular salaries, the courses taught there should equally be additional to those regularly taught, until such a time as demand is sufficiently large for these courses in Fall and Spring.
Action Plan: Implement in Interim/Summer 2013.

It is fair to say that, looking back from the summer of 2017, this strategy has worked—a strategy whose success was premised on the faculty all looking over data on credit hour production and thereby recognizing that they had shared values and a shared investment in the future of the department that, to whatever extent, were being undermined by shifting the burden of credit hour production to online instructors and non-tenure track faculty. This change ensured not only that new course development became a priority (which continues to this day)[8] but that (i) all tenured/tenure-track faculty each began teaching one lower-level, large enrollment core course each semester along with one upper-level seminar as well and it (ii) freed non-tenure track Instructors (the department usually has at least one such full-time Instructor along with up to three part-time instructors grading at least one of its online courses) to focus on core honors courses (this emphasis on offering three honors sections of our introductory courses per semester has proved to be an important recruiting sites for REL majors while also helping the College of Arts & Sciences to serve the needs of the Honors College). The effect of this new policy was apparent by the end of the first year in which it was implemented; for a total of 395 students were taught in 2012/13 by tenured/tenure track faculty while 665 were taught by tenured/tenure-track faculty in 2013/14 (a 68% increase). This means that while the total number of seats offered by REL in 2012/13 and 2013/14 was nearly the same, a significant shift took place in who taught whom. And that is a shift that continues (e.g., in 2014/15 460 students out of 1368 were taught by non-tenure track faculty, meaning that 908 students [or 66% of all students] were taught by tenure-track or tenured faculty members [497 of whom were taught by the senior, tenured faculty]); the full-time Instructor is now seen as a specialist teaching three honors intro courses per semester, which are capped at 25 students each, and, if at all possible, which are all scheduled on the same days/schedule, leading to three classes being but one prep. A fourth class in the person's specialty (or a team-taught religion and popular culture/film course in which they take the lead in organizing the class) rounds out his or her teaching duties. And, because full-time Instructors at the University of Alabama are now understood to be teaching 5/5 unless they are carry out departmental service (in which case they remain at 4/4), the department has devised a small number of focused, service opportunities (from which it benefits, to be sure) which it sees as manageable and thus fitting for Instructors to tackle—so as to ensure that their teaching obligations remain at no more than four courses per semester. As for online courses, 250 students were taught by means of that medium in 2014/15, constituting just 18% of all students taught by the department (approximately 20% of whom were distance learning [DL] students). None of the courses offered online competed with a lecture courses.

The moral of the story?

Well, as already noted, a department cannot set teaching loads for Instructors (i.e., we have no choice to recognize where we are in the hierarchy) but it can decide what courses they teach, how much to invest in the online environment, and how best to use the talents of the non-tenure track people it hires—to serve as important work experience for them (as well as possible sources of additional income) and to benefit the department's own overall goals. But, as argued earlier, doing this must be seen as but one aspect of a larger and coherent plan, which involves the entire department, rather than ghettoizing the Instructor(s) as if they work in some sort of ancillary unit set apart from the real department. Too often I've seen departments organized in just that fashion—departments which, on first glance, seem to be two separate units, in which students might graduate with a B.A. without ever taking a class with a tenure-track or tenured faculty member, inasmuch as these faculty members, based on subsidies provided by contingent faculty members, have the luxury of only teaching electives or specialized topics close to their own research interests. (At the graduate level I think of units whose faculty rarely teach an undergraduate student inasmuch as their doctoral students engage in the lion's share of that teaching, thereby subsidizing much of the department's credit hour production.)

It must be said, of course, that this one department is not singled out as having solved some large institutional problem. Instead, the above proposal is offered as a specific example of how the values of a department concerning the work of contingent faculty can be woven into larger goals of the entire unit, ensuring that all faculty members not only share in the vision that animates the department and the direction in which it moves, but equally share in the work needed to take it there (regardless their rank or the nature of their appointment). And so while every oar is obviously not the same—someone needs to organize the speakers series and someone else must be the advisor while yet another will monitor the social media or the student association—and while the faculty have little power in determining many of the constraints in which they carry out their work, they do have more control than might at first be imagined when confronting the many issues in higher ed that now loom over us—for a full-time instructor who might have taught four different large enrollment courses ends up, instead, teaching three sections of the same class on MWF and, perhaps, an evening seminar once a week in their specialty area. And so if everyone can perceive themselves as rowing together, while knowing that each contributes in a different but nonetheless much needed way (i.e., your work as advisor frees me to tackle something else that needs doing), it seems to me that departments can more collegially and productively approach such things as the labor needed to reproduce the unit from day to day—and I hope that it is clear by now that this includes, but is hardly limited to, making a difference in the lives of their non-tenure track colleagues. In this way, I think, one can exhibit both modesty (by knowing that, in every institution, there are things beyond our control) while also employing a strategic sense that allows you—recalling Gus's response—to give it a try.

Notes

1   A shorter version of this chapter was presented at the 2015 annual meeting of the American Academy of Religion, at a panel entitled "Creative Responses to Contingency," sponsored by the AAR's Contingent Faculty Task force, and was also published online as one of four pieces on "the contingent campus" at www.politicaltheology.com/blog/there-are-advantages-to-knowing-your-limits-in-making-a-difference-for-non-tenu re-track-colleagues-russell-mccutcheon (accessed June 29, 2017). My thanks go to Kelly Baker for her kind invitation to be part of this panel (and included among the pieces eventually posted at the Political Theology blog) and also for her leadership in helping the AAR to begin talking more explicitly about issues related to non-tenure track faculty. Of her own many pieces on this topic, see www.politicaltheology.com/blog/the-contingent-campus-adjunctification-and-the-growth-of-the-academic-precar iat-kelly-j-baker (accessed June 29, 2017). Aside: of note is that in 2017 the AAR voted to add a contingent faculty representative to its permanent board—the first of which is Kerry Danner, currently a lecturer with the School of Continuing Studies at Georgetown University.

2   Much earlier in my career, while an Instructor, myself and the other full-time instructor once added up the number of students we collectively taught and it was over half of what the 10 person department taught in any given semester. We knew ourselves to be lucky to have jobs, of course, but it was a sobering fact that we were not sure our colleagues recognized.

3   Some local details have been removed and some brief explanatory asides have been added to assist readers outside the department.

4   My hope is that readers understand that there are great freedoms and flexibility in our department in terms of what a faculty member teaches each semester, despite this document lending the impression of a rigid framework in which we do our work. That having been said, the structure in which we exercise our freedoms is certainly made apparent to all faculty members when each coming semester's courses are determined (i.e., faculty are queried each semester, when it comes time to set the next semester's schedule, for their requested courses and days/times); for certain areas must be covered (e.g., to make good on the tracks system that guides the B.A. curriculum) and certain types of courses must be offered regularly (e.g., honors sections, core writing and humanities sections, along with upper-level seminars and, as of the Fall 2017 semester, M.A. foundations courses). In the case of some departments I have the impression that while utter rigidity may govern the teaching opportunities and topics of contingent, or even tenure-track, faculty, utter freedom can characterize the teaching of some senior faculty—hardly the sort of balance on which a department's success is premised, in my experience.

5   The University of Alabama's Fall 2 and Spring 2 are shortened semesters that run each fall and spring, beginning several weeks after the fall and spring semesters start, and which rely on online courses. They are seen as giving an additional opportunity for students to enroll in courses even after realizing they needed to drop a fall or spring course.

6   The department's undergraduate curriculum had for some years—as in the case of many other departments—been organized around such things as Western or Eastern religions, etc. While making some revisions in that format, it was not until this time that a complete revision in its structure was developed by Profs. Merinda Simmons and Steven Ramey in which courses were arranged (and developed) around the previously mentioned cross-cultural, comparative tracks: Communication, Context, and Contest (each of which comprises an area in which students must specialize). The hope was that such a revised curriculum—which also allowed students, with the undergraduate director's permission, to transfer in a small number of courses, taken in other departments (where courses relevant to REL are regularly offered), to count toward their REL major—would encourage double majors to declare their interest in the study of religion, inasmuch as it complements and enhances work they are already doing toward their first major.

7   As it turned out, this thesis option was not developed until the Fall of 2015, and was first implemented in the Fall of 2016—during the same time as the department prepared its ultimately successful proposal to begin a new Master's degree. The BA thesis option, as designed by our faculty, requires students, with the permission of their advisor, to (i) designate one regular upper-level course as their honors seminar and to then (ii) enroll in 3 credit hours of honors thesis the following semester (ideally the seminar explores a topic related to their thesis interest). The thesis that results is intended to be an original research paper suitable for submission to an undergraduate journal for consideration. The final component of this honors track is that, in place of defending it before faculty, (iii) students present their findings publicly, and field questions, at our annual research symposium each spring semester.

8   Newly hired faculty are not asked to develop a new 100-level core course, let alone upper-level seminars, until their second or third year in the department, however, since the work of planning a new course takes a back seat to regularly teaching a small number of current courses (or using a current variable topics course number) that we hope will fill and thereby help to establish a student following for the new faculty member.

Chapter 8

Perhaps (Not) Love[1]

In 1981 Plácido Domingo released a duet with the late John Denver entitled "Perhaps Love." Written by Denver, it was composed during his separation from his first wife, Annie—also the inspiration for 1974's "Annie's Song," in which she is said to have filled up his senses, like, among other things, the mountains in springtime and a walk in the rain.[2] But by the early 1980s, with a divorce on the horizon, Denver's writing is far more modest, for the duet isn't quite sure what love is:

> Oh, love to some is like a cloud
> To some as strong as steel
> For some a way of living
> For some a way to feel
> And some say love is holding on
> And some say letting go
> And some say love is everything
> And some say they don't know

Here, in a nutshell—or, better put, in a pop lyric—we find the problem with this year's presidential theme. For this word love is a malleable, local term that, despite being used by a wide variety of people to talk about their own daily lives, *has no analytic utility whatsoever*. For if it can be defined in such a wide variety of possibly contradictory ways—does it mean holding on or letting go?—then it proves of no use to the scholar who is trying to offer empirically applicable generalizations about cross-cultural human behavior (presumably what we see ourselves to be doing, inasmuch as we have attended this conference).

So, as I see it, the problem with finding this category used as it is this year, by our field's largest professional association,[3] is the all too common failure to understand the difference between, on the one hand, *descriptions* of how some people happen to talk about their lives and, on the other, the requirement for scholars to develop a theoretically driven, specialized vocabulary capable of making those claims curious by *redescribing* them. In other words, we are not here to adopt just one group's way of talking about the world but, instead, *to study that very talk itself, alongside all the other ways that people talk and act and organize*. Yet our Academy often fails to entertain this difference, because, I would argue, doing so undermines its ambitions; for limiting ourselves simply to *studying* those who talk about the possible civic value of this thing they call love,[4] as opposed to taking love as a given and then debating its merits "as a public or political force," would undercut the common assumption that the work of a scholar of religion is omnirelevant; for we seem not only equipped to diagnose and cure what ails the city but, as exemplified by a recent theme, we even have a "role specific duty" to help solve climate change.[5]

Now, I think we come by this failure honestly—a failure in knowing our limits— for scholars are themselves human beings, of course, and thus often tempted to elevate their own commonsense view of the world into a self-evident human universal. I think here of the tourist's mistake of eagerly seeking out local words for what they themselves already know—"What's your word for 'avocado'?" The mistake is in failing to entertain that not everyone might arrange and signify the world in the same manner. Do you know the story of the Boston entrepreneur Frederic Tudor, and his early exports of that New England natural resource—ice— to Martinique? A shipload of it first arrived, in remarkably good shape, in February of 1806, but the Caribbean locals had no interest whatsoever in frozen water so most of it simply melted at the dock (Johnson 2014: 49ff.). As scholars of religion, I find that we often make this same error, since many of us presume that we're studying an eternally enduring and deeply significant element of the human. Sure, not everyone calls it religion—so some of us now allow that the word itself can be historicized, but we then go to the archives, or to our field notes, looking for a better word to name that mysteriously universal "it" that we somehow know to be present despite our nomenclature not quite putting it into words. So why wouldn't we claim to have valuable insights to help solve everything from global warming to social woes? For our relevance knows no bounds—case in point: scholars of religion now even claim expertise to study those who insist that they don't even have a religion.

So yes, I love my dog—Who wouldn't? Have you seen her on Instagram? But I also love my wife and I even love tortilla soup. But which of those idiosyncratic uses of this term will stand as a value in service of the city? Based on what (or should I say, whose?) normative criteria will we make that call? Not long ago I saw a montage of, at the time of writing this, President-elect Donald Trump's campaign speeches, where he proclaimed his love not only for this country but also for the old days, his company, building buildings, that sign, NASCAR, people who faint, his protestors, the military, China, the Hispanics, the Saudis, Israel, the evangelicals, the Mormons, and the poorly educated, to name but a few.[6] Now, do we, as scholars, embrace his (and our) incredibly nebulous category, love, and use it to make the city great again, or do we dismiss his claims as not quite a proper use of the term? For, thinking back to those opening lyrics, some might read his list as a politician's insincere expressions, while yet others might hear them and cheer "Lock her up."[7]

What I hope is becoming evident is that just because many of us use this term as we go about signifying our own worlds, it does not follow that it necessarily has utility to us as scholars who study *how* people signify their worlds. That some in this room (or roughly one in two, nationally—I admit, though, that I'm not confident that such a diversity of political opinion exists at the AAR[8]) likely have little difficulty understanding Trump's claims as mere rhetorical devices, useful in swaying a crowd, suggests to me that we are not incapable of taking the step toward seeing *all such uses* of this ill-defined sentiment, love, as being engaged in the same practice, though, to be sure, for a wide variety of effects—a step that we might take if we are prepared to hear our familiar uses as being just as curious as those that strike us as alien.

But that's a step that we find difficult to take; for when *others* project their local as if it is eternally relevant, we easily identify their ethnocentrism—i.e., when we look back and see the Victorians doing it we offer harsh rebukes for how they condescended to others by universalizing their own particular. However, that many of us fail to recognize similar problems when proposing the idea of love as having academic utility suggests to me a failure of the very critical thinking that we in the humanities often say that we teach to our students. So I want to be clear: it's not, as some have complained, that this year's theme carries with it an undisclosed Christian bias (one that might be corrected by bringing others to the table); rather, it's proposal is evidence of a failure to understand that, unlike the familiarity of campaign slogans, scholarship requires us to talk about the world in counter-intuitive ways. Sure, it's more than likely that most, if not all, of us here today, at some point or other, have talked about being *cozy*, but that does not mean that we ought to elevate this term to the status of a cross-culturally useful heuristic device so as to, let's say, study how coziness can somehow save the city. That some seem unable to make the same argument, draw the same limits, when it comes to that crazy little thing called love—not to mention the no less local but equally universalized category religion—is therefore the interesting thing, to me. For some familiar concepts seem to be too close to us and thus too important for us to see them as being local and therefore important *to us, for our purposes*. As I said to a colleague not long ago, this is all pretty good fodder for the cognitive scientists among us, inasmuch as it seems that we can't help but see the familiar everywhere that we look, much like those faces they say we're all cognitively compelled to see in the clouds.

Although I'm no cognitivist, I also happen to be interested in this topic: *why* so many people claim to see something they call religion wherever they look. I've argued that the subtle yet important shift from studying religion to studying the discourse *on* religion would help to address this problem by reinventing the field as a cross-cultural study of signification systems. At the University of Alabama we're trying to do just that and, despite the challenges that come with working in any competitive institutional setting, we've had some successes. But when our largest professional association proposes that our collective scholarly focus should be on how love can transform the world,[9] well, such representations slow our progress, by re-instilling a model of the field that's more akin to Eliade's New Humanism than what many scholars of religion are actually up to today.

Now, I realize that I've spent my time on only half of the theme. The other part is, of course, the adjective "revolutionary." In keeping with my opening, then, let me end by drawing on another pop lyric—John Lennon's 1968 B-Side to "Hey Jude" (but also credited to Paul McCartney): "Revolution." As some of you likely know, its opening lines go as follows:

You say you want a revolution
Well, you know
We all want to change the world ...[10]

Much like the folk notion of love, revolution is slippery as well, since our shared wish to change the world doesn't necessarily mean that we all want to change it in the same way—the bitter divides of this country's recent Presidential election should make this painfully evident. And so it strikes me that, inasmuch as we are gathered here *as scholars of religion*, and not in terms of the many other possible identities that we each surely operationalize from time to time (few of which we may all share), we should be a little more modest, we should entertain the limits of our expertise and our relevance, and leave changing the world for another occasion. For, as Wendy Doniger recently argued, with regard to what she describes as conservative faith-based groups infiltrating our profession:

> Scholars of religion must find the courage to defend the field and preserve its independence in the face of these threats. (Doniger 2016)

I find this to be very good advice—also when applied to incursions from closer to home and from the other end of the political spectrum; for it shifts the terrain to conversations about what is and what is not *our field*, challenging us to address why we even think that our profession might save the city. For, taking the recent election seriously means acknowledging that a fair percentage of the population actually thinks the city needs to be saved from people like us.

Postscript

An interesting thing occurred, I think, at the 2016 annual meeting where the preceding paper was presented (late on the closing day)—and deserves some comment here. I did not attend the session to which I'm about to refer, but I gather that it took place in the same room as the above-mentioned panel, though it took place much earlier in the conference and with far more popular speakers—since the 1,000 seat convention hall was, or so I'm told, filled (as opposed to the less than 30 people present for the my own session; I counted the number of attendees from my seat at the front of the room). At that other event, introduced by the AAR's then President Serene Jones (also president of Union Theological Seminary), Michelle Alexander offered a plenary address (at the invitation of Jones), involving an on-stage interview/conversation between herself and Kelly Brown Douglas (canon theologian at the Washington National Cathedral, director of the religion program at Goucher College, and author of the book *Stand Your Ground* [2015]).[11] Alexander, herself the author of widely praised book *The New Jim Crow* (2010), was introduced by Jones as a public intellectual who was, at that time, a newly appointed visiting professor at Union Theological Seminary (a position she will hold from 2016 to 2021); it was also noted that she was about to begin her own seminary studies (at Union as well).

Alexander's calls for a "revolutionary change in consciousness," as Brown Douglas put it during the event, concerning addressing such things as police violence toward minority members or the way in which the legal system disproportionately punishes minorities, was undoubtedly relevant for her invitation to speak at that year's conference, given Jones's selection of the already discussed conference theme. For, as Alexander said at one point in that plenary conversation:

> We are going to need to build a new moral consensus about who we are as a nation and what it means to be in right relationship with one another. And that is the work of revolutionary love.[12]

As she went on to explain (38:47), this notion of love "is not about emotion, but is about recognizing the divinity within the other; [unless] we come to recognize that we are all the children of God ... we are going to continue these patterns in the United States ..." Applause then happened throughout the hall.

What I find interesting about this event was not that openly Christian theology was so prominent; after all, as some of its members have long argued, liberal theology in general and, in particular, liberal Christian (and usually a specific type of liberal Protestant) theology, have been prominent in this professional association for many years—in fact, since its very inception, one could argue.[13] So, for members of this organization who are critical of this inclusion—and I count myself among this group, having been a member for 27 years (as of 2017)—this panel wasn't all that different from what they had heard in person or read in its journal on many past occasions. Instead, the curious thing was the manner in which some in attendance were either surprised or disappointed (perhaps alienated, maybe even angered, inasmuch as they perhaps unexpectedly felt excluded by some of the comments at a panel advocating for "a radical solidarity" [49:48]) to find such overtly theological, and specifically Christian, content—not only at the American Academy of Religion but explicitly sanctioned by its President. For what does one make of such a panel, and its presidentially sanctioned conversation, if one is *not* Christian, or *not* a believer of any sort, let alone if one was *not* the type of political actor who talks in just this manner, with just these interests and goals?

For instance, with such alternative audiences in mind, consider Alexander's response to Brown Douglas taking the conversation to the role to be played by the Christian Church and "the faith community," in bringing about the revolution that they both claim is needed. For after Brown Douglas received more applause for asking rhetorically whether the church had failed "in what it means to be church, what is means to join in the mending of this world, what it means to indeed join Jesus on the cross..." [49:16]), Alexander asserted that one can

> rail against the system, and call it out, and talk about the facts ... but in the end it is all sound and fury signifying nothing if it isn't really coming from that place of revolutionary love ... if you aren't offering a path rooted in the recognition of the divinity of each and every one of us ... (56:02)

She then added: "this project of trying to birth a new America, if it is not morally grounded, and if it is not deeply linked to a spiritual awakening ... I think we'll see ourselves replicating these patterns for many years to come" (57:15).[14] And, again, applause from the large audience followed. The session then ended with Brown Douglas summing it up by adding:

> That [i.e., the revolution of consciousness] must start within our faith communities ... We have to begin to see in the other, ourselves ... Every single solitary person, regardless, who has breath or had breath, is a sacred child of god and deserves to be treated as such.

Given the tightly focused nature of this rhetoric, and the affinity one might have for it only if one happens to be a member of a specific branch of Protestant Christianity (perhaps the group repeatedly applauding throughout the session), it's probably no wonder that some in attendance felt rather excluded—such as Laura Levitt, a professor of Religion, Jewish Studies, and Gender at Temple University, who stated, in a blog on the event that as posted just a week later: "Perhaps I was naive. In retrospect, that seems quite likely. I should have known this would become a Christian theological conversation ..."[15] As Levitt then went on to write, after Alexander "told the story behind her book":

> All of a sudden the revolutionary who had sung the praises of the Black Panthers, shifted gears. The revolution became spiritual, and, more specifically, a proclamation of the power of "the Church," of Jesus's suffering on the cross, on the brother/sisterhood of humanity, all of us "children of God." This was a decidedly Christian universal message. Just as Alexander proclaimed the bankruptcy of American democracy she proclaimed the revolutionary power of the Church. I could not help but hear a call to crusade, a sacred revolution in the name of Jesus Christ and I was no longer a part of this story. The discourse had shifted, profoundly. I was in a different universe.

As Levitt concludes, "[i]f this is radical love, I want no part." She elaborates:

> Here in the words of this most compelling social critic, I no longer felt welcome. The universal proclamation of this session and its revolutionary love had no place for Jews or Muslims, for Hindus or Buddhists, and certainly not for the many atheists and agnostics of any and all stripes who are part of this scholarly organization. In our bounded differences from these well-meaning and progressive Christians, we were, it seems no longer welcome.[16]

Those interested in identify formation would therefore do well to study this event, for despite the apparent presence of many overlapping practical interests (i.e., shared political viewpoints), the rhetoric of Jesus on the cross, at least for some in attendance, divided as effectively as it functioned to unite yet others in that 1,000-seat room.[17]

Now, even for one who has grown cynical about the role that a certain sort of participant claim or viewpoint continues to play in the academic study of religion, this session was sobering—not only in its explicit anchoring of social change in a philosophically idealist version of the Protestant social gospel but also in its normative stand on the shape that society ought to take. While personally sharing dismay at the presence of what at times certainly seems to be utterly unbridled police violence in the streets of many U.S. cities—aimed specifically at members of minority groups—along with how the U.S. has transformed into what some now regularly refer to as the carceral state—the question, for me, is whether, *as a scholar of religion* (for this all took place, one cannot forget, at an annual scholarly conference for those who study religion) I have any necessary or special insights into either of these developments. Now, as a politically liberal person one may, of course, assume one does and such a person may even feel compelled to speak out on the issue and organize forms of resistance; but, again, *speaking as a scholar of religion*, it seems fair to me to inquire as to our place and role in such debates. (Question: do politically engaged mathematicians, astronomers, or oncologists feel compelled to engage in such discourse at their conference's plenary sessions?) For if we are free or even expected to enter them with an authoritative voice (based on the imprimatur of our diplomas and research specialties, presumably—thereby becoming public intellectuals, I guess) then are there not a host of social ills for which we might also advocate, on behalf of people who occupy far different places along either the political or theological spectrum? But I find it difficult to imagine the American Academy of Religion—either as a body or as the result of its President's interests or actions—feeling either free or compelled to take a stand on the realization of such other concerns. I won't offer many examples here, to flesh out my argument, since it should be rather easy for a reader to imagine a position on an issue that they may themselves abhor but which is nonetheless advocated—sometimes vehemently and even righteously—by some religious group, somewhere in the world.

The question, then, is what the scholars of religion's role is when it comes to such issues.

Given that, as best I can tell, its institutional mission is not to adopt, pursue, or normalize politically and the theologically liberal causes,[18] it continually amazes me how the AAR (as evidenced in that plenary panel) so easily slides into just this role—though the amazement is something I state merely for rhetorical effect, since the field is not only understood by the AAR extremely broadly (thereby making it a home to outright theologians, humanists, and social scientists alike) but the field is also self-selecting for those who align themselves in particular ways when it comes to a variety of issues. Case in point: those who study world religions in order to, let's just say, demonstrate and then advocate for the inherent superiority of one among the many will likely not find much of a home in this professional association, let alone the field of Religious Studies, in which such research is normally focused on ascertaining the cross-cultural and trans-historical similarity that underlies them all.[19] Simply put (to offer buy one example), it strikes me as unimaginable to have an AAR event, much less a Presidential plenary address, devoted to the topic of advocating in favor of, say, not just the constitutional right of the members of the Westboro Baptist Church to protest at people's funerals but also one that both adopts a normative stand concerning the truth of their view of the universe along with the advocating for scholars of religion *qua* scholars to help realize their worldview—for, agree with them or not, their members are presumably just as legitimately an example of religious actors as are any other.[20] For adopting the stance of religious actors, and pursuing their goals, is precisely what we found in the plenary session described above, though the favored position is far more dominant, and thus accepted than Westboro's—though certainly it is not without its more conservative critics in the current U.S., to be sure. In fact, the distance between supporting Jones's, Brown Douglas's and Alexander's shared viewpoint, on the one hand, and supporting that of the Westboro Baptist Church, on the other, is probably so great that my use of the two as if they count as comparable examples may strike some readers as ridiculous (at best) or pernicious (at worst).

Yet, for the scholar of religion whom I have in mind as constituting a colleague, both instances would qualify as examples of data, i.e., both are ways that human beings articulate, authorize, and implement a view of the world and their place in it. Which of these is correct or more persuasive is, I would add, *a judgment best left for scholars to make on their own time*, while they occupy any of the many other subject positions we each surely also occupy, and thus not a position they should advance in the guise of scholar of religions (such as in the classroom or during their professional meetings).

This, I maintain, was the point that I tried to make in my above presentation however, the distinction in roles and discursive settings was, apparently, heard differently by some of my co-panelists. Seemingly in response to my own brief summarizing comments during our panel, after all of the five papers had been delivered,[21] Sarah Eltantawi, a professor of comparative religion and Islamic studies at Evergreen State College, replied (looking at me, at the far end of the panel, as I recall):

> Well, I don't feel that I have the luxury ... if only I could walk into the classroom and be seen completely for my credentials ... This distinction is not a reality for me, you know, that somehow I'm limited to my credentials ... (1:06:50)

Noting that she is seen by many students as a Muslim woman and a Muslim in her classes, I heard her as pushing back against the position for which I had argued—though, from where I sat, she struck me as providing an ideal example of the challenges that, in varying ways, *we all face* in trying to ensure that, when they are in our classes, *students learn and then play by the discursive rules of the game called scholarship*. (That we will not always be successful in this exercise goes without saying, and that the challenges will always be present—in more or less ways, depending on the setting and who our students see us to be—is equally obvious, I would hope.) For despite her apparent disagreement with my position, she then went on to say:

> It doesn't mean that I run my classroom as a confessional space or my own personal therapy session ... My job is to educate; I consider my job [is] to complicate the Islamic tradition; so I do what I can to disrupt easy answers ... Which I'm credentialed to do, I guess. (1:07:48)

While unfamiliar with her work, having just met on the occasion of this panel, I'd agree wholeheartedly with her; for it strikes me that her comments on her role in the classroom are an excellent example of a professional persevering despite unprofessional assumptions that are undoubtedly brought to her classroom by some (or even many) of her students—natural assumptions, or perhaps better put, assumptions that are to be expected, perhaps, given some of those students' probable life experiences, and thus something to be identified and addressed in the class, in an effort, as I would phrase it, to create an institutional and discursive space in which we might begin to attempt to carry out some counter-intuitive, critical thinking so as to, in her words, disrupt the easy answers (foremost among them, perhaps, might be how we stereotype others in our effort to make sense of them and ourselves).[22] It's a disruptive activity that our students will hopefully entertain doing because, I would further argue, of the confidence created by the training and the patience that we each exhibit in the classroom while leading them through such exercises (which is never easy, no matter who you are, I'd hasten to add—though, to be sure, the inevitable gap between students' ideas of an authoritative professor and their perception of each of us does afford many of us with luxuries that are not universally shared by all of our colleagues).

So, despite the appearance that we disagree, I think that we actually agree on much and would, perhaps, both be discouraged or, perhaps frustrated, to find the rhetoric (which was no doubt sincerely spoken—but sincerity is not the issue, of course...) of Jesus on the cross receiving enthusiastic applause at an AAR Presidential plenary address. For we seem to share the position that the space in which we work, as professionals, is *not* confessional and it is *not* a therapy session. As a scholar of religion I am *neither* here to sing the praises of love nor am I here to birth a new nation, since I'm not so confident that the city *as I wish it* to be is *the city as it ought to be*. Instead, exhibiting rather more humility, we recognize that we are here, with reference to the conference theme we were asked to examine, to study how competing and possibly contradictory ways of using that term, love, along with a variety of alternative and cross-culturally evident civic models, are each authorized and what happens when they bump up against one another.

Notes

1   This previously unpublished chapter was presented as part of the Roundtable Panel, "What's Love Got to Do with It? Critical Appraisals of Love as a Civic Value," organized by the Committee on the Public Understanding of Religion, American Academy of Religion, in November 2016. Its concern was addressing what that year's AAR President, Serene Jones, had selected as the conference theme: revolutionary love. The papers from the session were filmed and are all available at www.youtube.com/watch?v=ccDzQecGuMk. For additional responses see the various posts, including one from then AAR vice president and incoming president (for 2018), David Gushee, at http://bulletin.equinoxpub.com/?s=revolutionary+love%3A+scholars+respond+to (accessed June 10, 2017).

2   It was a separation that, in 1982, ended in a divorce with a settlement that is said to have so enraged Denver that he cut their bed in half with a chainsaw: see "Dropping

In: John Denver's Moral Victory" at www.skinet.com/ski/resorts/2005/12/dropping-i n-john-denvers-moral-victory (accessed October 15, 2016).

3   The program units of the AAR had received the following email notice (sent to them on December 9, 2015) form the President, in request for them to consider how to incorporate the upcoming 2016 theme into their unit's call for papers:

> This year's annual meeting theme is **Revolutionary Love.** Neither word captures the complexity of the theme, but I use the word "love" in the broadest possible sense, including love as a social and political force, a structural reality, a collective endeavor, a shared social practice, a language, a relationship, a moment, a gesture, an identity, a quest. The membership of the AAR includes scholars who study religious traditions and historical moments of enormous variety. It's hard to imagine any area of study, however, that does not reflect on the topic of "love"—again, defined as broadly and creatively as possible—in one form or another. I use the term "revolutionary" next to "love" to turn our attention to love that seeks to transform the world, which includes love that both tears down and builds up. To provoke our thinking, let me offer the prophetic words of James Baldwin, *"I use the word love here not merely in the personal sense but as a state of being, or a state of grace— not in the infantile American sense of being made happy but in the tough and universal sense of quest and daring and growth."*

I quoted the above text in a brief post, not included here, posted in December 2015 at: https://religion.ua.edu/blog/2015/12/10/revolutionary-love/ (accessed July 1, 2017). Of interest is that the email went on:

> Next year's theme [i.e., 2017], under [then incoming President] Eddie Glaude's leadership, is going to be **Religion and the Most Vulnerable**, and many of these same ideas will be continued. Please take special note that we anticipate hosting plenary sessions for the next three years on the theme **Religion and Hatred**—in an effort for the AAR membership to continue thinking together about the role religion scholars have to play in engaging the growing and fierce "hatreds" of our present political moment.

4   By the way, the apparent choice not to refer to it by the far more common terminology of "civic virtue" is itself interesting to me—as if the change to "value" signified some less theologically-invested language, perhaps.

5   See McCutcheon (2015: 176), where I quote the instructions sent to chairs of program units that year, concerning operationalizing the 2014 conference theme: "Climate Change and the Coming Global Crisis: Religion and Responses."

6   The montage of Trump campaign speeches was created and posted on March 23, 2016 by *The Jimmy Kimmel Show*: www.youtube.com/watch?v=rXj_yrEkFJI (accessed September 27, 2016).

7   The latter is, of course, a reference to the chant heard throughout at the 2016 Republican national convention, and other rallies, with reference to Hillary Clinton.

8   Anecdotally, I can report that fairly uniform and open laments were expressed, overheard either in hallways between sessions or as explicit part of panel papers, at 2016's conference concerning Donald Trump's very recent (and to many here, surprise) presidential election victory.

9   Mind you, it's a transformation probably not inclusive of the so-called "Love-Sick Romeo" who hijacked that EgyptAir flight, late last March, and took it to Cyprus in order to, or so it was reported at the time, give his ex-wife a letter; see www.mirror. co.uk/news/world-news/egyptair-plane-hijack-love-sick-7646259 (accessed April 13, 2016).

10 "We'd all love to change the world" is the lyric in some versions (e.g., the video version of the song, directed by Michael Lindsay-Hogg in 1968).

11 This plenary was also filmed and can be found at www.youtube.com/watch?v= L0fEMFtOn4E (accessed June 26, 2017).

12 See the plenary's video in note 11 above, at 37:37. For subsequent references to the video I give timings within the text.

13 For those unfamiliar with either the derivation from the AAR from the National Association of Bible Instructors (NABI), following the latter's 1963 self-study, or with critiques of the legacy of Christian theology within this Academy of scholars, see chapters 14 and 15 of Wiebe 1999—Against Science in the Academic Study of Religion: On the Emergence and Development of the AAR and A Religious Agenda Continued: A Review of the Presidential Addresses of the AAR—along with an update of the latter essay in Wiebe 2006.

14 I will not even mention the manner in which such a plenary excludes the many non-U.S. citizens who annually attend—since the AAR is, after all, a specifically U.S. scholarly association. But, given its global aspirations—and thus the number of international scholars who annually attend (such as the many Canadians, not to mention the Brits, Germans, South Africans, Koreans as well as Dutch and even Japanese scholars who regularly participate each year)—the AAR's growth has created conditions in which it aspires to be something other than what it is, leading to a situation in which a call to "birth a new America" likely falls on many ears which do not have this particularly nationalist affinities.

15 Find the post at: http://bulletin.equinoxpub.com/2016/11/revolutionary-love-and-th e-colonization-of-a-critical-voice-an-outsiders-reflections (accessed June 27, 2017).

16 For more, see also the opening segment, which is a conversation between Levitt and Mike Altman and which directly addresses this AAR plenary session, of the third episode (entitled "The Conference") of our own department's podcast, posted here: https://soundcloud.com/studyreligion (accessed June 27, 2017).

17 See Merinda Simmons's comments on the conference for a related critique: https:// edge.ua.edu/k-merinda-simmons/love-in-a-time-of-scholarship (accessed July 1, 2017). There she concludes as follows: "Critical theory surely has devastating implications for logic structures that would reductively—often fatally—ascribe an essence to something called 'race.' But that fact is too often forgotten, it seems, even now in this academy wherein talk of 'critical theory' proliferates but wherein its implications are curiously absent. Scholars thus do themselves (not to mention the publics they study, if taking many stated motivations into account) no favors by simply pointing to a different 'phenomenal reality' (to use Joyce's phrase), professing their love for it, and calling that progressive academic work. What we are left with, in that case, are dueling essentialisms in the service of respective passions. And that's a whole lotta [*sic*] love that race studies could do without."

18 The AAR's statement of purpose reads: "The purpose of the Academy derives from two principal goals: (1) To promote understanding of and critical reflection on religious traditions, issues, questions, values, texts, practices, and institutions. To this end, we foster communication and exchange among teachers and scholars, and the public understanding of religion. (2) To serve the professional interests of members as students, teachers, and scholars" (see www.aarweb.org/about [accessed June 20, 2017).

19 Curious was how candidates for the AAR's Vice Presidency, just a couple years ago, focused on this very issue, saying, basically, that the mission of extending invitations to liberal theologians must now be matched by including more conservative positions

as well within the Academy. As the eventual winner of the vote, David Gushee (who was also on the panel at which this chapter's paper was originally presented) phrased it in his election statement (see www.aarweb.org/sites/default/files/pdfs/About/Elections/2015VPStatements.pdf): "Ensuring that AAR is perceived as a valuable, central context for every kind of scholar in religion. I think we have reason to be concerned that for many scholars the annual AAR meeting is becoming primarily important for its auxiliary or related meetings rather than for the AAR meeting itself. To the extent that this occurs because AAR is seen as not particularly hospitable to, say, confessional or constructive theology, or more conservative religious viewpoints, this is a matter worthy of our attention." See also Mike Altman's post on this election: https://michaeljaltman.net/2015/10/15/the-aar-vice-presidential-election-and-the-illusion-of-choice (accessed June 27, 2017).

20 As background, the Westboro Baptist Church (whose URL is, believe it or not, godhatesfags.com) was founded in 1952 by the late Fred Phelps (1929–2014), and is self-described as an old-school, or primitive Baptist church. "We adhere to the teachings of the Bible," they note on their website, "preach against all form of sin (e.g., fornication, adultery [including divorce and remarriage], sodomy), and insist that the sovereignty of God and the doctrines of grace be taught and expounded publicly to all men" (www.godhatesfags.com/wbcinfo/aboutwbc.html, accessed June 27, 2017). It is nationally-known in the U.S. for their far right politics and habit of picketing such things as funerals or LGBQT events ; you can obtain a copy of their picket schedule here: www.godhatesfags.com/schedule.html.

21 As part of my brief, follow-up comments I said: "I think I've been invited here because of certain credentials I do or don't have ... I think I'm here in a very particular role. I think we all have many very particular roles ... And I fear a rather large mistake is being made if I presume that whatever role I happen to have at this moment is omni-relevant ... I think it's a misplacement of authority ... So that's an important self-limitation, perhaps; I might be criticized for that. I certainly have strong views on how the nation ought to work but I don't think those strong views are credentialed by my diploma from the University of Toronto, that helps to credential me and put me on this panel" (1:24:47).

22 See what I consider still to be an important essay on this very topic, published by Martin S. Jaffee in *MTSR* some years ago (1997)—in which he makes plain that, when he taught, he would often make his own visual appearance as a rather Orthodox-looking Jewish man as a piece of data for his students to consider how identification functions. In fact, it was on the basis of this essay that, just a few years after, we invited him to inaugurate an annual lecture series at the University of Alabama.

References

Alexander, Michelle (2010). *The New Jim Crow: Mass Incarceration in the Age of Colorblindness*. New York: The New Press.

Doniger, Wendy (2016) "The Repression of Religious Studies," *The Chronicle of Higher Education*, April 20. Retrieved from http://chronicle.com/article/The-Repression-of-Religious/236166?cid=at&utm_source=at&utm_medium=en&elqTrackId=69866972078141e7b7807ac6cb0054fd&elq=98a4c3d31675436eab0511ea5b8074f8&elqaid=8744&elqat=1&elqCampaignId=2954 (accessed February 22, 2018).

Douglas, Kelly Brown (2015) *Stand Your Ground: Black Bodies and the Justice of God*. Maryknoll, NY: Orbis Books.

Jaffee, Martin S. (1997). "Fessing Up in Theory: On Professing and Confessing in the Religious Studies Classroom," *Method and Theory in the Study of Religion* 9/4: 325–337. https://doi.org/10.1163/157006897X00313

Johnson, Steven (2014). *How We Got to Now: Six Innovations That Made the Modern World*. New York: Riverhead Books.

McCutcheon, Russell (2015). *A Modest Proposal on Method: Essaying the Study of Religion*. Leiden: Brill.

Wiebe, Donald (1999). *The Politics of Religious Studies: The Continuing Conflict with Theology in the Academy*. New York: Palgrave.

—— (2006). "An Eternal Return All Over Again: The Religious Conversation Endures," *Journal of the American Academy of Religion* 74 (3): 674–696. https://doi.org/10.1093/jaarel/lfj091

Chapter 9

So You're Not a Priest?
Identifying the Scholar of Religion[1]

In an effort to discuss how it is that scholars of religion might identify themselves to others—given how often we're mistaken for something other than what we are (e.g., as if we're training to be religious functionaries or ritual specialists), such as on a flight when our happenstance seatmates invariably ask us what it is that we do—I'd like to open by citing something that I wrote a while ago concerning how colleagues react when they find out that you're interested not in religion but, rather, in the very category religion itself and thus the fact that we call certain things religious or spiritual. For, writing in the introduction to *Manufacturing Religion*, I phrased it as follows:

> For some scholars of religion, such a metatheoretical focus will no doubt be troubling or possibly even perplexing. I say this because, on a number of occasions, I have been asked by colleagues, "But where do you get your hands dirty?" I take it that they are asking me what historical religion, which specific myth, or what particular ritual do I study. No doubt after coming clear as to what the book is concerned to address, some readers will still be asking what I simply refer to as the "dirty hands" question. "All this is fine and good, but what has it got to do with religion?" Another form of the question revolves around talk of hard data: Where is your hard data? Have you been in the field? Where is your ethnographic evidence? The prominence of this sort of questioning in the discourse has direct relevance for the critique I develop, for it presumes that religion, myths, and rituals are simply and self-evidently "out there," unique and easily identified, like ripe fruit on a tree just waiting to be picked. (McCutcheon 1997: 6)

I then concluded that making the discourse on religion one's data "is generally not received very well by some scholars" (ibid.: 7). Hence my early career choice of a quotation from Pierre Bourdieu's *Homo Academicus* (his study of French academia itself) as an epigraph to open that book: "the sorcerer's apprentice who takes the risk of looking into native sorcery and its fetishes ... must expect to see turned against him the violence he has unleashed" (Bourdieu 1988: 5).

As Bourdieu went on to write immediately after, though which I did not quote in that epigraph:

> Karl Kraus [the early-twentieth-century Austrian satirist] was well placed to formulate the law according to which objectification is all the more likely to be approved and acclaimed as "courageous" in "family circles," the more distant in social space are the objects to which it applies ... [H]e says that anyone who rejects

the pleasures and easy profits of long-distance criticism, in order to investigate his immediate neighbourhood, which everything bids him hold sacred, must expect the torments of "subjective persecution." Thus we have been tempted to adopt the title, *A Book for Burning*, which Li Zhi, a [sixteenth-century] renegade mandarin, gave to one of those self-consuming works of his which revealed the rules of the mandarins' game. We do so, not in order to challenge those who, despite their readiness to denounce all inquisitions, will condemn to the stake any work perceived as a sacrilegious outrage against their own beliefs, but simply to state the contradiction which is inherent in divulging tribal secrets and which is only so painful because even the partial publication of our most intimate details is also a kind of public confession. (Bourdieu 1988: 5)

I quoted this very early in my career and, though the language of persecution and torment certainly now strikes me as rather over the top—at least with regard to the responses I've sometimes had upon revealing some of our field's trade secrets—the lines still resonate with me, now that I've been at this for two and a half decades; for, as Bourdieu makes evident, turning our analytic skills on ourselves, rather than reserving them for our studies of the exotic other—whether we admire or are puzzled by those others—can come with consequences.

One of my first experiences of just such a poor reception—to which I refer in that above quotation, but where I provided no real details[2]—was when I was first asked that "dirty hands" question: it was during a job interview at the American Academy of Religion (AAR), in one of those curtained-off convention cubicles in a hotel ballroom; it was for a tenure-track position at Western Michigan University (an opening, as it was then described in the ad, specifically aimed at hiring in the area of method and theory). I was pretty new to the interview game back then and this may have been my first experience in person with a hiring committee. It was November of 1995, as I recall; I was an Instructor, at the time, at the University of Tennessee (I'd been hired over the phone for that position), and I had successfully defended my dissertation up in Toronto the January before (and the MS had been contracted but would not be published for another 18 months or so).[3] What made all of this unique was that Western Michigan was hiring in an area that almost no one took seriously, at least back then—long before all those now mandatory "method & theory" courses were invented in grad schools across the continent and, so, well prior to many people in the field starting to list on their CV "method & theory" as one of the competencies. So for that rather small group of us at the time (many of whom were, indeed, trained at the University of Toronto, some intersecting, to one degree or another, with the orbit of Don Wiebe) who had come to identify with what was then a pretty new specialty in our field, it was a little exciting to see such a job ad.[4] Jump ahead a bit and we eventually learned that the search was cancelled (a so-called failed search) and the position was then re-advertised and filled the following year, with the qualifier "method and theory" now merely listed among the various things the successful applicant might be able to do.

So I'm guessing that, like so many other occasions in my experience, "m&t" had probably been the occasion for an internal arm-wrestling match in that department—it's a hunch based not just on how the ad changed over the course of a year but also on the evidence provided by that dirty-hands question that I was asked in that brief interview at a conference (the sort of twenty-minute interview that helps a search committee narrow down the applicants to those they'd like to invite to campus later). For I was asked that question by faculty who, as it occurred to me at the time, didn't seem to understand what they had advertised for—or who, of course, might have been using the occasion of an interview to contest an ad with which some might have disagreed. "So and so in our department works on Japan, so and so does Africa, I do such and such—so where do you get your hands dirty?" was how I remember the question being posed to me. My answer concerning studying methods and theories, and thus studying the works of scholars of religions themselves and doing fieldwork at conferences and in journals—an answer that I paraphrased in the introduction to *Manufacturing Religion* but, again, without referring to the occasion of its composition[5]—didn't go over so well, at least according to my recollection of the event, for it just elicited a paraphrase of the same question, asked of me yet again, as if repeating it— much like the tendency to talk loudly and slowly to a foreigner—might help me to understand it better. Not unlike an interview I had many years later, to be dean of an honors college (at which the search committee exclusively asked questions about recruiting, such that I had to pause and ask if this was indeed an interview for the position of dean), I was then asked so many questions about what religion I actually studied that I paused and, as I still recall rather clearly, sought clarification by asking something like: "This is a position in method and theory, no?"

Needless to say, I didn't get the job.

But a friend in my program at Toronto was invited for an on-campus interview, though, if memory serves, and based on her reports when she returned, she didn't fare much better. And so, as noted above, the search was mounted again the following year, and it succeeded by looking mainly for someone with an expertise in a tradition—something like religion in North America, as I remember it.

While it's pretty obvious that none of this rises to the level of the violence of which Bourdieu wrote, failing to obtain a way to feed yourself because your interests and the place where you put your comparative and explanatory skills to work deviated from the norm is as close as I think anyone—at least myself—would like to come to it in one's professional life.

So yes, seated on a plane, trying to explain to your seatmate what being a scholar of religion entails, as opposed to being a theologian, for example—or, maybe, doing so at a family gathering with Great Aunt Edna, let alone answering queries from parents or siblings—sometimes presents some challenges; but it's understandable, of course, given the prominence of how people in our society use the term religion in everyday life. Whether church attendance is declining or not, virtually everyone is skilled in the widespread folk uses of the term and therefore have no difficulty identifying, say, a religious story on the evening news in distinction from one that's more about politics or sports. So I think that the challenges of talking to someone on a jet, about our work, are understandably and pale in comparison to the difficulties entailed in trying to explain to some colleagues—*colleagues*, which implies that we are people who work together, supposedly sharing common tools and intellectual interests—that one studies the fact that some people (including them, perhaps) call certain things religious (or not). Trying to elaborate on this in a job interview—especially when they're looking for someone who works in methods and theories—is, at least in my experience, even worse.

Given the ease with which we know that we're not studying, say, mana, but, instead, *studying people who happen to talk about mana*—and thus rather easily making the shift to seeing our work as anthropocentric as opposed to, say, mana-centric—suggests that, if pressed, these colleagues should be able to figure out that the shift from religion to "religion" is not that difficult to make. For as the case of mana so nicely illustrates, just because people themselves talk about something as a feature of their world does not necessarily mean that we, as scholars, must naively or uncritically accept its existence and, as the people themselves may see it, its ontological status or role as the basis for offering explanations about other things in their world. After all, there's all sorts of people who claim to be masculine or feminine but there's also plenty who are interested in studying gender as an historical or social phenomenon itself—it's not that controversial, at least to many scholars today (in fact, it's now even a little passé to some). But tell another scholar in our field that you study the category religion itself and, well, there's a pretty good chance that they'll roll their eyes, tell you you're "obsessed with the category religion" (as someone once did with me, looking over my online CV at an NEH event where I was a guest) or maybe, as a scholar more senior than I did not so long ago, tell you in an email that people are worried for you because you're in a rut. As I've noted on other occasions (i.e., the introduction to McCutcheon 2014), so-called ruts and obsessions are understood as expertise when they are in the "correct" areas (thus, such judgments are, of course, in the eye of the beholder), for who would suggest that, for example, Peter Brown was obsessed with antiquity or that another book on Hinduism by Wendy Doniger was evidence of the rut she'd gotten herself into? Perhaps critics might even blurb a book in which your work appears and use their few sentences on the back cover as a chance to undermine the point of the essay you wrote for the volume. I should add that, yes, this happened and that after I notified the press of what seemed to me like an unprofessional jab—not asking for its removal but simply alerting them to what I saw to be going on—that blurb was changed (I'm unaware how or why) before the book got into print.

None of this is outright violence, for certain—if by that we mean bloodshed; but each is a curious moment of disciplining, a situation in which your research interests are not misunderstood but, because the threat they seem to pose *is understood all too well*, it is actively contested and undermined by colleagues. And so, the arm wrestling of that early job interview never really went away; it's just that the power imbalance of that prior occasion has been moderated, somewhat.

So when it comes to making the shift from religion to "religion"—to being interested in the possible motives or effects of using that legally sanctioned term in either this or that manner—it's still fairly controversial work. I think here of the recent rejection of a co-written essay (written with Aaron Hughes), by the *Journal of the American Academy of Religion*, because—or so we were told in the rejection notice—the essay (which was on the gatekeeping role played the rhetoric of collegiality in our field) was not either on world religions or methodologies used in their study (supposedly the two foci of the journal, according to its online mission statement, which was cited in the rejection).[6] If this indeed is the focus of the journal—an excessively narrow understanding of the field that, in my reading, never characterized it before and hardly characterizes all of its contents now—then most of my writing career now seems to have been classified as outside the academic study of religion.

That I've persisted in this apparently unorthodox interest seems to have made me, and not just my work, a little controversial as well—for example, apart from being told I'm in a rut it has gained for me the reputation that I'm out to kill religious studies departments or the field as a whole. In the early years I always thought that it was an association that had something to do with my friendship with such colleagues as the late Gary Lease, who played a central role in the demise of the program at Santa Cruz (for more, see his essay in the special issue on the then state of the field in *Method and Theory in the Study of Religion* [7/4 (1995)]; see also the papers in his honor in a special 2009 issue of *Method and Theory in the Study of Religion* [29/2]). But since I've been working in a department that has so successfully reinvented itself since 2001 (e.g., we've more than doubled, since then, the size of our tenure/tenure-track faculty and, began offering a rather novel MA in the fall of 2017) it still puzzles me that this impression continues. (Just how much of my work has someone with such an impression actually read, I sometimes ask myself ...) In fact, people who get jobs working at Alabama are routinely quizzed, or so they later report to me, by friends elsewhere who want to know what it's like working with someone who's trying to eliminate the study of religion; perhaps it's because we've succeeded by being a different sort of department, turning our gaze and our social theory tools inward, to some extent, and thus the fear these queries actually signify is for the future of a very particular version of the study of religion, when the study of religion was practiced as what at least Wiebe would simply term a crypto-theological endeavor.

But critiquing that pursuit hardly prevents us from redescribing the field and doing it in a different way.

So I find that in the midst of some conversations not with seatmates or extended family (and, yes, I've had my share of those moments too) but with colleagues—colleagues who may be self-conscious, and thus on the offensive, inasmuch as they fear becoming data, perhaps—there's sometimes a lot of background noise, baggage, or whatever one wishes to call it, that impedes a quick description of what it is that I actually study. Defying the boxes into which we usually place ourselves comes, at minimum, at the price of raised eyebrows or, when the stakes are higher, with rejection letters for either articles or jobs;[7] it really would be so much easier if someone in my position could just say that they study Buddhist rituals or Native American origins stories.[8] But even for those who seem to think that they get it, they often assume that it's just the word, religion, that a scholar such as myself studies, as if things have natural lives without words to name them. (Wasn't that Wilfred Cantwell Smith's point in asserting that faith pre-dated the so-called cumulative tradition? And is this not the drive behind the advice, quoted by Brent Nongbri [2015], to change the word religion to something else in translations of texts from antiquity?[9]) "Surely people were religious even if they didn't have the word religion, no?" It's a remarkably anachronistic and Platonic, though commonsense, approach if you think about it, one that many would see as sadly outdated if applied to other topics, but this essentialist viewpoint still reigns in our field. "Sure there's no functional equivalent to 'religion' in this or that language," someone might admit, "but of course those people were religious. They believed in gods, didn't they?" But what if by words we instead meant the terminological tips of socio-semantic icebergs, the frameworks that enable us not just *to identify* something but, as part of that process, *to distinguish* this from that and then *to rank* that over this, all in an effort to make sense of where we happen to find ourselves? For then to say that one studies the word religion says far more than some tend to think when they first hear it. For now we study not the term, religion, as if it is separate from some pan-human quality or deeply personal disposition that might have been called virtually anything else, but, rather, we examine the very fact that we (and, yes, sometimes it is all about us) come to know others, and thus ourselves, by applying this word (and all that comes with it) in discrete situations, as if it names something deep in the human heart (or brain, maybe the genes?). Perhaps it's a little too grandiose to phrase it this way, but now the study of "religion" is but one way into the study of identification and signification, linking us closely to such other cutting-edge fields as semiotics and identity studies.

While I could cite, as an example, what I consider to be one of Smith's more important later essays (2004), on how the U.S. Supreme Court has used the category religion, in two specific cases, to navigate the way the nation ought to understand behaviors that seem to deviate from accepted norms (the cases, one a free exercise and the other an establishment case, involve Santeria sacrifice in Florida, on the one hand, and Christmas displays sanctioned by a city in Rhode Island),[10] instead consider a more recent, but no less significant, effect of being able to classify one's preferences as religious, at least as we see it played out here in the U.S. It doesn't just mean that you may be able to obtain a tax advantage (by being exempt from paying property tax, for instance) but it means that you might be privileged with regard to the application (i.e., limitation) of some federal laws. Citing the importance of not undermining people's "deeply and sincerely held beliefs," we can easily find a variety of recent laws, proposed or passed at the state and federal level, which exempt so-called religious people from behaving toward others in ways that are normally policed (at least when the motives are not classified as religious—such as declining to rent someone an apartment or terminating their employment). Based on the free exercise clause of the U.S. Constitution's First Amendment, in which citizens are able to practice their religion without fear of interference from the government, such laws are often portrayed as protecting the devoted from secular intrusions—such as the recent legalization of same-sex marriage in the U.S.[11] For example, consider the state of Mississippi's Protecting Freedom of Conscience from Government Discrimination Act (signed into law by the Governor on April 5, 2016).[12] According to the law:

Section 2
The sincerely held religious beliefs or moral convictions protected by this act are the belief or conviction that:
  (a) Marriage is or should be recognized as the union of one man and one woman;
  (b) Sexual relations are properly reserved to such a marriage; and
  (c) Male (man) or female (woman) refer to an individual's immutable biological sex as objectively determined by anatomy and genetics at time of birth.

Therefore, as stated in Section 3:

  (1) The state government shall not take any discriminatory action against a religious organization wholly or partially on the basis that such organization:
    (a) Solemnizes or declines to solemnize any marriage, or provides or declines to provide services, accommodations, facilities, goods or privileges for a purpose related to the solemnization, formation, celebration or recognition of any marriage, based upon or in a manner consistent with a sincerely held religious belief or moral conviction described in Section 2 of this act;
    (b) Makes any employment-related decision including, but not limited to, the decision whether or not to hire, terminate or discipline an individual whose conduct or religious beliefs are inconsistent with those of the religious organization, based upon or in a manner consistent with a sincerely held religious belief or moral conviction described in Section 2 of this act; or
    (c) Makes any decision concerning the sale, rental, occupancy of, or terms and conditions of occupying a dwelling or other housing under its control, based upon or in a manner consistent with a sincerely held religious belief or moral conviction described in Section 2 of this act.

Because of what comes to be understood as ones "sincerely held religious beliefs" (and that there is no test for sincerity is a crucial element of all this, of course, and we all know how easy it is for yet other belief systems *not* to be classed as religious but as extremist or cultic, such as the Russian court that, in the fall of 2015, ruled that the Church of Scientology, was not a religion; see AFP in Moscow 2015) one is therefore free of a variety of hiring and discrimination laws.[13] That those on the opposite side of this debate would reclassify these actions as bigotry should be obvious; this makes profoundly evident that, depending on one's goals, strategically using the classifier "religious" can have significant implications in U.S. law—motives and implications that strike me as worth studying without the scholar worrying about whether these really were sincere or properly religious beliefs.

But that's just not the right approach for those who wish to study the sacred—either to embrace it or debunk it (the two positions that still seem to define many of the debates in the field). This third option—the very ability to signify something *as* sacred, *as* set apart, *as* inviolable, etc.—strikes me as a far more interesting route, ensuring that we have productive, interdisciplinary conversation partners all over the university, united not by our object of study but by our shared curiosities and the common tools that we use to satisfy them—curiosities such how internally divided and hierarchically arranged social groups go about authorizing and contesting the norms that they work to put into place, norms that they then use to define themselves as a group or to define others as outsiders.

So sitting across from those faculty at that job interview, well over 20 years ago, reading that recent email in which I'm told I'm in a bit of a rut, or learning that an association with you might jeopardize someone gaining employment as a professor, are not examples of such conversations. In fact, if anything these are all examples of an ongoing contest in our very own internally divided group; for, not so dissimilar from the way the category religion is used in our wider society, to manage identities, behaviors, and resources in daily life, within our academic field one's place can be determined by how closely ones object of study fits the dominant or traditional use of the term. And so contests over "religion" in the academic study of religion are simply contests over the way the field ought to work and who should be allowed into it.

I think here, for instance, of David Robertson's recent work on conspiracy theories and his articulate arguments for why such an object of study ought to be considered a credible area in which a scholar of religion can work (e.g., Robertson 2016, 2017). As he phrases it in the conclusion to his 2017 article at the online *Religion Compass*:

> Is it our job as scholars of religion to tell people what they should think? Or rather, is it to observe and report with as much objectivity as we can the weltanschauung of others? Anthropologists have long treated the beliefs and practises [sic] of communities in exotic parts of the globe with respect, and attempted to explain the inner logic of their thinking, even when certain aspects are somewhat offensive to Western sensibilities—witchcraft, cannibalism, circumcision, and so forth. Even so, in most cases, the critique that their society is primitive compared to our modernity is clear, whether implicitly or explicitly. We do not tend openly to mock their irrationality, their paranoia, their lack of judgement, however—but this is precisely what the majority of academic work on conspiracy theories does. (Robertson 2017)

Our inability to study, in a serious manner, such so-called conspiracy theories (seeing them as part of a worldview that is either expressive or constitutive of a group) is therefore evidence of how we, as scholars, are working *to normalize our own social world*, in distinction from these others, by drawing lines and policing boundaries—much as how we (not to overlook how it is also done by the media and politicians, of course) normalize certain groups as orthodox or mainline and yet others as extremists or cults. A scholar such as Robertson, however, prompting us to consider the provocative similarities between, for instance, claims concerning the existence of UFOs and claims concerning the existence of angels, provides an ideal example of a site where reconsidering the usually taken-for-granted boundaries around our category religion may have the benefit of opening up fields of study previously unheard of.

And this strikes me as a good place to close—by bringing the work of another unorthodox, and entrepreneurial early career scholar onto the stage;[14] for the anecdotes from this chapter are hardly unique to me; were they then there'd be little use in writing about them other than some sense of self-satisfaction. Instead, the limitations of the field and the challenge of rethinking it have been experienced by a wide variety of people, in the generation before myself (such as mentors who report being fired from theological colleges, where they once worked, for, of all things, heresy) to academic generations after my own, who continue to read widely, think creatively, and press the field in new directions—yet experience resistance all the same. So I'm hardly alone in getting the push-back of that dirty hands question and, undoubtedly, many others' answers in similar situations have prompted a few raised eyebrow (let alone rejection letters). But despite these challenges, the long term health of our collective intellectual and institutional pursuit depends upon novel ways in which we identify our objects of study, not to mention how we then identity as scholars of religion—the efforts of our late-nineteenth-century predecessors, many of whom frequently gave large public lectures to persuade their audiences of the gains that could be made by what was then a newly established comparative science, make plain that these challenges are hardly new. But what will always be new is how each of us will choose to address them when someone leans over either an airline seat's armrest or an interview table, and asks us what we do for a living.

Notes

1   An earlier, shorter version of this unpublished chapter appeared as part of a series of invited posts at the blog for the *Bulletin for the Study of Religion*; find others in the series at http://bulletin.equinoxpub.com/?s=so+you%27re+not+a+priest (accessed May 15, 2017). Given that almost all of the posts in this series concerned how one describes one's work to people outside our field (such as friends or relatives who might presume that studying religion means preparing for the clergy—a presumption most in our field have likely experienced), it seemed to me to be a productive move to consider instead the difficulties that some of us sometimes have when asked to talk about our work to people who work in the same field.

2   Frankly put, it did not strike me as self-beneficial, at that time and at that point of what I hoped would be my career, to provide too many insider details about this particular occasion. As readers might guess, I feel rather differently now—though I still am discrete, to some extent, in relaying the story.

3   Publishing aside: I edited the MS very little after defending the dissertation, and sent it directly to a number of publishers; being content with the MS as it was, I reasoned (and was likely advised) that I shouldn't invest time in making revisions unless directed to do so by a publisher. The book was contracted fairly quickly (after being rejected by

all but one of the twelve or so publishers to which I had initially sent the prospectus), but, once the final MS was revised and off my desk it took about a year to see the copyediting; so a book that I had finished in the fall of 1995 wasn't published until later in 1997. I find this to be a useful story to bring to the attention of some early career scholars so that they fully recognize the sometimes surprisingly long timetable of the publishing industry.

4   Bear in mind that *Method and Theory in the Study of Religion*, a now well-established, international peer-review journal in the field, was founded at Toronto, by graduate students, in just 1989, and at the time of this interview it was in only its early years with an academic publisher (what was then Mouton de Grutyer); see the introduction to Hughes (2013) for more background on the journal.

5   As I later recorded how I re-phrased that conference answer there: "Because I study the ways scholars construct religion, I do fieldwork in publications and at national and international conferences on religion, where the methodological and theoretical hegemony in the field is often most evident. So, to the question, 'Where do you get your hands dirty?' I can honestly answer that I do it as a participant-observer-analyst of the scholarly profession of constructing and studying religion in North America" (McCutcheon 1997: 7).

6   For more on this episode, see the postscript to the forthcoming chapter by Hughes and myself, to be included in Leslie Dorrough Smith's forthcoming edited collection of papers from the 2017 meeting of the North American Association for the Study of Religion (NAASR).

7   I could also relate the time when someone reported to me that they were cautioned that a certain department would never hire someone associated with myself or my particular approach to the field. As readers might guess, the recipient of such information is put in a rather delicate position—though it would not be the first time that I had discussed with scholars at earlier career stages than myself, those who may have sympathies concerning the critique some of us have offered of our field, the need to be tactical in disclosures of their affiliations and interests. For, as per the above-mentioned paper on collegiality that I co-authored with Aaron Hughes, it would be naïve to assume that hiring committees are always focused on merit—or, come to think of it, that this quality that we call "merit" was itself an easily and uniformly defined measure.

8   As a follow-up to the previous note, I have regularly cautioned grad students who consult me about their work or the field that, even if primarily interested in theoretical topics, they more than likely need to be able to portray themselves credibly, to eventual colleagues and hiring committees, as "having a tradition." (This advice is based on my own experiences, of course, but also on insights gained from friends who, over the years, have trained in thoroughly cross-disciplinary units, such as Santa Cruz's well-known History of Consciousness program, where students may need to be quite intentional about crafting their training and CV so as to be understood, eventually, by others as an Historian or Anthropologist, etc.; for, while trained in an interdisciplinary unit one will more than likely seek employment in a unit that defines itself by means of rather traditional disciplinary boundaries.) Since any theoretical or methodological interest sensibly needs a place where that work is carried out or exemplified, developing a specialty in that e.g., such that one does the fieldwork or learns the languages, means that one can legitimately represent oneself as a content specialist in that specific area—thereby possibly satisfying a dominant discourse that still effectively guards the gates of employment and publication in the field.

9   I find this suspect advice to be realized in Barton and Boyarin's (2016) nonetheless important contribution to the study of religion in antiquity (see McCutcheon forthcoming for a chapter devoted to examining their book). For the time being, suffice it to say that what is worth attention is how—or so I would argue—the discursive domain that a word, used in a specific manner and in relation to a host of other terms, judgments, practices, and institutions, establishes is subsequently taken for granted, as if it pre-dates the (as I'll call it) socio-semantic effects of the designator and will naturally remain once the word is abandoned. As noted in a previous publication of mine, this is the realist, Shakespearean approach that we still find all throughout the field: as if the self-evidently fragrant rose would smell as sweet whether or not it was were called a rose (see *Romeo and Juliet*, act II, scene II).

10   Respectively, the cases were *Church of the Lukumi Babalu Aye, Inc. v. Hialeah*, 508 U.S. 520 (1993) and *Lynch v. Donnelly*, 465 U.S. 668 (1984). What is significant about Smith's essay is that he has no interest there in adjudicating what religion really is or whether the Court was correct in its decisions; that is, he assumes nothing about religion, but, instead, shifts the ground to examining the Court's use of the classification religion itself. So the essay nicely illustrates how, in order to come to the decision that they do, the majority in each case must moderate relationships of similarity and difference so as to apply what it takes as settled knowledge from the domain of the familiar (i.e., past cases [i.e., precedent] or what might even be termed commonsense) to that of the strange (the practices brought before the Court). Case in point, if, as Smith argues, the Court and popular culture at large both uncontroversially understand Roman Catholicism as a religion and African traditional practices as religious (and thereby rightly deserving the protections of the First Amendment's free exercise clause) then how can something that scholars understand as a syncretistic mixing of the two (i.e., Santeria, as described in the *Encyclopedia of Religion* article quoted in the majority decision) not also be a religion (making the city's actions to outlaw their sacrificial practices unconstitutional)? It is therefore *the logic by which the decision is reached*—again, a classic comparative approach dealing with issues of similarity and difference—and thus *the social utility of this category religion*—that interests Smith. This essay, delivered prior to publication as the second annual Ninian Smart Lecture (in September 2003), can be viewed online at www.uctv.tv/shows/God-Bless-This-Honourable-Court-Religion-and-Civic-Discourse-7910 (accessed June 28, 2017).

11   Find the June 26, 2015 U.S. Supreme Court decision (in a 5 to 4 vote) at www. supremecourt.gov/opinions/14pdf/14-556_3204.pdf (accessed June 25, 2017).

12   Find the bill's text at https://legiscan.com/MS/bill/HB1523/2016 (accessed June 25, 2017).

13   In the summer of 2016 a federal district judge had issued an injunction against the law, but on June 22, 2017, the U.S. Federal Appeals Court for the 5th Circuit lifted the injunction because, or so the three judge appeals panel found, the plaintiffs challenging it do not have standing. (In U.S. law one must be able to demonstrate that one is injured by an action in order to have legal grounds to contest it.) At present it is unclear if the plaintiffs will appeal this verdict. Find the Appeals Court's decision at www.ca5.uscourts.gov/opinions/pub/16/16-60477-CV1.pdf (accessed June 25, 2017).

14   I say entrepreneurial because, while a doctoral student, and along with Christopher Cotter, Robertson co-founded the Religious Studies Project, a now well-known podcast in the field, that now involves a large number of other early career people, in the UK and beyond; visit it at www.religiousstudiesproject.com.

References

AFP in Moscow (2015). "Russian Court Bans Moscow Branch of the Church of Scientology," *The Guardian*, November 23. Retrieved from www.theguardian.com/world/2015/nov/23/russian-court-bans-moscow-branch-church-of-scientology (accessed June 25, 2017).

Barton, Carlin A. and Daniel Boyarin (2016). *Imagine No Religion: How Modern Abstractions Hide Ancient Realities*. New York: Fordham University Press.

Bourdieu, Pierre (1988) [1984]. *Homo Academicus*, trans. Peter Collier. Stanford, CA: Stanford University Press.

Hughes, Aaron W. (ed.) (2013). *Theory and Method in the Study of Religion: Twenty-Five Years On*. Leiden: Brill. https://doi.org/10.1163/9789004257573

McCutcheon, Russell T. (1997). *Manufacturing Religion: The Discourse on Sui Generis Religion and the Politics of Nostalgia*. Oxford: Oxford University Press.

—— (2014). *Entanglements: Marking Place in the Field of Religion*. Sheffield: Equinox Publishers.

—— (Forthcoming). *Fabricating Religion: A Fanfare for the Common e.g.* Berlin: Walter de Gruyter.

Nongbri, Brent (2015). *Before Religion: A History of a Modern Concept*. New Have, CT: Yale University Press.

Robertson, David G. (2016). *UFOs, Conspiracy Theories and the New Age: Millennial Conspiracism*. London: Bloomsbury.

—— (2017). "The Hidden Hand: Why Religious Studies Need to Take Conspiracy Theories Seriously," *Religion Compass* 11/3–4. Retrieved from http://onlinelibrary.wiley.com/doi/10.1111/rec3.12233/pdf. https://doi.org/10.1111/rec3.12233

—— (2017). "Am I a Religious Studies Scholar?" in Russell T. McCutcheon (ed.), *Fabricating Identities*. Sheffield: Equinox Publishing.

Smith, Jonathan Z. (2004). "God Save this Honourable Court: Religion and Civic Discourse," *Relating Religion: Essays in the Study of Religion*, 375–390. Chicago, IL: University of Chicago Press.

Smith, Leslie Dorrough (forthcoming). *The Architecture of the Academy: Processes, Institutions, and Power in the Academic Study of Religion*. Sheffield, UK: Equinox Publishers.

Chapter 10

Why I Blog[1]

[H]is tone was that of an expert, yet his talks were still accessible to the general public. (Louis-Jean Calvet 1995: 85)

If Roland Barthes (1915–1990) was alive today, I'm convinced he'd be blogging.

But let me back up a bit and first say that I'm not sure how I originally came across his work—specifically, his influential collection of short pieces entitled *Mythologies* (as well as the follow-up English collection, *The Eiffel Tower*)[2]—a deceivingly little book, with short chapters on a series of seemingly mundane topics, which a biographer, also cited in the epigraph just above, aptly described as "a kind of ethnography of society through an analysis of the signs that society produces" (Calvet 1995: 147). My now worn copy, with my name and "U of T '92" written in the front, along with a quote copied from the book ("… to deprive it of its history"), is the 1973 Paladin edition, with Richard Hamilton's 1956 collage on the cover—the one with the housewife vacuuming, the stripper wearing pasties and a lampshade on her head, and the muscleman holding an oversized (and rather phallic) Tootsie pop in his hand.[3] In a catalogue, from a 1990–1991 exhibition of his work that traveled in Germany and Spain, Hamilton (1922–2011) described the work's aim as being "to throw into the cramped space of a living room some representation of all the objects and ideas crowding into our post-war consciousness" (Hamilton et al. 1990: 44). If we were to make explicit in the collage's already crowded living room (which, among other items, also contains a romance novel cover, a canned ham, and a reel-to-reel tape recorder) the economic status and future hopes of the bourgeoisie half a century ago—the people who were newly able to buy all those "convenient" canned hams—then we would arrive at what was a rather fitting choice for *Mythologies*' cover image, inasmuch as Barthes makes quite plain that what his translator characterized as his "highly poetic and idiosyncratic" book (Barthes 1973: 7) was concerned with offering an ideology critique of what was then emerging as what we today might call mass-culture. For as Barthes later explained in a TV interview: "[t]he purpose of *Mythologies* is to tackle systematically, as a block, a kind of monster which I have called the 'petite bourgeoisie' (even if this does tend to mythify it) and to tirelessly chip away at it" (quoted in Calvet 1995: 101).

In my memory it was through Bruce Lincoln's own influential essay collection, *Discourse and the Construction of Society* (1989), that I first came across Barthes, but then I realized that my copy of that book's first edition has "UT '94" on the inside the cover (the T now signifying Tennessee [and not Toronto, where I earned my

Ph.D.], where I worked for three years at the start of my career—a lesson in not always trusting one's memory as a verbatim repository of the past. So if not via Lincoln, then it was likely through my doctoral supervisor, Neil McMullin, in the early 1990s, that I first came across the book, probably during my prep for comprehensive exams, when he had me reading works that went on to have considerable influence over my thinking—books such as Jameson's *The Political Unconscious*, Lentricchia's *Criticism and Social Change*, Eagleton's introduction to literary theory and his then new book on ideology, Anderson's *Imagined Communities*, LaCapra's *Soundings in Critical Theory*, de Certeau's *The Practice of Everyday Life*, not to mention a variety of works by Derrida and Foucault (all of which provided the methodological framework for my first book [which was my revised dissertation], *Manufacturing Religion* [1997]). In fact, I cite my edition of *Mythologies* in both my dissertation and in *Manufacturing Religion*, briefly, along with *Discourse and the Construction of Society*, to tease out an alternative notion of myth, one that I found handy when examining the work taking place when we read such authors as Mircea Eliade or Joseph Campbell discuss the deep meaning of this or that origins narrative (a theological/humanistic approach that we still find in the field today). In fact, some years later I expanded on his understanding of myth to structure my own essay on that topic in the *Guide to the Study of Religion* (2000).

But the book became important to me for more than just its rather expansive notion of myth (understood not by its content [i.e., origins tales] or simply as a literary genre [alongside but distinguished from legends and folk tales] but, instead, as a socio-rhetorical mode by which we authorize our significations); and so, throughout my career, I've worked with *Mythologies*, read other of Barthes's works, and used them in classes from time to time; some of the students who have studied with me, over the years, have purchased the book and mulled over why, for example, the rear fins on a 1957 Chevy might have once looked "sleek" whereas they now look "clunky" or how divergent or even directly competing ways of viewing the world can each be seen by their supporters as normal, authoritative, and right—to the exclusion of all others. Although I certainly wouldn't go so far as to call myself a semiotician, the intersection of studying signification and identity (or, following Jean-Francois Bayart [2005], something I'd just rephrase as acts of identification) has increasingly come to shape my work—thanks, in part, to that early exposure to the misleading simple chapters of *Mythologies*.

And I'd say that, in a roundabout way, it also led me to start blogging.

Now, I'm self-aware enough to know how I write and what motivates me to write; as might be apparent to any readers who may be familiar with some of my work, much of my early writing was propelled by, shall we say, a strong dissatisfaction with how the academic study of religion had been (and, I might add, still is being) practiced. And that motivation resulted in a flurry of publishing activity (from, say, 1993 to 2003, including the pieces collected together in *Critics Not Caretakers* [2001] and *The Discipline of Religion* [2003]); as I'd phrase it now, each of these essays was a discrete attempt (i) to illustrate, at a specific site, what I considered to be an instance of a wider theoretical or methodological problem in the field and, despite those who continue to characterize my work as being nothing but negative critique, (ii) to offer an alternative, for those who were equally dissatisfied, concerning how we might instead proceed.[4] Although I didn't realize it at the time, looking back I think the format of the essay, allowing a series of strategically selected juxtapositions (i.e., of common practices versus alternative), was useful inasmuch as each provided a small, bounded Petri dish where an experiment in thinking could take place—a way of understanding our work that I eventually picked up from Jonathan Z. Smith (who, making use of the idea of a thought experiment more than you might at first realize, has argued that comparison is as close to a controlled scientific experiment as those in the human sciences can get).[5] Given my rampant dissatisfaction with the field, the essay (coupled with increasingly more deliberate choices for the targets that I selected) was thus the ideal format to adopt. It also suited the various other commitments any early career person also has.

So, with my rather eager approach to writing in mind, when computer memory, along with processor and internet speeds, all increased, and blogging became a thing (or a more popular thing, such as in the late 1990s), I recall purposefully avoiding it (much as I avoided Twitter when it was first launched), knowing that, given my rather enthusiastic approach to writing, this was one rabbit hole down which I probably should never go; after all, Facebook (which I joined back in the summer of 2005) soon became enough of a distraction. But, as Sean Connery learned, one should never say never;[6] for when our department, then under the direction of my colleague Ted Trost, decided to establish a blog, in the late Spring of 2012—to provide an online venue to discuss the coming academic year's series of speakers, all addressing the relevance of the humanities—I began to write online for the first time.

But it took some convincing, since from May 7 until August 27 that year only my colleague, Steven Ramey, wrote on the site; he had set up the WordPress template and was managing the blog, and so, throughout the summer, he was the sole member of the faculty to write for the site, producing thirteen posts, all addressing the upcoming lecture series' broad theme and trying to prompt a conversation among readers.[7] Knowing that one colleague shouldn't solely be responsible for generating the content for a department-wide initiative, I wrote my first post on September 25, 2012, in reply to the first of four guest lecturers we had visit our campus that academic year, all asked to address the same theme. The 1,200-word post, entitled "Turtles All the Way Down" (a phrase I've used earlier in this book), read (in full) as follows:

> It's the day after our inaugural lecture in 2012–13's series on the place of the Humanities and Social Sciences in the contemporary university and I'm troubled by the student feedback that I've heard so far. It's come from some of our undergraduate majors, who attended, as well as from an assortment of students enrolled in my 100-level introductory course who also attended. ("Write me a one page description and you can earn some extra credit in the course"—the professor's old trick to get students new to the university to think a few new thoughts, and, as we used to say, expand their horizons.) Whether or not it was the intended message of the speaker—Prof. Gregg Lambert from Syracuse University—the students seem

to have heard a message of lamentation for the future of the Humanities—not a description of how we got here or a renewed defense of our relevance but, instead, a (to their ears at least) dire message from a senior professor concerning the fact that they may be deluded to think that grad school might be for them (since they'll possibly be mired in student debt that will take them decades to repay—making grad school sound like a bit of a scam); because they're all just human capital, spewed into the global market from a never-ending pipeline, why continue in their studies? As one first year student who attended the lecture said to me today, sounded both intimidated and incredulous: "Declaring a major may be the most important decision of my life?!"

Now, this is not necessarily the lecture that I heard (e.g., the pipeline imagery was directly contested by our speaker, but the image remained nonetheless), but I can understand why certain parts stood out for them—the shocking often proves the most memorable. And maybe that was our lecturer's intention—a little cold water to wake us from our dogmatic slumbers. Perhaps these sobering words caught some of our students off-guard because we, as their professors, have not hammered home often and loudly enough that education is now (whether it always was, and we just had the luxury to pretend that it wasn't, is a discussion that we ought to have) a part of the cost/benefit economic system as much as anything else. Given the uphill argument that we, in the academic study of religion, feel that we have in helping students (and, more importantly, perhaps, their families) understand that this undergraduate major is as relevant as any other (did you ever wonder why is "If you're not going to become a History teacher, then why major in History" is not a question for people in that field?), you would think that our students, perhaps more than anyone else's, had already done some of the hard-nosed decision-making long before declaring their REL major. And given the complex careers that some of us have had (yes, I know what it is like to be an Instructor and to consider the hard truth that, having earned a Ph.D., I had not also earned the right to feed and clothe myself by means of those skills), we are particularly cognizant of these issues and try to make sure students know too. But perhaps they need to be told again: structural factors well beyond your control kicked the sand out from under so much of the national and global economy in the late-2000s that it may take decades to recover (if recovery is even the right word).

But tied to that structural level analysis there needs also to be one that focuses attention on individual agency—and I wonder if this is what the student also needed to hear. Now, I'd likely never be accused of erring on the side of the rugged, can-do lone individual, boldly making meaning in the world—so fear not: I am not descending into some argument for the self-evident, intangible value of the Humanities for the noble self. No, not at all. Instead, I'm taking a basic insight from structuralism seriously and noting that, while we may emphasize one or the other for analytic purposes, no analysis of a binary pair is sufficient if is neglects the other side of the coin. After all, the way that the Other-in-our-midst is silenced or at least ignored (whether it's worth recovering is, of course, another conversation) is a basic building block of the critical theories that have shaped so much of our work in the academy over the last generation or two—from the work of Social Historians to postcolonial theorists. So, taking a page from our own critical thinking playbook I think that, while focusing on structure, we also need also to draw attention to the agents within that structure; for the system did not invent itself (and it isn't homogenous either) and neither did the agents invent themselves from whole cloth—none of us would be here without the mating rituals that were not of our parents' own making, though they tweaked the rules and each other, to be sure.... And around and around it goes: structure made by agents made by structure made by... Turtles all the way down. That's how the critical thinker in me sees it.

And this is the part of the message that our students didn't hear: that they are agents within that structure, determined by many factors well beyond their influence, yes, but that they are nonetheless agents who, by their very activity, affect the structure (isn't this the moral of the double slit experiment?); they collaborate and thereby continually re-make it.

I'm no Pollyanna, of course, and I'm certainly no Dr. Pangloss—no one is going to pull themselves up by their own bootstraps, despite how popular the "I made it myself" sentiment is right now in the current US Presidential election. But I would also not like to erase the presence of the actors in these structures, those who made the rules, benefit from them, labor under them, and who can and will change them—how, we have yet to see.

So this is not some dreamy-eyed message of hope—I'll also leave spinning that tale to the political campaigns. But it is a message to our students to pay attention to the wider, structural circumstances in which you do your work—the structures that work on you: all those turtles above you and below—but also to know that those social worlds did not spring from the ground like a mushroom overnight; instead, people—huge numbers of people, people who didn't know each other, people collaborating, competing, and contradicting each other—made them. Since you're people (good people, salt of the earth people) maybe you can re-make it.

So be modest. Be strategic. Know that your good looks will only get you so far. Know that, at times, you're an almost powerless item exchanged in a network of international capital—but, then again, you knew that as soon as you walked into The Gap, watched MTV, faced ever-rising tuition rates, or sat and respectfully listened to tenured professors lamenting over the job market. But also know that you have agency...—within structure within agency within structure, etc., etc., all the way down. And knowing your place within this never-ending system of reciprocal actors in situations-not-of-their-making means that you have what the ancient Greek called mêtis (μῆτις): cunning intelligence.

So never forget: you're a tactical turtle. Cowabunga! (McCutcheon 2012)

The intended audience was clearly our own discouraged students. (Several had talked to me after the lecture, expressing their dismay at what they heard as its message, and thus my inaugural post was born.) As with anything one writes, I'm not sure what effect it had. (I recall Bruce Lincoln once saying that he saw writing as akin to putting notes in bottles and throwing them into the ocean, not knowing where they would or wouldn't land.) Did readers even get my Teenage Mutant Ninja Turtles reference at the end? The plugin that keeps track of traffic on the site failed early on, and had to be reinstalled, so our data now reports that it has been accessed only 83 times; but whether or not it was read by anyone else, for me it was still an important initial foray into writing for a far wider readership than I normally had.

As I've noted elsewhere, sometime ago I came to realize that the imagined, intended audience of my scholarly writing was myself twenty (or now 30) years or so behind where I am now: younger scholars, maybe doctoral students, who are dissatisfied with the field they're entering but who, also, were not sure how else to do their work. Whether or not they followed my lead (and, say, began to problematize the category religion itself), they would at least find a model for how someone who has made a career as a scholar of religion *but who does not study world religions* thinks things could be otherwise—which might be useful to them as they figure out how they want to tackle things. (Or, to rephrase, I've long understood that the position against which my work argues is extremely well entrenched and I'm therefore not likely going to change the minds of more senior scholars who disagree with my approach.) But this first blog post, an even more refined and delimited experimental setting than a scholarly essay, was an exercise in writing succinctly for a rather different sort of reader—not just the undergrad reader who I imagined when writing the introductory book (2007) I've already discussed in an earlier chapter; instead, being posted in public with the click of a button, on what we used to call world wide web (Aside: does the younger genera- tion know that's what the www in the URL stands for? Come to think of it, do they know what URL signifies...?), it had to be legible (whether agreeable or not) and available to almost anyone who happened upon the site—it's a topic Ramey and I have discussed on many occasions, as we both invented online writing personae: how brevity can be more effective than one might think. While I'm not sure that I succeeded at that this first time (the 83 hits suggests otherwise), it was, at least for me, an important first step into a new genre.

Which brings me back to Barthes's *Mythologies*.

For not everyone may know that his book is a collection of short pieces that he originally wrote, each month, throughout the early/mid-1950s, for a small variety of French arts and literary magazines, such as *Esprit* (founded in 1932), *France-Observateur* (founded in 1950 and later renamed *Le Nouvel Observateur* or *L'Obs* for short), and *Les Lettres Nouvelles* (founded in 1953). As narrated by his biographer, Barthes—then working for the Cultural Affairs section of the French Foreign Office, "where he dealt with missions and the teaching of 'French as a for- eign language'" (Calvet 1995: 97), and while moonlighting with various research projects (such as helping to begin work on what became the *Dictionnaire du français fondamental*)[8]—was recruited in 1950 to help produce the literary supplement for what was then the newly founded *L'Observateur Politique, Économique et Littéraire*. Soon Barthes became a regular contributor there and elsewhere, such as his reg- ular column in *Les Lettres Nouvelles*—writing there on "whatever subject he chose" (Calvet 1995: 100). As his biographer goes on to recount:

> He had just published a piece in *Esprit* in October 1952, an ironic glance at that par- ticular Olympus of the gods of the ring in which he had explained that wrestling was not merely a sport but a spectacle in which everything was a sign, a signifier. He decided to continue to write in this vein. (Calvet 1995: 100)

As already noted, in 1957 a collection of these ironic glances was published in France, comprising the original edition of *Mythologies*.

They are, again citing his biographer, pieces distinguished by their "combination of erudition and popularization" (ibid.: 85)—a style Calvet suggests was linked to experiences Barthes had had a decade before, while working in Bucharest, Romania, as the librarian at the French Institute. He began that job in 1947 (traveling and living there with his mother, in fact) and, as Calvet details, soon began offering evening lectures, for locals interested in French history and contemporary culture. "It was a style developed," Calvet argues,

> because of the place where he was speaking. If he had taught at a university, he would have adopted a different tone, moulded his discourse into the forms of classical academic discourse. At the institute, however, speaking to a cultured but non-specialist audience, he perfected in oral form what was later to become his style of writing. (Calvet 1995: 85)

While I had no idea of the details of his little book's style and composition when I first read it, I tend to think that my early exposure to Barthes's writing style and targets/data, coupled with the broad theme of the department blog (at least in the early years), along with my sense that the next generation of scholars, if they were anything like I was at their stage, might find it handy to have a few alternative models for doing their work, along with my own particular setting (i.e., working at that time exclusively with undergraduate students) all created the conditions in which blogging could be seen as a desirable choice. (That many academics still look down on it—"Why do you invest so much time on that" I'm sometimes asked—is worth noting here; such commentators would have probably reviewed *Mythologies* harshly had they been there when it was first published—"a book about margarine and plastic?!") While I've certainly not stopped writing and publishing research essays, book chapters, or review essays since that first post in September of 2012, I have tossed quite a few pithy, experimental glances into the virtual ocean over the past several years—most posted at either our department blog or at the site for Culture on the Edge, a research collaborative of which I'm a member.[9] All told, to date I've posted 363 blogs of varying length and substance at the former site and another 439 at the latter (along with a smaller number of guest posts at a variety of other sites, such as at the *Religious Studies Project*, *The Immanent Frame*, *Political Theology Today*, *Engaging Religion*, and, of course, the blog for the *Bulletin for the Study of Religion*). Though the topics of those posts vary widely, I think what unites them is also evidence of the influence of Barthes on my thinking: they all try to examine how the world we take for granted works, doing so at a specific site that might otherwise not attract our attention (e.g., a nonchalant photo of a young Buddhist monk drinking from a bottle of pop or the misleadingly simple phrase, "I believe you"[10]). While having no interest to reproduce or mimic Barthes's now classic book, blogging—coupled with my desire to provide readers with a succinct e.g. with which to mull over a possible shift in the way they carried out their own work as scholars of religion—offered new challenges for me as a writer (my reputation for long, unwieldy sentences, with asides such as this very one, had to be rethought in light of a blog's requirement for far pithier writing) and offered the possibility of new readers. For while people still read (or, in light of online pithiness, should I now say wade through?) books and peer review articles, of course, I have a sense that changes in both the work conditions of the institution that is the modern university and the attention span of some early-twenty-first-century readers have created a situation in which a 750- or 1,000-word blog post, easily accessible through a social media link that quickly circulates online, may now be some people's preferred (or maybe even their only) venue for finding intellectual provocation.

Which, again, brings me back to the brief, monthly columns, on seemingly random pop culture topics, that were to become the chapters in *Mythologies*.

So although it's based either on utter speculation or self-beneficial projection, I'd like to think that, were he alive today, Barthes would also be enjoying the tremendous freedom that the virtual medium affords while using it in the rather precise, controlled manner required of experts aiming to talk plainly, succinctly, yet persuasively to the public.

That I came to this, shall we say, self-conscious awareness of the uses for a pedagogical writing style rather later in my career than Barthes did in his (if readers will forgive me comparing myself to Barthes) is not insignificant, of course; that my first academic book was lucky enough to have been published by a press with an enviable reputation, and that I eventually landed tenure-track work (after three years as a year-to-year instructor) meant that I had freedoms for some of my subsequent work, to be sure, inasmuch as those preoccupied with imprimaturs seemed to have been satisfied when they looked at my CV and saw Oxford University Press's brand listed there. For whatever reason, as already noted above, I became an essayist after that first monograph was published, though I was fortunate enough also to have been involved in editing journals (such as twelve years with *Method & Theory in the Study of Religion* and five years with the now defunct *Bulletin of the Council of Societies for the Study of Religion*) as well as handbooks, anthologies, and essay collections. Blogging, then, despite how some devalue it, was something that I realize I could afford to tackle, given that I happen to be of a generation who was able to turn to it after already many years of writing, peer review publication, and teaching under my belt. And given the—at least some would surely say—rather unorthodox approach of my work, the blog's pedagogical writing style made sense to me; for when you don't agree with your field's widely accepted first principles (e.g., that religion is a uniquely distinguishable and fundamentally important and deeply meaningful aspect of the human that is only secondarily expressed outward, into the world) you quickly learn that each piece of writing must work from the ground up, attempting to persuade either novice or reluctant readers to rethink basic assumptions that they take for granted. (It's for this reason that I've always questioned the common distinction between research/publishing, on the one hand, and teaching, on the other—instead, it's pedagogical all the way down, something not always apparent to those who only preach to the choir in their work.) Writing, then, was a form of ideology critique, if by that we at least mean an approach that invites readers to reconsider the self-evident (i.e., to regain its history, to paraphrase the above-cited quote from Barthes in the front of my copy) and, instead, come to see it as happenstance—an approach that, again, has roots in *Mythologies*'s attempt to, paraphrasing Barthes's 1957 preface, rethink the naturalness with which we regularly portray our own historically determined world.

But, as noted above, Barthes, of necessity, confronted the challenge of combining erudition with popularization far earlier in his career than I—and this difference is probably something not lost on the generation now either going into or just coming out of graduate school.

Case in point: as mentioned in earlier chapters, I had the good fortune a couple of years ago to go up to the University of Chicago to lead a workshop in their Divinity School's The Craft of Teaching series.[11] While there I met with some old friends, schemed on a project or two, and presented a paper and participated in a discussion with about 25 people on teaching the introductory course (almost all of whom were current M.A. or Ph.D. students [Chapter 6 in this volume is a revised version of the paper that I gave on that occasion][12]). Of course I had to eat too and so I went out to some nice dinners with a couple different groups of students and faculty and it was there that some of the more interesting conversations took place. Among the questions that I was asked one evening was one concerning whether early career scholars, who are about to go onto the job market, should have an active social media presence, whether that means being on Twitter or blogging ...?

Apart from four years away from it (from 2009 to 2013), I've been a department chair in a large U.S. public university since 2001 and have been in on interviewing and hiring many people during that time, so I've seen lots of CVs over the years, and—like a lot of topics—I've got an opinion on that question.[13]

Although only one person asked me that question about social media, I heard it as a variation on a number of the questions that I fielded from grad students while I was up north, or when talking at other campuses—questions not just about whether they should be blogging but also about whether they should be writing book reviews, submitting their work to peer review journals, trying to present at conferences, etc. And, in programs like Chicago's (or, maybe I should say, unlike Florida State University's doctoral program in the study of religion), where grad students don't have all that much opportunity to teach their own undergrad class (contra to FSU's model of getting grad students in front of undergraduate classes right from the outset), some also asked how they could put their best pedagogical foot forward when applying for jobs in which other applicants may have considerable teaching experience. Basically, the questions concerned the attention they should (or should not) give to items other than their dissertation. As a person who spent a fair bit of time, much earlier in my career, writing to the book review editors of journals in attempts to review books (in hopes that review essays and maybe peer review essays might later follow), it seems that the strategy I once used to gain writing experience is rather alien to what some of these students are now being told by their graduate directors and supervisors.[14]

An informal dinner with students, while visiting a campus, isn't the place to definitively answer each of these queries in detail (and, yes, "Do it all" is hardly a sufficient answer) and far be it from me to assume that a strategy I attempted to employ, in the early 1990s, has continued relevance today; so I tried my best, in person, to provide as many reasons (and anecdotes) as I could to illustrate why I happen to think this and not that when it comes to some of these issues. But with the question about online skills/presence in mind, for now just consider this: who would ever ask if you need to know how to use a word processor in order to get a job these days? It's a silly question, right? For within just a couple decades that once exotic technology, mastered initially by just a few, has become such an integral part of what we do that we don't even call it "word processing" any more—we just call it "writing."[15] So ... in preparation for a job application, might one ask what role does social media play in the department to which you're applying for a position? Or might the answer to "Where do you think the future of the web is going in higher education?" inform how you prepare yourself for the job market? That is, might being conversant with the virtual world, having a professional presence in that world, and knowing your way around various software and hardware that make it possible, be not only beneficial to your application but something you wish to represent as a commonsense skill that you, of course, possess?

Each person must answer such questions for themselves, to be sure, and the answers likely depend on the sort of program to which you're applying (Ivy League program with grad students or small liberal arts college with no major?); but addressing such questions strikes me as one among the many items that a strategic young scholar ought to be thinking about, since the structure into which one steps upon entering the academic job market is so fraught and beyond ones control that taking a firm grasp on whatever factors you *can* determine, or at least influence to whatever extent, is likely a sensible move. For, if nothing else, as I recall Adam T. Miller rightly chiming in when this topic came up on my visit to Chicago, the decision to try blogging does help to get us writing regularly and that's got to be worth something when you're trying to produce a dissertation that, sooner or later, will surely become a rather onerous and maybe even boring task.[16]

Moral of the story? The decision to invest time in one or more aspects of social media can have unexpected outcomes.

Speaking of decisions: in the background of many of the questions that were posed to me on that campus visit was a broad choice that (some? many? all?) graduate programs/supervisors seem to have made, a choice that created the structure in which people were formed into a specific sort of grad student (with specific skills and concerns) and thus from out of which they posed their questions: are graduate schools training scholars or colleagues?

It doesn't have to be mutually exclusive, sure, but in my experience it often is.

While it's understandable for a school to have the ambitious goal of getting their grad students to write dissertations that will revolutionize the field (as their supervisors' expectations are sometimes communicated to me by those posing these sorts of questions to me, either on campus visits or social media messages)—thereby seeing their work as producing erudite scholars—speaking from a large state university department chair's point of view, I may be more interested in hiring a colleague: someone who, yes, does innovative, original, and rigorous academic work, but also someone who is prepared to do that work next door to me and the other people with whom I work.

That is, the work of being a university professor is often somewhat more than just being a good or careful scholar (which, of course, can be a perfectly solitary life in which any effort devoted to blogging or writing book reviews can be seen as time stolen away from one's more important academic tasks), for it means working as part of a group to achieve collective goals that transcend one's own research and writing—like, say…, the goal of successfully reproducing (who knows, maybe even expanding) the unit in which we each carry out our own individual research and teaching. So, whether they disclose it or not, many departments are probably looking for more than cutting edge research or the dogged ability to chase down the details in the footnotes. While both are desirable, sure, many would also like evidence of teaching ability, e.g., can you successfully mix the expertise with roughly equal parts generalizing, popularizing, and infectious enthusiasm, so that you can effectively talk to a 19 year old who is in your class not because of the inherent interest the topic holds? After all, how else do we get majors in the study of religion other than by students stumbling across us in satisfying their Gen Ed requirements? (For, unlike other fields, which have versions of themselves in the high school curriculum, the academic study of religion is generally a novel experience for university students who enroll in our classes to satisfy a general education requirement. In fact, isn't that how many of us became scholars of religion in the first place? We were all—or almost all of us—19 and uninterested at some point …). Departments would probably also like to see evidence of an understanding of the service required of a faculty member and thus the need to be able to juggle a variety of balls without dropping (m)any (or at least show evidence of knowing which will bounce and which will shatter if dropped); service to the profession is important, sure (such as serving on a program unit at the national scholarly association or editing a journal), but more importantly perhaps, there's the often unheralded service to the local unit (i.e., who will advise our student association, plan our guest lectures, develop new courses, organize new course proposals, hold the movie nights, serve on this or that college or university committee, chair the Tenure and Promotion Committee, decide how we use our scholarship funds, be in charge of the website and maybe even create a blog or a podcast…?). A great scholar, in my experience, is not necessarily someone who also has these various institutional needs in mind let alone someone who has the necessarily skills to contribute to satisfying them.

As I believe I said one evening while at dinner in Chicago, most chairs and hiring committees also probably hope that the people they hire will succeed in their new positions, eventually earning tenure, a hope that makes a hiring decision also a bold speculation on whether that candidate will eventually make a successful career out of that appointment—which, despite having little control over this particular situation, puts the job applicant in a perhaps unanticipated driver's seat; for they now need to come up with ways to communicate as much strategic information as possible to the hiring committee, to help them make that speculative leap, to help them feel good about the risk we all take when we bring someone new aboard.

So, through a cover letter and CV, a statement on teaching and writing sample, and, if lucky enough to travel to campus, a sample teaching, job talk, and countless meals with other faculty members (and, often, students as well), applicants can paint for their interviewers a picture of someone who will contribute and succeed, who will enhance what a department's members already happen to do but also take them somewhere new. Simply put, they are in the position to make sure interviewers know what else, apart from completely their dissertation, they've been doing with their time as a grad student for, if hired in the sorts of departments in which I've happened to work, they'll surely be asked to do plenty more than just work on their own research as a professor.

The question, then, to return to that dinner in Chicago, is whether blogging is part of that picture? Is writing a blog one among the many balls that we're managing to keep aloft all at the same time?

That there are few positions in the country now in which faculty have the luxury of focusing almost exclusively on teaching specialized graduate students and writing their next so-called "field-changing book"—the inverse of that statement is to take seriously how many two- and three-person departments of philosophy/religious studies there are in the country or how many positions there are in which someone teaches 3/3 or 4/4, with all classes being a different prep...—indicates to me that those who have influence over grad programs in our field would be well advised to be a little more nimble than they seem to be currently, to help their students prepare to be colleagues and not just scholars. For while we all might want to reshape the field, it's departments that pay our salaries and it's the students whom we teach there (many of whom are undergraduates in general education classes) that largely justify our existence as university professors. (To rephrase: few in our field justify their existence based on the research overhead that their grant dollars bring in.) And besides, given the time it takes to research and then write a book, have it refereed externally and then revised, contracted, copyedited, proofed, indexed, published and eventually (if you're lucky) reviewed in a few reputable places and maybe adopted in courses, then read more widely, let alone the years that it takes for its argument to slowly percolate throughout the field so as to—*in the rare, best case scenario*—change it, you'll need to figure out what else to do with yourself in the meantime. And so having a job in the field, working with other colleagues, is not a bad place to start.

So ... should you be blogging as a grad student?

To answer that (though I feel as if I already have) I can reflect a little more explicitly on why I blog.[17] For perhaps that might shed some light on the effects it, or some online activity akin to it, might also have for others. (For those wanting the other shoe to drop now: of course you should, in moderation of course, since grad students have many responsibilities; though, it should be said that, apart from a good dose of sheer luck, developing the skills to juggle them all is precisely what is needed to succeed in this career, making blogging a useful ball to have.)

As noted above, our department started its blog (in 2012) as a place where faculty and students, not to mention the invited lecturers, might interact in the attempt to get people talking about the relevance of the humanities, as a counter-narrative to the one most frequently cited and repeated in the media—trying to make evident that since we all have a stake in this debate we likely ought not to rely on the ordained big shots writing in *The Chronicle of Higher Education* to be the only ones discussing it. That the blog then soon grew into the department's venue for publicizing the broad work of its own students, grads, and faculty—implicitly keeping its eye on making evident the applicability of what we do in our classes and thus, yes, the wide relevance of the liberal arts—should be pretty apparent to anyone who is even just acquainted with it. So, as a faculty member at that time, and then beginning in 2013 as the chair of the department once again, I saw it as a worthwhile use of my time to begin blogging pretty regularly.

After all, like anyone who has been at a job for a while, I have a story or two in my back pocket—who wouldn't after teaching for even just a few years. For it seems to me that good teachers have their fair share of "go to" analogies and examples that they've learned to draw upon in the classroom, to demonstrate a principle or to try to persuade students on a point. So why not put a few of those into print and then hit the "Publish" button? Assuming future students aren't yet perusing the blog, you can still use them in a lecture or two some other day and, today, they might serve as a useful e.g. for a reader who is starting to amass some anecdotes of their own.

So, for starters, I blog, and support students and grads posting their own work there, in the hope of benefiting my department.

One of those benefits to the department is that students and former students can see their writing appear in public, online and linked on the department's Facebook and Twitter sites (yes, I'd argue that departments need to be well represented on social media), maybe even liked, reposted, or commented on by people elsewhere in the country or elsewhere in the world (and your mom too, why not?); when their writing appears in a blog post students see the direct impact of classroom efforts on the so-called real world (on friends and family or whomever clicks the link to see what's new at Alabama), thereby narrowing that presumed gap between what we once called town and gown by demonstrating that the tools we teach allow students to say new and hopefully interesting things about the world in which we live. It's also a venue for grads (who either miss what they once did in our classes or who still wish to apply those skills to the worlds in which they now live and move), to continue to contribute to what we do. (Lesson: not every valuable alumni contribution is a financial gift.) And it allows faculty who post their own work to be seen by grads and students as pitching in to the same collective projects (one such project is for the members of all of these constituencies to use a widely available digital platform and its text to imagine into existence that shared thing we call "the department" [with the appropriate hat-tip to Benedict Anderson's analysis of the nation-state as but one among many imagined communities, of course]).[18] Sure, profs have a little more experience and a few more moves up their sleeves, but the gulf between us and students is often not as large as we'd sometimes like to think (often it's more like a channel or a canal), suggesting that any time we can make evident that we are all working on the same shared problems, and doing so in common venues and with similar tools, is not time wasted. After all, as their teachers we're in the business of modeling for students a way of talking about the world, a way of problem-solving, and a way of reasoning, so how better to do that than by sharing and building a common venue, in plain sight, where we read and comment on each other's work?

But I'm not (that) selfless and so there are other reasons too. For I work in that very department—one among many on my campus, and, you may or may not be surprised to learn, it is not the only one where classes focus on the role of religion in human affairs; so anything that helps our department's faculty and students to coalesce, making it a place not only with which students and grads identify but also one identified by other profs, in other departments, or by administrators at various levels of the hierarchy, able to see us as a cohesive site of innovative and earnest (yes, at times, fun) activity, well..., that benefits me pretty directly; for, like my colleagues, I enjoy doing what I do and so I'd like to see this unit stick around for a good long time. (I speak here as someone who came to this department, back in 2001, when it was slated to lose its major and, possibly, be closed.)[19] For as many of us agree, social groups (from nations to university departments and even families) don't exist of their own inner moment or self-evident value. The blog is therefore one among many interconnected sites where we not only study social formation but carry it out. (The old proverb from Luke 4:23, "Physician, heal thyself" could be rewritten: "Social theorists, apply your tools to your own situation.)

But it benefits me in other ways too; thinking back to Miller's comment at dinner one night in Chicago, it gets me writing pithy posts (i.e., controlled experiments) on a fairly regular basis and I've subsequently spun a variety of them into other projects—case in point: this very chapter. And, while some of my work in journals and books is known already to some readers, the online venue also benefits me by bypassing the bureaucracy of publishing (it takes months or years to get some pieces into the hands of readers) by providing me with a direct and instantaneous publishing venue. Sure, I don't have a copyediter (wink) and it's not peer-reviewed, but blogs ought not to be confused with a book or an academic essay[20] and, besides, one can find that literature elsewhere if that's what you wish to read. And who knows, maybe that's where some enterprising readers will go when they log off the computer after having read a post that got them thinking about something. "I wonder what else he's written ...?" or "There must be people who disagree with this guy—what have they written?"

Yet another reason why I blog concerns an intentional effort to provide other instructors with a pithy argument, application, or illustration that they might be able to use in their own classes. It happens infrequently, for all I know, but periodically one learns that a colleague was able either to one of your blog posts in a class, to illustrate a point, or, especially when the topic of the post is something in the current news, the post brings an e.g. to someone's attention that assists them to make a pedagogical point of their own. For, as noted above and in previous chapters, the work conditions of the modern university have changed, when compared to just decades ago, since teaching loads have increased in many places and a far higher percentage of those who are teaching undergraduates are not themselves in any university's tenure-track system—in fact, they may be lecturing part-time at two or more schools in the same semester. So blogging is a self-conscious attempt to provide a service to the field—however, of what use these bottled message are is, as noted above, always difficult to determine; but given the amount of time required to prepare lectures, it may be a small favor to someone, teaching who knows where or how much, that they come across a post on their Facebook wall or Twitter feed that leads them to a nicely framed, 750 word commentary on, say, the difficulty of defining religion or the implications of standpoint in how people talk about or interact with the world. In this way, one can understand seeing blogging as a service activity or perhaps even a branch of teaching.

But I blog for yet another reason.

Over the past couple of years there's been an increasing emphasis on the problems created by pay walls at online, for-profit academic journals, portraying them as impediments to the (literally) free exchange of ideas. While I'm not going to single-handedly overturn the industry that is print capitalism (an industry that I, as a published author, participate in, to be sure; for who doesn't want to see a royalty check, no matter how small, no matter how much it fails to symbolize the work that went into the piece or how small a share of the piece's total earnings it represents ...?), I made a conscious decision to spend at least a few years putting sustained energy into professional but public, online writing, as bit of an experiment in its own right. As noted above, there's just over 800 posts of mine floating out there in cyberspace, many are substantive but others are far briefer (maybe a provocative image juxtaposed with a poignant quote from an author in our field), but the vast majority are (following Barthes's model) discrete, bite-sized examples of the sort of scholarship I've argued for all along, making each a little exercise in how to handle an e.g., how to see our objects of study as (again, with Barthes in mind) normal and mundane rather than unique and essentially or inherently interesting. So whether they're read or not, it helps my other work (my academic writing *and* teaching) to do these little writing exercises and, who knows, it might be just the sort of accessible, quickly read model that some readers need to help them to connect a few dots of their own, to get them moving along a different way of talking about how to study the world.

But as I said earlier, what the gain of posting this work online will be is not clear to me now, though it's at least been my attempt to take seriously that while there are books that cost money there's also research, written in a different, more colloquial voice (one that, more and more, seeps back into my other writing, as you have surely noticed) that I'd like to think of as being no less useful or innovative but which is just posted in public, free of charge, for anyone to read (so long as they have a computer and decent internet access). But, ironically perhaps, I find that, even for those who take seriously the need for open source publishing, blogging is still often seen as the lesser cousin to "serious" scholarship; it was with this in mind that the previously mentioned research collaborative in which I do some of my work, Culture on the Edge, two years ago, reinvented its blog as peer-review, and began soliciting/accepting/mentoring submissions from outside the group, in an effort to assist early career writers with some feedback on their work, provided by one of our members, and thereby also to give them a CV line that others might see as having greater worth, inasmuch as it might be distinguished from the sort of self-serving op-ed that characterizes some personal blogs.

That I've already jumped many career hoops and carry a variety of (for good or ill) imprimaturs on my CV (i.e., he worked there, he's published here, etc.), means, as I indicated above, that I have some freedoms with what I do with my time and writing that others don't have. I know that.[21] (Aside: although a department chair, with a lighter teaching load but with a variety of service obligations on campus, I have other constraints on my time that others likely don't have—meaning that it all might be a wash at the end of the day and that we're all busy no matter how you slice it. For example, this morning, before getting to this chapter's revisions, I wrote a hiring proposal, dealt with fall enrollment numbers, wrote captions to a variety of posts on the department's Facebook page, and worked on budgets and endowment projections for 2017/18.) But, yes, if I was much earlier in my career I'd likely not be posting as energetically as I did for the past few years—but, thinking back to the (as the old timers might say) "fire in my belly" that I had in the first decade of my career, maybe I would have embraced blogging then, had it existed. But we also can't lose sight of the fact that, at least at present, the profession doesn't award tenure and promotion for posting a witty gif or a timely two or three paragraphs on something in the news. Whether it should is another conversation (personally, as you might have figured out already, I see blogging as a service to the department and the field and, along with a variety of things, worth recognizing among our many other service contributions), but that doesn't mean that blogging and social media in general are irrelevant or a distraction and thus a waste of professional time. Rather, I see them as helping us to become professionals. Consider that already published volumes that I've edited are collections of rewritten blog posts from the members of Culture on the Edge, each of which is followed by an original and substantive commentary written by an early career scholar who, in almost all cases, I first met when they friended me on Facebook—having read me in class they found me online. Several of them regularly blog too. So I was able to identify a group of almost near strangers as contributors to books through reading their blogs, their online comments, and by messaging with them about what they worked on (see McCutcheon 2015, 2017).

So, why do I blog?

Simply put, it seems to me a logical extension of what I do in the rest of my professional life: working with others to model a certain way of thinking about human subjects, what they do and what they leave behind after they're gone; teaching is already a way of doing that modeling on a public catwalk, where a smaller group can be the judges (our work is judged not only by the peer review process). Moving to writing for far wider audiences means working with less and less of a net, of course, since we control much of the discourse in the classroom, let alone in our scholarly writing aimed at specialists; so blogging (or engaging in what, more generally, some now call the public humanities—a term that is, in part, a response to the debate on the relevance of our work [what our department's blog started out addressing back in 2012]) comes with risks, certainly—some of which are rather greater than just the time taken away from your own "serious" research and writing. Concerning those more significant risks, consider, most recently, the experience of Sarah Bond, an assistant professor and classicist from the University of Iowa, whose June 7, 2017, online article on the anachronistic link some (such as earlier generations of colonialists or contemporary white supremacists) make between, on the one hand, the white marble of Greco-Roman statues (which we fail to realize has lost the pigments in which it was originally painted) and what others would take to be the rather racist standards of beauty and worth, on the other, caught the online attention of far right readers, resulting in death threats.[22] As the *Inside Higher Ed* article on the episode puts it in its opening paragraph:

> Scholars vary in how and to what extent they engage with the public. Sarah Bond ... works at the high end of the engagement spectrum, via a blog, other use of social media, a column in *Forbes* and more. She's described her efforts as a way of making antiquities accessible to all, but recent threats she's received demonstrate the potential perils of that outreach. (Flaherty 2017)

It's a risk we're bringing to the attention of our own graduate students, since our department's longstanding focus on making full use of the digital medium—an initiative begun back in 2001 with careful attention to our web presence—has, to a surprisingly large extent, resulted in a graduate program (launched in the fall of 2017) that trains M.A. students to be scholars of religion conversant in both the use of social theory *as well as* the digital skills necessary for effective work in the public humanities.[23] Recognizing that some may wish to obtain a graduate degree but pursue careers outside academia, the program aims to train students for further doctoral work, certainly, but also for futures in any number of other fields where effective communication and analytic skills are relevant and valued. So, regardless the field into which our graduates go, making them aware that reader response theory is not an idle intellectual position but that it can help a writer to understand the many unanticipated ways in which readers can take their work—not to mention to have them consider that reacting to a piece of writing does not require one actually to read it[24]—things that anyone writing in public likely needs to consider seriously. After all, as I cited in an epigraph two decades ago (to an essay on the scholar of religion as a public intellectual—one which, by the way, also cited *Mythologies*):

> The moment you publish essays in a society you have entered political life; so if you want not to be political do not write essays or speak out." (Said 1996: 110)

Which brings me all the way back to Barthes—for while it would be incorrect to suggest that I was self-consciously aware that some of his writings structured my work over the years, and even seem to have influenced some of the initiatives we've tackled at the University of Alabama, looking back at my worn copy of *Mythologies* and thinking of our effort to make the relevance of our work apparent for people well beyond our students, it's now clear to me that his effort to bridge erudition and popularization in that little book has had a tremendous impact on me and even our department. For while we didn't start blogging simply because of Barthes (that would be a far too simplistic origins narrative, of course), I think it fair to say that because of such things as his provocative, monthly essays on the complexity of the mundane we were inspired to start thinking well outside the box—whether that box be our classroom's walls or the assumption that a scholar of religion only has something to say about some set apart and sacred domain known as religion. Instead, if we understand the things that we routinely call religion (even the fact of naming some things as religious!) as being no less ordinary than anything else people do, then maybe we too have skills that will allow us to take a glance at detergents, steak and chips and the world of wrestling—or maybe a young Buddhist monk drinking a coke or someone saying "I believe you ..."—and find something curious there that's worth our time.

Notes

1   Given this volume's goal of offering some practical feedback in at least half of the book, that dovetails with the theoretical position outlined in the opening four chapters, and given that I have spent a fair bit of my time, in the past several years, writing online, it seemed a profitable exercise to reflect self-consciously on the reasons for investing time and effort in that activity—and to take seriously early career concerns about the utility of investing in the online medium. This chapter, which is previously unpublished, though which draws on portions of two blogs I have written (which is noted in the text at the appropriate place), therefore resulted. My thanks to doctoral students Travis Cooper (Indiana), Adam Miller (Chicago), and Andie Alexander (Emory) for their very helpful comments on an earlier draft.

2   *Mythologies*'s original Éditions du Seuil edition of 1957 included 53 chapters, only 28 of which were selected by Annette Lavers, Barthes's translator, and published as what we have come to know as the English edition of *Mythologies*. The remaining chapters from the French original, along with five brief essays also published at that time but in other French periodicals (e.g., the essay after which the collection was named), were eventually translated in English as well and published first by Hill and Wang (a division of Farrar, Straus and Giroux) as *The Eiffel Tower*. According to Calvet, upon learning that his publisher wished to publish a slimmer version of the French original, Barthes made one stipulation: "that 'Le monde où l'on catche' ('The world of wrestling') not be cut" (Calvet 1995: 143).

3   The work, entitled "Just What Is It That Makes Today's Homes So Different, So Appealing?," is part of the Zundel Collection at the Kunsthalle Tübingen art museum, in Tübingen, Germany; it is often credited as being among the first works of what we might now call iconic post-WWII pop art.

4   I have come to think that the much repeated claim that my work offers no way forward—which I take to be an unhelpful caricature of deconstruction that is often called upon by its critics—is because the proposed, redescriptive alternative (e.g., as exemplified in Chapter 4 of this current collection or in McCutcheon 2003: ch. 7) regularly shifts the ground by studying so-called religious discourses as a way people work out everyday disputes. And because this move, premised on a theory of "religion"

as a mundane social technique, is unsatisfying for those who wish not to (as we once used to say) reduce religion to a non-religious source, the alternative that I propose is not seen as a legitimate alternative and so it is never entertained—thereby leaving the impression that my work offers no constructive proposals.

5   See Smith's comments on comparison at www.chicagomaroon.com/2008/06/02/full-j-z-smith-interview/ (accessed June 21, 2017). This interview is included in a collection of transcribed interviews and one original essay of Smith's to be published in 2018 (see Braun and McCutcheon 2018).

6   I'm referring, of course, to the title of his 1983 Bond film, *Never Say Never Again*, which was supposedly a reference to his own words, reportedly uttered after filming 1971's "Diamonds Are Forever," that he would never play that character again.

7   As I understand it, Ramey has long had an interest in communicating with audiences wider than just our classrooms, such as his earlier involvement with workshops for school teachers—a discussion topic in our own department, over the years, as the faculty strategized with possible department-wide initiatives. Whether this was among his conscious motives for beginning to blog, I'm unsure, but I'd be overlooking another important source if I did not recognize his interests as having a lasting effect on my own work.

8   Begun in 1950, this basic French lexicon collected and defined the two thousand or so most common words used by French speakers.

9   As described on its blog: "Culture on the Edge is a scholarly working group centered at the University of Alabama and begun in the spring of 2012. Its aim is to use social theory to offer more nuanced understandings of how those things that we commonly call 'identities' are manufactured, managed, and continually reproduced. This blog and its supporting sites do more than merely publicize the group's findings; they comprise, instead, a public site where the group carries out its collaborative work— both through scholarly blog posts as well as through conversations sparked in the various comments sections, where you are invited to participate, as well" (see https://edge.ua.edu/identity/; accessed June 19, 2017).

10 Concerning these two posts, see https://edge.ua.edu/russell-mccutcheon/kids-drink-pop-so-what/ (posted on June 11, 2013) and https://religion.ua.edu/blog/2017/06/12/the-problem-of-belief/ (posted on June 13, 2017; both accessed June 17, 2017).

11 As a practical demonstration of the relevance of blogging, the following portion of the chapter is adapted from an April 9, 2015, blog post entitled "Scholars or Colleagues" and posted at https://religion.ua.edu/blog/2015/04/09/scholars-or-colleagues (accessed June 16, 2017).

12 Four Chicago doctoral students—Emily Crews, Drew Durdin, Kelli Gardner, and Adam Miller—later wrote responses to the paper. With an introduction from Aaron Hollander, who arranged for my visit, the set was published as "Crafting the Introductory Course in Religious Studies" in *Teaching Theology and Religion* 19/1 (2016) and my paper appears in this volume.

13 As a result of that question, I was later able to learn why a few earlier career scholars blog themselves—see, for example, Thomas Whitley's answer here: www.thomaswhitley.com/blog/2015/4/13/why-i-blog (to make more professional connections, to widen the audience that might find his research, and to work in a medium over which he can exert a larger degree of control are among his readings; accessed June 19, 2017) or consider Ken Chitwood's answer to the why question (he describes it as following Stephen Prothero's lead, to combat religious illiteracy, in his case) in his "Bloggng Like an Academic" posted at www.hastac.org/blogs/kenchitwood/2015/10/08/

blogging-academic (accessed June 27, 2017; thanks again to Travis Cooper for the latter reference).

14 For example, between 1990 (two years after enrolling in Toronto's doctoral program) and the year in which I defended my dissertation (1995), I published 14 book reviews, whether appearing in general humanities periodicals or such more central journals for our field as *Religion, Journal for the Scientific Study of Religion, Review of Religious Research, MTSR*, and *Studies in Religion/Sciences Religieuses*. This, of course, was in the days prior to journals—as some now do—limiting or policing the involvement of graduate students in writing book reviews. As I've discussed elsewhere, this strategy led to my first review essay (1993) for a journal for which I had already reviewed on two previous occasions (in 1990 and 1992); that essay was directly related to my dissertation research and a revised version was included in my dissertation though, on the direction of the external reviewer, not in the published version of the book.

15 I was hardly at the front of the line, but I recall getting my first desktop computer in 1985, complete with large floppy disks that I was tirelessly changing in order to do anything on it. But that signaled the end of adding page 212a to a dissertation MS so that a short revision could be included without re-typing all of the previous 212 pages.

16 Since then Miller has ended his own personal blog but has become affiliated with managing the blog for the *Bulletin for the Study of Religion*—an ideal example of how one might move ones interests in the direction of more branded sites that may be of greater professional consequence to one's career one day.

17 The following portion of this chapter is revised from "Why Do I Blog?," posted on April 10, 2015, at https://religion.ua.edu/blog/2015/04/10/why-do-i-blog/ (accessed June 16, 2017).

18 As Travis Cooper (quoted in the introduction to this volume) insightfully commented, when reading an earlier draft of this chapter: "If anything, curmudgeonly voices who disparage blogging are ignorant on even the most basic and rudimentary media studies tenets. Communication matters. Textual circulation matters. Blogging matters. Social media matter."

19 For more on the background of our department, and strategies we've used to reinvent it, see my afterword in Ramey (2015).

20 In fact, there is some debate now as to whether social media, of various forms, are more akin to oral literature; see for example, the June 2011 article, "Is Twitter Writing, or Is It Speech? Why We Need a New Paradigm for Our Social Media Platforms," posted at www.niemanlab.org/2011/06/is-twitter-writing-or-is-it-speech-why-we-need -a-new-paradigm-for-our-social-media-platforms/ (accessed June 27, 2017; my thanks to Travis Cooper for this reference).

21 My colleague at Alabama, Michael Altman (currently in his fourth tenure-track year and who has recently established our department's podcast), was a more active blogger as a doctoral student than as an assistant professor, and he's given some careful thought to the change; see his post at: https://michaeljaltman.net/2015/04/15/ why-i-dont-blog-as-much-anymore (accessed June 19, 2017.)

22 For her original article, see https://hyperallergic.com/383776/why-we-need-to-start-seeing-the-classical-world-in-color (including the online comments); concerning the reaction of some readers, see www.chronicle.com/article/For-One-Scholar-an-Online/ 240384 and Flaherty (2017) (all accessed June 19, 2017). Bond's own blog is at: https:// sarahemilybond.com.

23 For more details on the rather organic development of this program, and its twin foci, see McCutcheon forthcoming.

24 As the closing lines to the above-cited *Inside Higher Ed* article put it: "Perhaps most distressing about Bond's case, she said, is that 'it seems quite clear that the people who have had the most violent reaction to her essay are the ones who have not actually read it,' relying instead on 'distorted and misleading summaries'" (Flaherty 2017).

References

Anderson, Benedict (1991) [1983]. *Imagined Communities: Reflections on the Origin and Spread of Nationalism*. London: Verso.

Barthes, Roland (1957). *Mythologies*. Paris: Éditions du Seuil.

—— (1973) [1957]. *Mythologies*, trans. Annette Lavers. Hammersmith: Paladin.

—— (1997) [1979]. *The Eiffel Tower and Other Mythologies*, trans. Richard Howard. Berkeley, CA: University of California Press.

Bayart, Jean-Francois (2005). *The Illusion of Cultural Identity*, trans. Steven Rendall, Janet Roitman, Cynthia Schoch, Jonathan Derrick. Chicago: University of Chicago Press.

Braun, Willi and Russell T. McCutcheon (eds.) (2018). *Reading Smith: Interviews and Essay, 1999-2013*. New York: Oxford University Press.

Calvet, Louis-Jean (1995) [1990]. *Roland Barthes: A Biography*, trans. Sarah Wykes. Bloomington, IN: Indiana University Press.

Certeau, Michel (1988). *The Practice of Everyday Life*, trans. Steven Randall. Berkeley, CA: University of California Press.

Eagleton, Terry (1989). *Literary Theory: An Introduction*. Minneapolis, MN: University of Minnesota Press.

—— (1991). *Ideology: An Introduction*. New York: Verso.

Flaherty, Colleen. (2017). "Threats for What She Didn't Say," *Inside Higher Ed*, June 19. Retrieved from

www.insidehighered.com/news/2017/06/19/classicist-finds-herself-target-online-threats-after-article-ancient-statues#.WUeTL5wWX2c.facebook (accessed June 19, 2017).

Hamilton, Richard and Dieter Schwarz, Stephen Bann, Lynne Cooke, and Sarat Maharaj (1990). *Exteriors, Interiors, Objects, People*. Stuttgart: Edition Hansjörg Mayer.

Jameson, Fredric (1988). *The Political Unconscious: Narrative as a Socially Symbolic Act*. Ithaca, NY: Cornell University Press.

LaCapra, Dominic (1989). *Soundings in Critical Theory*. Ithaca, NY: Cornell University Press.

Lentricchia, Frank (1985). *Criticism and Social Change*. Chicago, IL: University of Chicago Press.

Lincoln, Bruce (1989). *Discourse and the Construction of Society: Comparative Studies of Myth, Ritual, and Classification*. Braun, 1st ed. New York: Oxford University Press.

McCutcheon, Russell T. (1993). "The Myth of the Apolitical Scholar: The Life and Works of Mircea Eliade," *Queen's Quarterly* 100/3 (1993): 642–663.

—— (1997). *Manufacturing Religion: The Discourse on Sui Generis Religion and the Politics of Nostalgia*. New York: Oxford University Press.

—— (2000). "Myth," in Willi Braun and Russell T. McCutcheon (eds.), *Guide to the Study of Religion*, 190–208. London: Bloomsbury.

—— (2001). *Critics Not Caretakers: Redescribing the Public Study of Religion*. Albany, NY: State University of New York Press.

—— (2003). *The Discipline of Religion: Structure, Meaning, Rhetoric*. New York: Routledge. https://doi.org/10.4324/9780203451793

—— (2007). *Studying Religion: An Introduction*. New York: Routledge.

—— (2012). "Turtles All the Way Down," posted on September 25. Retrieved from https://religion.ua.edu/blog/2012/09/25/turtles-all-the-way-down (accessed June 18, 2017).

—— (ed.) (2015). *Fabricating Origins*. Working with Culture on the Edge, vol. 1. Sheffield: Equinox.

—— (ed.) (2017). *Fabricating Identities*. Working with Culture on the Edge, vol. 3. Sheffield: Equinox.

—— (forthcoming). "Learning to Code: Digital Tools and the Reinvention of an Academic Discipline," in Christopher Cantwell and Kristian Petersen (eds.), *Introduction to Digital Humanities: Religion*. Berlin: Walter de Gruyter.

Ramey, Steven (2015). *Writing Religion: The Case for the Critical Study of Religion*. Tuscaloosa, AL: University of Alabama Press.

Said, Edward (1996). *Representations of the Intellectual*. New York: Vintage.

Part III

In Praxis: Responses to "Theses on Professionalization"

Whether at the level of individuals or nations, the "immaterial" rests on very real structures, such as education systems ...

Pierre Bourdieu, in *Firing Back* (New Press, 2003)

Preamble

Russell T. McCutcheon

As noted in the introduction to the book, this third part of the book features not my writing (other than this brief preamble) but that of twenty-one different early-career scholars, all of whom are responding to something that I wrote over ten years ago, looking at items that I then thought that all early career scholars in our field ought to be thinking about as they considered transitioning from being graduate students to the scholars they had long hoped to become—and by scholars I mean full-time, employed faculty members.

That the humanities job market has been poor for decades should not go unnoticed as we focus on this issue; for, if asked, many senior scholars who today seem successful and prosperous will more than likely share their own war stories from the trenches of applications, searches, and limited term sessional positions with no job security (what we now collectively call contingent labor). In fact, I now find myself to be someone who has somehow turned into one of those senior people—time flies, as they say—and I've not been shy, on previous occasions, to try to use anecdotes from my own career as stepping stones toward saying something more broadly about the job market in our field, on how I think that searches ought to be conducted and job ads written, etc. The trick is not to use the anecdote as evidence of some sort of exceptionalism or special pleading but, instead, to see it as an e.g. that opens a discussion on a far wider topic that has plenty of examples elsewhere as well. For I know of scholars well ahead of me in the game, who have now retired, who could tell a tale of two of their own, about having no academic work for years on end, moving great distances for the sake of an undesirable job, partners who had to make tough choices, etc., all making evident the sacrifices that they and their families made for their careers.

I say this because I fear that current early career scholars today sometimes fail to understand that the practical, institutional context in which they find themselves is hardly unique, and thus that they more than likely have allies in the senior scholars whose careers they may inaccurately think were immune to pressures beyond the individual's control. But, in writing that sentence, I also wish to retain a very clear awareness, in myself and my readers, that the situation in which young scholars now find themselves is also different from that of their predecessors. (After all, as Jonathan Z. Smith taught us on not a few occasions, any two things can be both similar *and* different, and it is therefore important not to overlook one set of relations while examining the other.) For the continually increasing pressures on the humanities job market, that can be traced back to the early 1970s, has reached a peak, fifty years later, that makes the situation of looking for work twenty, thirty, and forty years ago surely seem to be highly appealing to today's job applicants. Speaking from my own setting, in the U.S. public higher ed system, the portion of tax dollars going to support universities has consistently lessened over the years (what voter doesn't want to hear politicians talk of tax cuts, after all?), such that not only individuals (and, to be sure, their families) bear a far larger percentage of the costs of their education (i.e., constant tuition increases) but there is a far greater incentive on the part of university administrations to hire far cheaper part-time labor to do the job once done by self-governing tenured faculty members. The number of full-time job openings therefore has plummeted over the years. So given the stresses of today's job market, it's to their peril, I would argue, for now senior scholars not recognize that, although they themselves surely have a tale or two to tell about the high prices that they and their classmates once paid, the students whom they are currently credentialing in the graduate programs that their generation now runs are entering an extraordinarily harsh environment whose costs are tremendously inflated over once they once were.

Simply put, we all pay prices; but, depending on your standards or when you came into the game, some of those prices may not only be far more exorbitant than others but the prices others end up paying may not even be noticeable to us given our own focus on a different set of criteria for navigating costs and benefits. (I think here of the time someone in the profession once told me that they envied my not having children and thus all of the time that I could put into my research and writing—a comment that, from where I sat, disastrously failed to consider that the prices they saw themselves paying as a parent might strike someone else, such as myself, as gaining for them highly desired ends. But of course, they were oblivious to the fact that *we're all paying costs*—different costs, yes, but costs nonetheless ...)

So although it will not miraculously change what faces those now looking for employment as professors, my interest to continue to help promote the writings of earlier career scholars suggested to me that this book, given its focus on some of the practical issues in the field, was an ideal opportunity not only to help publish and thereby promote some of their good work but also to keep the conversation going on what currently faces them when they go looking for employment. What's more, using my own "Theses on Professionalization" (McCutcheon 2007) to set the table (which open each of the twenty-one pieces that follow) struck me as a way not just to reinforce what I once wrote and still advocate but, more than likely, also as a way to demonstrate how some might think that decade-old piece may miss the mark today (as some of the respondents point out), given what all has transpired between then and now (the world economic collapse of 2008 for starters). But more than this, for in light of reports that I heard about the animated discussion that took place after a November 2017 panel of the North American Association for the Study of Religion (NAASR), which in part focused on early career/job market issues, and which made evident a clear generational divide among some of those in the room (in which senior and younger scholars differed in how they discussed these issues), it seemed to me that ending this volume not with my own Afterword but, instead, with over twenty other, different voices, all tackling these practical issues as they see fit, and in most cases, doing so from within the current trenches, would be fitting and, I hope, consequential for both ends of the generational spectrum. For while not wishing to dismiss the very real costs paid by my own seniors or those in my academic generation (and, having moved countries to get what was only promised to be a 9 month position, back in 1993, and then living apart from my wife, while we both pursued our careers and tried to gain employment at the same university, for a total of 12 years, I can certainly identify with some of those costs myself—for, given my own choices and the structured settings in which I made them, I too have stories of being absent and far from home during crucial times in my own family), I aim here to shine the light on those currently making cost/benefit analyses of their own. I therefore see the following short essays as providing crucial information for those now supervising graduate students' training and interviewing them for positions but also as helpful demystification offered by the peers of those who may pick up this book prior to venturing onto the job market themselves.

For, as the old saying goes, forewarned is forearmed ...

Reference

McCutcheon, Russell T. (2007). "Theses on Professionalization," in Mathieu E. Courville (ed.), *The Next Step in Studying Religion: A Graduate's Guide*, 41–45. London: Continuum.

Introduction

Matt Sheedy

> It doesn't look good captain, but we've come too far to turn back now ...

The above epigraph sounds like something I've read in a book or heard in a movie. While I don't know its origin, whether I'm paraphrasing something or whether I'm inventing it from whole cloth, the sentiment is real.

It wasn't until the economic crisis of 2008 that I first began to consider the possibility that an academic job might not be so easy to come by once I completed my Ph.D. Despite this bourgeoning awareness, it was all an abstraction back then as I knew very few people on the other end of the degree who had struggled to find a job and was constantly assured by my senior colleagues that I'd do just fine so long as I kept pace (e.g., presenting at colloquia and at conferences, writing book reviews and, eventually, publishing essays, taking on editorial roles, etc.). As I began paying closer attention to the job market in the years that followed, there didn't seem to me to be all that much panic among the academic ranks, even in the wake of the Occupy Wall Street movement in late 2011, which saw unprecedented global protests in response to bank bailouts and housing foreclosures (in the U.S.), among a host of other issues, and where talk of "austerity measures" from governments and news pundits became a daily affair the world over. Austerity measures, if I may offer a stipulative definition, reflect a process whereby governments, in conjunction with corporate power (a variable that's sometimes overlooked, as was common with the Tea Party movement in the U.S.), cut-back on spending and investment in whatever is perceived to be excessive, wasteful, redundant, or even harmful to state economies increasingly subject to the pressures of market forces (sometimes referred to as neo-liberal ideology).

It didn't take long, however, for those in the humanities and social sciences to express their concern over what all this might mean for their future and for the future of their disciplines—after all, what is it that we produce that can be sold as a viable commodity? And where's "the next Steve Jobs" in all of this? Thus it began to occur to many of us (myself included) that the adage that what we do is a necessary social good is perhaps more an ethos of decades past than a present reality.[1]

It wasn't until around 2012/13 that I began to see regular articles from younger academics, ABD's (i.e., All But Dissertation) and recently minted Ph.D.s,[2] starting to cast doubt upon the future of the humanities,[3] including think pieces from professors on how to reinvent the wheel,[4] or, just as common, instructing students to avoid graduate school altogether.[5] One of the better-known voices coming out of the study of religion was (and remains) Kelly J. Baker,[6] who appears in this collection of responses (see Response to Thesis 15), and has written extensively about her decision to transition out of academia, most recently in her book *Grace Period: A Memoir in Pieces* (Blue Crow Publishing, 2017).

Another personal narrative that struck me within my academic circle of friends was the announcement on Facebook by Kate Daley-Baily (a brilliant and highly motivated scholar of religion) that she could no longer continue with her graduate work due to a lack of resources and teaching opportunities. In the lead-up to her decision Daley-Baily wrote a two-part series in the *Bulletin for the Study of Religion* blog in 2014, entitled "A is for Adjunct,"[7] in an effort to speak out about then-current conditions. This was followed by an essay entitled "For the "Good or the Guild: An Open Letter to the American Academy of Religion" in 2015,[8] which prompted a series of responses that also appeared in the *Bulletin* blog, including one from then-Executive Director of the AAR Jack Fitzmier.[9] In addition, the *Bulletin* also ran a three-part series called "Life After Religious Studies"[10] in an attempt to provide some personal narratives on why people chose to leave the discipline and how they've reinvented themselves in their (academic) afterlife.

It is beyond my recollection to say exactly how the idea to have twenty-one responses to McCutcheon's "Theses on Professionalization" came about (which originally appeared on the *Bulletin* blog, and which I facilitated as editor). Suffice it to say that these ideas and concerns were in the air.[11] Having written the "Theses on Professionalization" in 2007,[12] prior to the economic crisis and its aftermath, it seemed fitting to invite twenty-one early-career scholars to respond to McCutcheon's suggestions some eight-years on (the series started in the summer of 2015 and all appear in an updated form here), reflecting on how they've experienced things by comparison, while adding new perspectives in light of changing conditions. McCutcheon has consistently engaged with questions of the state of the field in the study of religion throughout his career (perhaps more than anyone else in the last two decades), and has, moreover, been a consummate mentor in helping students and early career scholars navigate their way through the disciple's many weeds. It should come as no surprise, then, that this collaborative endeavor has come to pass.

Of course some of the concerns in the theses and replies are not new, and it is instructive to look back on the experiences of scholars in previous decades in order to compare and contrast their own particular battles in the academic trenches. Here it is worth reproducing a question that I asked Scott Elliot in an interview with him on his edited volume *Reinventing Religious Studies: Key Writings in the History of a Discipline* (Routledge, 2013), which is a compilation of pieces from what was once the *Bulletin of the Council of Societies for the Study of Religion* (1969–2009). As I put it to Elliott back then:

> In the second to last section of the book, entitled "Religious Studies and Identity Politics," scholars such as Russell McCutcheon, Darlene Juschka, and Gustavo

Benevides take up the problem of the role of market forces in the 1990s in shaping the perceived value and direction of the human sciences. It may come as a surprise to many younger scholars such as myself who are experiencing the sting of a poor job market that these issues were being raised back then. What are your thoughts on the relevance of these earlier debates in relation to the study of religion today and what they might suggest for possible solutions? Here I am thinking, for example, of Tim Jensen's essay on how he and his colleagues in Denmark have worked directly with business and government on matters pertaining to religion while at the same time using a deconstructive approach that rejects the idea of religion as *sui generis*.[13]

If there is a lesson here, then perhaps it's that the grass in the past was not as green as many of us had thought (at least since the 1990s), and that thinking about structural conditions in different countries (such as Denmark) is an important part of engaging with the question of professionalization in our current moment, regardless of whether we find only cautionary examples or, perhaps, alternative models that might be adapted in different places.

In the following replies to McCutcheon's twenty-one theses there are at least (by my estimation) twelve main themes that arise:

- The role of apprenticeship in academia.

- One's Ph.D. specialty training vs. adapting to market demands.

- Expectations regarding how long it can take to find an academic job.

- Balancing your research time vs. earning money.

- Institutional reputations and how to work with (or around) them.

- Structure vs. agency (i.e., knowing what you can and what you cannot control).

- Being enterprising outside of the usual channels.

- Being aware of what teaching needs are in demand and developing new courses.

- Publishing in journals and attending conferences.

- Where to look for jobs and strategies for promoting yourself.

- On learning how to juggle it all.

- Life-work balance and the limits of sacrifice.

The range of contributions here provides enough of a representative sample of current scholars of religion (and one scholar of literature and sexuality studies, Katelyn Dykstra) to offer a glimpse into the storm, stress, and occasional success of academic life in the trenches of late graduate and early career life. In the interim since 2015, when these were first being posted, a few of these authors have moved on from academia (either permanently or for the time being), while others wrote their replies having recently acquired a tenure-track position. Others still find themselves in the trenches, working to complete their Ph.D.s, working as adjuncts post-Ph.D., or finding post-docs and visiting professorships, both in North America, Europe, and even Southeast Asia, as newer communication technologies open-up access to academic networks that were (relatively) closed to generations past.

For most of us who have come this far, we're here because we love what we do ... and what we do with what we do, well, that's the question at hand.

Matt Sheedy (Ph.D.) is visiting professor of North American studies at the University of Bonn, Germany, and is the associate editor of the *Bulletin for the Study of Religion*. His research interests include critical social theory, theories of secularism and atheism, as well as representations of Christianity, Islam, and Native American traditions in popular and political culture. He is currently working on a manuscript that provides a critical examination of Jürgen Habermas's theory of religion in the public sphere.

Notes

1 See for example Bill Readings's analysis in *The University in Ruins* (Cambridge, MA: Harvard University Press, 1997).
2 See https://chroniclevitae.com/news/95-my-post-academic-grace-period. Note: all subsequent links, cited in each of the replies to follow, were current as of January 2018.
3 See, for example, the widely circulated YouTube video, "So You Want to Get a Ph.D. in the Humanities," from 2010, at www.youtube.com/watch?v=obTNwPJvOI8.
4 See www.chronicle.com/article/The-Future-of-the-Ph.D./131749.
5 See www.chronicle.com/article/Graduate-School-in-the/44846.
6 See Baker's important commentary charting her transition and its implications for the humanities over several years at Chronicle Vitae: https://chroniclevitae.com/people/1467-kelly-j-baker/articles.
7 See https://bulletin.equinoxpub.com/2014/04/a-is-for-adjunct-part-1.
8 See https://journals.equinoxpub.com/index.php/BSOR/article/view/29036.
9 See https://bulletin.equinoxpub.com/2016/03/for-the-good-or-the-guild-scholars-respond-to-kate-daley-bailey-2.
10 See http://bulletin.equinoxpub.com/?s=life+after+religious+studies.
11 As a follow-up series, the *Bulletin* blog also ran a series in response to the Theses series entitled, "If I Only Knew Then: Tenured Scholars on Professionalization," offering a look from those further along in the game: http://bulletin.equinoxpub.com/?s=if+I+only+knew+then.
12 McCutcheon's "Theses on Professionalization" originally appeared in Mathieu E. Courville (ed.), *Next Step in Studying Religion: A Graduates Guide* (London: Bloomsbury, 2007) and was reproduced in 2012 on the Religious Studies Project website: www.religiousstudiesproject.com/2012/02/29/russell-mccutcheon-theses-on-professionalization.
13 See http://bulletin.equinoxpub.com/2013/12/reinventing -religious-studies-an-interview-with-scott-s-elliott-part-2 .

Response to Thesis 1

Matthew Dougherty

Thesis 1: Academia is unlike other professions in that the pre-professional period of training, which includes coursework, dissertation research and writing, and teaching assistantships—is not akin to an apprenticeship. Accordingly, there is no direct linkage between the accumulation of credentials and admission to the profession, no necessary relationship between feeling oneself to be qualified and the ability to obtain full time employment as a university professor.

When I first read this thesis as a doctoral candidate, it struck me that most graduate students I knew were already aware that the credential they hoped to earn would not be enough to gain them academic employment. My cohort has, after all, come of age in an era when the number of credentials that guarantee employment seems to be shrinking fast. The doctoral students I studied with were dogged by the feeling that there was always something we could be doing to better our chances on the job market: cultivating an online presence, talking to potential collaborators at conferences, publishing articles, or finding mentors to help with our self-identified weaknesses. At the root of all this activity was the belief that, ultimately, doctoral students are responsible for our own education and professionalization.

Approaching graduate school this way held both promise and peril. On the one hand, it encouraged us to think intentionally about our doctoral training. When we learned to direct our careers and research while there were still mentors readily accessible to help, we better prepared ourselves for a life in or outside academia. On the other hand, the attitude that there was always "more" that we could be doing did not necessarily lead us to spend our time wisely. We were just as likely to respond with frenzied activity directed at helping us "stand out" as with a plan for our development informed by a clear sense of our weaknesses and strengths.

Although born of anxiety, students' reflexivity about their development can be directed in helpful ways when graduate mentors and programs clearly identify the skills they want their graduates to have beyond those necessary for the credential and integrate those skills into graduate curricula and classrooms. As this thesis makes clear, there is nothing that either graduate students or their mentors can do to change the job market such that the credential guarantees employment. Concentrating on developing skills useful for being on the market or working as an early-career academic will not fix the central problems of academic underemployment, but it allows those with charge over graduate students' development to respond to the situation as it stands.

The role of mentors is particularly crucial here because not all graduate students have equal amounts of time "free" after teaching, coursework, and research to spend on plans for professionalization that might or might not pan out. For example, those with family responsibilities such as young children or aging parents—a group that includes disproportionate numbers of women and people of color— have significantly less extra time available to spend on strategically professionalizing themselves after hours and on the weekends than those without.

Neither do all graduate students, even as separate Master's degrees become more commonplace in our field, arrive in doctoral programs having had equal amounts of exposure to academic culture and knowing equally well where to direct their energies. Knowing what conferences are most relevant to one's interests, how to write a book review, or how to craft an academic CV are all necessary skills for success in our field. Some doctoral students will have acquired many of these skills during their undergraduate years, but others will not. Often, this is a result of class divisions: colleges and universities that don't expect many of their graduates to go into academia will be much less likely to offer opportunities to learn skills relevant to that field.

With that reality in mind, although graduate students can be expected to take responsibility for directing their own education, they cannot be expected to learn to do so without help. Given that graduate students seem, in general, to already know the truth McCutcheon's thesis points out, from my perspective it now has the most value in the reminder it gives to faculty of the realities that graduate students on the market face. It ought to help them to be clear to their students about both the chanciness of the market and about how to develop skills that might improve one's chances the most. Sending, even by omission, the message that the Ph.D. alone is enough does the most harm to those students with the least free time or prior knowledge of academia.

Fortunately, not all professionalization has to happen entirely under students' own steam. I took graduate seminars that required students to create syllabuses or write book reviews—assignments that teach research and argumentation while having a more direct relationship to daily life in academia than does the traditional seminar paper. New student orientation in my program included frank discussions of the job market and advice on assembling a teaching portfolio. Many of the professors I assisted with courses took the time to observe me teaching and to discuss strategies for improvement with me. These were all concrete decisions that the professors in my program made to help their students keep sight of their professional development rather than focus only on coursework and teaching. Given that, as this thesis points out, there is no way to guarantee that a Ph.D. leads to a job, it is even more important now for mentors of graduate students to make choices that foster the growth of specific professional skills that help ease the transition into the market and, hopefully, into a job without assuming that work on professionalization must compete with the normal demands of a graduate program.

Matthew Dougherty graduated from the Department of Religious Studies at the University of North Carolina at Chapel Hill in 2017. He studies religion and empire in early America. More details about him and his work can be found at https://unc.academia.edu/ MatthewDougherty.

Response to Thesis 2

Tenzan Eaghll

Thesis 2: A Ph.D. is awarded not only as a mark of intellectual competence and disciplined method but also as a professional credential that signals one's eligibility for employment as a researcher and teacher within academia. Although these two aspects of the degree can complement one another, they can just as easily conflict, as in when one's research expertise fails to overlap with ever changing employment needs.

There is a gap between what we specialize in during our graduate studies and what we are required to teach once we are employed, and during the completion of my Ph.D. this gap worried me tremendously. My concern with this gap didn't arise because I felt unprepared. I mean, I had been studying religion for over a decade and felt confident in the subject matter. It is just that the gap between my area of expertise and the demands of the job market were so big as to make the latter seem like a foreign territory. Moreover, given the state of the academic job market at the time—which continues to be difficult to this day—this 'foreign territory' seemed like a place that I may be exiled to for a very long time. With the shrinking pool of tenure-track jobs and the rise in the amount of poorly paid adjunct positions, I was worried that I might get stuck in the adjunct loop for years to come.

Early on in my studies, I had assumed that by developing intellectual competence in one particular area of religious studies I would naturally be preparing myself to teach both my topic of expertise and more general introductory classes in the field, but I eventually came to recognize that this is incorrect. Part of the reason for this was because my area of expertise is Continental philosophy, which doesn't see a lot of job postings, but also because, like most Ph.D. grads, I was not trained to be an expert in any of the "bread and butter" classes on which religious studies departments depend. As anyone familiar with the religious studies job market knows, most entry level positions require teaching a whole slew of introductory classes that most Ph.D. grads have only basic knowledge in—Introduction to World Religions, Nature of World Religions, Introduction to Christianity, etc.— and although I had personally served as a teaching assistant and course instructor in some of these classes during my Ph.D., I was never tested to prove my competency in any of these particular subjects. In order to attain my Ph.D. I only had to pass comprehensive exams that tested my knowledge within the fields of study related to my dissertation topic. Never once was I tested in my knowledge of "Hinduism," "Buddhism," the "religious experience of mystics," or even the broad history of "Christianity," yet those are the topics I knew that I would be expected to teach with sublime proficiency once I entered the job market.

Of course, I am not suggesting that there should be exams for these general subjects in all Ph.D. programs, but simply that the particular reasons for which a Ph.D. is awarded doesn't necessarily overlap with the demands of the job market. Moreover, I am trying to point out that the gap between intellectual competence and employment opportunities is a systemic problem in religious studies. In Thesis 2, McCutcheon calls attention to this problem because it is important *to remember that* Religious Studies is not a discipline with a rigidly defined phenomenon of investigation, and that the leap from graduate research to the job market can be difficult to navigate.

At the moment, I think the only remedy to this problem is for graduate students to be mindful of the gap and to prepare themselves accordingly. Graduate students should read widely in the field, familiarize themselves with critical scholarship beyond their own narrow area of study, and find ways to engage with other scholars on a wide range of issues. Throughout my Ph.D., I tried to meet these demands by spending much of my free time reading literature on diverse topics, writing blogs on numerous issues, and engaging in debate with leading scholars. I found all of this helped to prepare me for the job market by broadening my general knowledge of religious studies beyond my narrow field of expertise and learning to speak about "religion" in a jargon-free manner.

All of this proved immensely valuable once I was on the job market because I wasn't hired by a department that needed a specialist in Continental philosophy. In fact, during the hiring process my area of specialty was actually an impediment to getting the job. The department that hired me was actually looking for a specialist in Buddhism, but they took interest in me because of my ability to teach a wide range of undergraduate classes and my familiarity with contemporary debates in method and theory. Just as McCutcheon warns in Thesis 2, I found that *my research expertise was actually in conflict with the job market, and it was only because I had been proactive and tried to cover this gap that I didn't get stuck in the adjunct loop.* Moreover, now that I am actually teaching undergraduate and graduate students, I find all my extra-curricular grad work paid-off because I can instruct and communicate with my students on a wide range of issues, both popular and academic. This extra-curricular grad work even helps me interact with faculty members who have different methodological approaches than my own, as I can contribute to departmental debates about course modules or the future of the field, all while maintaining a sense of critical integrity.

Obviously, being proactive in this regard doesn't ensure that a Ph.D. grad won't get stuck in the adjunct loop after finishing their degree, but by reading widely in the field and engaging with other scholars on various methodological issues, they will be putting themselves in the best possible position to navigate the gap between their area of expertise and the job market.

Tenzan Eaghll completed his doctorate at the University of Toronto in 2016. He teaches courses on religion and philosophy at the College of Religious Studies, Mahidol University (Thailand). His writings have appeared in such places as *Religion Compass*, *Implicit Religion*, and the Bloomsbury Critiquing Religion series.

Response to Thesis 3

Shannon Trosper Schorey

Thesis 3: Pursuing a Ph.D. purely for the "love of learning" is one among many legitimate reasons for graduate studies. Pursuing such studies for both intellectual stimulation and eventual employment requires candidates to be as intentional as possible about opportunities to increase their competitiveness on the job market.

Many who pursue a Ph.D. do so because they love their research. Their passion and curiosity for their chosen subject is offered as the primary reason they endure years of long research and teaching hours, an extended period of meager pay and low (or no) benefits, family planning complicated by a variety of professional taboos and lack of resources, and the stress of an ultra-competitive and unpredictable job market. As the adjuncting[1] crisis[2] looms larger than ever, more grads are accepting contingent positions to make ends meet as they struggle to land a tenure track position.

I read Thesis 3 to be a call away from this standard narrative of the relationship between graduate studies and the job market. While "love of learning" is a popular and widely accepted reason to pursue graduate studies, this phrasing often delimits our imagination of what "success" looks like after the Ph.D. With no guarantee of the higher education equivalent of the "American dream," Thesis 3 asks grads to be more reflective and self-directed in both their training *and* imagination of what may constitute the job market. While this may mean adopting a wide variety of strategies as one completes their training, I offer three reflections here:

Firstly, graduate departments would be well served by offering platforms (whether in the form of lectures, open table discussions, job fairs, conferences, etc.) for graduate students to engage a wider variety of career options and training for positions outside of the academy. Most immediately, this might mean paying attention to job opportunities that emphasize research, writing, and teaching skills more broadly. Academic training can help prepare grads for a variety of careers that can be intellectually satisfying while, arguably, reaching much wider audiences than that of the average article or academic press monograph. Journalism, web writing, non-profit work, marketing, teaching, editing—these are just a few of the career options that run parallel to humanities grad training. "Love of learning," if it is a priority for you, should be rescued from the toxic and overly narrow definition the academy offers.

Secondly, for grads to "be as intentional as possible about opportunities" they should weigh carefully the marketability of their chosen research areas with the very real political mechanisms by which the academy reproduces itself. The job market reflects contemporary trends of intellectual inquiry as much as it annually re-affirms the deep patterns of the field's self-identification. Key terms serving at the heart of the field—ritual, text, world religions, etc.—are the most marketable because they are the most easily recognizable. Such terms are able to retain their social capital despite the important work deconstructing these categories precisely because they immediately orient one's research into a wider pattern of comparative data and allow the "importance" of one's research to be readily recognizable to university administration and students. It is a shorthand that attempts to collapse intellectual inquiry into niches that can be worked to identify what sort of scholar a department should hire. But over-reliance on keywords stresses the content of a person's research—Hinduism, early Christianity, religion and science—over other sorts of criteria, thereby privileging certain and pervasive implicit assumptions about what kinds of content seem to *essentially* matter in the study of religion.

In practice this sort of shorthand makes sense, but grads must be willing to think critically about their own positionality and participation in the construction of our field's peripheries and centers. I offer as an example the study of new religious movements—a subfield that, not long ago, was reserved for "playful" intellectual inquiry post-tenure. The implication was that these movements were neither serious nor important subjects of research, despite any potential methodological or theoretical framing. When, as an M.A. student, I announced that this was one of my chosen research areas I was strongly encouraged to work on classical texts or more readily identifiably "important" subjects so that I might land a position in a doctoral program and then a job. I am happy with my own decision to ignore this advice—a decision fueled by the important conversations about the canon of Religious Studies and its attendant colonial, political, and historical consequences (King, Masuzawa, McCutcheon, Styers, etc.). Yet at the same time I recognize that as a scholar I also have a duty to make my research relatable and part of a broader conversation that moves our field and re-makes it.

This leads me to my final reflection: "intentionality" here should be as much about the ways in which grads are able to translate their own professional identities as researchers, thinkers, and teachers as it should be about what kinds of opportunities and skill sets grads establish as they keep an eye on the job market(s). Grads should work closely with trusted advisors—both junior and senior— about how best to negotiate their interests with the languages and priorities of the contemporary market. Grads should also recognize the enormous skill set that accompanies the completion of a Ph.D. So many grads enter the market from a position of fear, when instead they should feel empowered by their training to make choices and pursue possibilities that are the most interesting to them.

What seems to be missing is not translatable skills but training and attention to how best wield that skill set in non-academic positions (this seems to me to also be part of our field's struggle to identify what we offer undergraduate students as well). Unfortunately, for many grads the work of finding alternative career paths is placed on them alone.

Shannon Trosper Schorey is a content strategist in the tech industry. She is a Ph.D. candidate at UNC Chapel Hill. Her dissertation explores issues at the intersection of technology, religion, and media.

Notes

1   See https://chroniclevitae.com/news/762-the-adjunct-crisis-is-everyone-s-problem.
2   See www.chronicle.com/article/OveruseAbuse-of-Adjuncts/143951.

Response to Thesis 4

Caleb Simmons

Thesis 4: Applying for full-time employment prior to being awarded the Ph.D. degree (i.e., when, after successfully completing comprehensive or general exams, one holds the status known as ABD [i.e., All But Dissertation]) is not uncommon; however, failure to gain employment at this stage must not undermine one's confidence. Apart from extraordinary circumstances (e.g., the so-called "fit" between your expertise and a department's needs), the doctoral degree remains a necessary condition for entrance into the profession.

The religious studies job market can be daunting. According to the Society of Biblical Literature and the American Academy of Religion's annual job advertisement data, there has been a steady decline of religious studies positions available since 2008 during which there has been an increase in Ph.D. degrees awarded.[1] Understandably, this can produce anxiety towards the end of graduate school as the whirlwind of writing and defending meet the flood of economic realities of unsecured income, student loans, etc. This raises the question: "when do I need to start applying for jobs?"

McCutcheon's Thesis 4, "the doctoral degree remains a necessary condition for entrance into the profession," remains accurate as "holding a Ph.D." continues "to be ranked highest among skills and/or experiences desired or required by hiring institutions" in the field of religious studies.[2] However, the numbers released by the SBL/AAR that cover 2005–2012 suggest that it is not uncommon for ABD job candidates to receive job offers. According to the data released in the 2013–2014 SBL/AAR job data:

> Less than five percent of hired candidates interviewed more than one year in advance of completing their Ph.D. 32.7% completed their Ph.D. the year after interviewing. 28.2% completed their Ph.D. during the year in which they interviewed or within one year prior to interviewing. 34.3% completed their Ph.D. two or more years prior to interviewing.[3]

These data suggest that 37.5 percent of hires did not have their doctoral degree in hand when they started their position and another 17.1 percent were interviewing in the year when their degree was expected to be awarded. Therefore, the majority (54.6%) of candidates hired in Religious Studies from 2005 to 2012 were not Ph.D.s when they received their job offers.

There are, however, problems with putting too much stake in these numbers. The same SBL/AAR report includes competing statistics with 81 percent of hiring institutions stating that the candidate that was hired had completed their Ph.D.[4] Additionally, this report provides no data for the degree status of applicants for each position (though average number of applications is provided); so one cannot know how many ABDs or Ph.D.s were unsuccessful on the job market.

The biggest risk for the ABD job candidate is adding the inevitable rejection that comes with the current job market into the tumultuous emotional field that accompanies the final stages of the doctoral process. As McCutcheon states, "failure to gain employment at this stage must not undermine one's confidence." That is the last thing one needs while walking into your dissertation defense.

There is, however, another option. Part of graduate school that is often neglected in our focus on research is professional development. While some of us teach while in graduate school, many other aspects of our future careers are unknown and are learned "on the fly." Unfortunately, for many of us the job application process is one of these overlooked components, even though at the end of the day it very well might be the most important. Testing the job market early in the doctoral process provides a way around this lacuna. With the help of trusted advisors, the green ABD Ph.D. candidate can develop the professional skills required to be successful on the job market: how to write a good cover letter, prepare an effective CV, and perform in an academic interview. By engaging the market earlier than later, the candidate has the opportunity to learn from their mistakes when the stakes are lower, knowing that there is still a year or two before the rubber really meets the road.

I entered the job market early. This was not with any sort of foresight regarding professional development, but through the process I have been convinced that these experiences helped me develop the skills necessary to be successful when I eventually became a viable candidate further along.

When I passed into doctoral candidacy, the joy of this rite of passage was short-lived as immediately I realized that my life had become a complex balancing act of time and funding and the ultimate goal of gainful employment seemed farther away than when I had entered my Ph.D. program. Luckily, at the University of Florida, my advisors were extremely upfront about the job market and the uphill battle that I might face coming from a school with a young doctoral program and lacking the "name-brand" in my field (South Asian religions). With this in mind, they paid special attention to my professionalization, including teaching, publishing, presenting at conferences, etc. The last piece of the puzzle, however, was actually getting a job.

I had the great fortune of receiving a visiting faculty position only a month after becoming ABD. I had applied because the position was close to my hometown and the call seemed like it was written exactly for my expertise. While this was a great opportunity both personally and professionally, it thrust me prematurely into the job market. I'd had a taste of being a professor and didn't want to go back. And for some reason, I thought I was ready for a tenure-track position. I wasn't.

I was lucky again because my mentors could recognize that I felt like going back to University of Florida would be a step backward, but they also knew that I was unprepared to compete for most (if any) tenure-track jobs. Through our many discussions, we decided that I should apply for jobs that seemed like a perfect fit keeping in mind, however, that I was not really ready. For the next two years while working on my dissertation, I applied selectively to several jobs receiving a few conference interviews each year, but without any real success. When I felt like an interview went well and heard nothing back (it is far too common that an interviewee never hears back from prospective employers), it hurt my ego. But that too became part of the professionalization process—rejection is probably the most consistent aspects of the job market. Through this process I not only developed a sense of the interview process, but I was able to get used to the inevitable rejection when the stakes were much lower (i.e. I still had time and funding to finish my Ph.D.).

In 2013/14, I went back on the market with my dissertation research completed and the writing process nearly over. I was still ABD, but I was only months away from my defense and was a very different scholar than I had been when I accepted the VAP position three years earlier. Because of the accumulated experience of writing cover letters, constructing CVs, and being interviewed, when it came to the final year of my doctoral program I felt thoroughly prepared for the job market process and was more comfortable and confident as I spoke with various search committees. At the end of the process, I ended up accepting a position at an R-1 university (University of Arizona). I can't help but think that part of the reason for my success was my experience stumbling and bumbling through previous interviews (not to mention being prepared for the suffocating anxiety that fills the bullpen in the SBL/AAR Employment Center). While it had certainly led to periods of self-doubt, in the end just like the other aspects of professionalization for academia, the application and interviewing process is a vital component for success within our profession.

Caleb Simmons (Ph.D.) specializes in religion in South Asia, especially Hinduism. His research specialties span religion and state-formation in medieval and colonial India to contemporary transnational aspects of Hinduism. He has edited (with Moumita Sen and Hillary Rodrigues) and contributed to *Nine Nights of the Goddess: The Navaratri Festival in South Asia* (SUNY Press, 2018) and recently completed his monograph manuscript *Devotional Sovereignty*.

Notes

1   See "Employment Trends" at www.aarweb.org/node/62 and www.aarweb.org/sites/default/files/pdfs/Career_Services/AARSBLJobsReport2015-2016.pdf.

2   See "Job Advertisement Data 2013-2014: Society of Biblical Literature and American Academy of Religion" at www.aarweb.org/sites/default/files/pdfs/Career_Services/AARSBLJobsReport2013-2014.pdf, p. 3. In the most recent data published in 2017, 93.3% of employers listed Ph.D. as a desired or required skill. See www.aarweb.org/sites/default/files/pdfs/Career_Services/AARSBLJobsReport2015-2016.pdf.

3   See "Job Advertisement Data 2013–2014: Society of Biblical Literature and American Academy of Religion," pp. 3, 35 (Table 29). This data has not been included in either the 2014–2015 or 2015–2016 AAR/SBL Job Advertisement Data reports.

4   See "Job Advertisement Data 2013-2014: Society of Biblical Literature and American Academy of Religion," p. 35 (Table 28).

Response to Thesis 5

Matt Sheedy

Thesis 5: Whether as an ABD or after having been awarded the Ph.D., some candidates accept year-to-year work as a full-time instructor or lecturer (sometimes also called a sessional position or a part-time temporary instructor). Such positions often entail teaching loads that are heavier than tenure-track or tenured faculty members and, depending on the salary offered, may necessitate supplemental teaching (e.g., evening or summer courses) for one to earn sufficient income. Although the benefits of teaching experience and an academic home can be invaluable to an early career person, the costs such temporary employment entails for one's ability to carry out research and writing can be high. Navigating these costs/benefits is no easy task; for instance, one might learn that, sometimes, time is more valuable than money.

I am reminded here of the now-infamous remarks by Mitt Romney during his presidential bid in 2012, when he stated the following on how college students struggling with debt might find a way out of their predicament:

> We've always encouraged young people: Take a shot, go for it, take a risk, get the education, borrow money if you have to from your parents, start a business.[1]

While borrowing money from one's parents is not an option for many, the idea that those with an advanced education (either pursuing or having recently completed a Ph.D.) could be strapped for cash seems to be at odds with what many perceive to be a path of privilege that leads to the ivory tower, and not, as is often the case, a narrow, unpaved mountain road that knocks many off the edge along the way.[2] The 2015 student strike[3] and arbitration settlement for TA's at the University of Toronto is but one of numerous examples of present challenges.

All of which is to say that we must acknowledge the larger issues at play effecting departments in the humanities—political, economic, and structural—giving rise to both creative solutions,[4] entropy (left unlinked for professional reasons), downsizing or mergers (both with other departments in the humanities or, in the case of the Study of Religion, with departments of classics, philosophy, history, theology [or some kind of realignment[5]]), and death.[6] Although McCutcheon's "Theses on Professionalization" was written before the economic crisis in 2008, and thus before the most recent round of belt tightening effecting the academy, such realities are nothing new.[7]

To whatever extent creative solutions might aid this current lull, it cannot be overlooked that the primary reason for the plight of sessional and part-time temporary instructors has much to do with larger social forces and the glut of recently minted Ph.D.s trying to fill fewer positions in a highly competitive market.[8] Unless these problems are addressed, time will be a commodity only available to a privileged few who are able to avoid the need to teach more courses (assuming, that is, that there are courses to teach in the first place) than a productive scholarly life can easily afford.

I find myself in a similar situation to that described in Thesis 5, though with several important caveats that, I hope, offer a useful point of comparison.

I defended my Ph.D. in January 2015, waded through three months of bureaucracy to finalize the process, and convocated in May of that year. Having been without the official Ph.D. stamp throughout most of the application process for positions starting in 2015–2016, I was (arguably) at a competitive disadvantage and did not secure anything for the 2016–2017 academic year. Despite these obstacles however, my position is an extremely fortunate one ... for the time being.

For some years now I have taught an online course at my current university, which is part of a public–private partnership, and thus offers a different pay-scale than in-class sessional positions that fall under collective bargaining agreements (the pay for in-class sessional appointments is approximately one-third of online courses). This has, in certain years, provided me with more money than my yearly fellowship (which was good for four years) and has allowed me to keep my financial head above water without having to search out a heavy teaching load or (as is not uncommon) to find part-time work outside of the university.

Massive Open Online Courses prior to the parenthetical abbreviation (MOOCs) notwithstanding, I know of no other Ph.D. student who has held such a position, and therefore see my experience as an anomaly and not a path toward the future. This is doubly fortuitous in my case since recent cutbacks at my institution left me with no in-class courses to teach during the 2015/16 academic year. Add to this the fact that I am located in Winnipeg, Manitoba, which, unlike Southern Ontario or, say, the Eastern Seaboard of the United States, does not have many other universities in close proximity where I can find part time work.

As editor of the *Bulletin for the Study of Religion* blog, I have been afforded numerous opportunities to gain contacts and establish professional relationships. I'd like to think that those who have contributed to the *Bulletin* over the years have also been able to establish contacts through this forum, contributing not only the occasional blog post, but also essays that have appeared in the *Bulletin*'s journal. Likewise, my tenure as editor has given rise to opportunities for collaboration with other scholars on any number of projects, and the *Bulletin* has benefited greatly from its affiliation with the North American Association for the Study of Religion (NAASR). All of which is to say, there have been numerous opportunities outside of research and teaching that I have been fortunate to tap into that have aided my own professionalization.

In the coming six months (circa August 2015) I have three conference presentations (two at the upcoming NAASR/AAR conference in Atlanta), a few book projects that I am planning to edit, two essays slated for books, and at least three essays to submit to professional journals. On top of this, I will be chipping away at the dissertation-to-book process, and fielding the firestorm of job and post-doc applications that come my way starting in September. This will be a grueling period, to say the least, and one that aim to conquer with shinny gold stars.

If I were saddled with three or more courses to teach during this time (I will be teaching one on-line course in the fall), as some in my position are, methinks that premature wrinkles and grey hair would be sure to follow. Indeed, for many early career academics, myself included, time is more valuable than money.

Addendum: Since October 2017, I have been the visiting professor in the Department of North American Studies at the University of Bonn, Germany, and remain as a lecturer at the University of Manitoba, teaching on-line and in-class during the summer. The decision to take this position in Germany, which is possibly renewable for another two years, was not a financial one (I could not have taken it, in fact, had I not been able to keep my on-line courses in Winnipeg), but one of building my CV, expanding my range of academic experiences, and developing professional contacts. This visiting professorship has not, at least in the short term, opened up more time for research, though I deem it crucial for remaining competitive in a still-bloated market. One caveat that I might add to McCutcheon's Thesis 5, then, would be that sometimes taking a temporary position (whether abroad or closer to home) is more important than time ... if you can afford it.

Matt Sheedy (Ph.D.) is visiting professor of North American Studies at the University of Bonn, Germany, and is the associate editor of the *Bulletin for the Study of Religion*. His research interests include critical social theory, theories of secularism and atheism, as well as representations of Christianity, Islam, and Native American traditions in popular and political culture. He is currently working on a manuscript that provides a critical examination of Jürgen Habermas's theory of religion in the public sphere.

Notes

1 See www.huffingtonpost.ca/entry/mitt-romney-students-otterbein-university-borrow-money_n_1460097.
2 See, for example, www.theguardian.com/higher-education-network/blog/2014/may/23/so-many-Ph.D.-students-so-few-jobs.
3 See http://rabble.ca/blogs/bloggers/campus-notes/2015/03/what-university-toronto-isnt-telling-you-about-ta-strike.
4 For example, https://blogs.religion.ua.edu.
5 See https://zwingliusredivivus.wordpress.com/2014/06/04/ripp-departmen t-of-biblical-studies-university-of-sheffield.
6 See volume 7, Issue 4 (1995) of *Method and Theory in the Study of Religion* at http://booksandjournals.brillonline.com/content/journals/15700682/7/4.
7 See "Part VI: Religious Studies and Identity Politics" in Scott S. Elliott (ed.), *Reinventing Religious Studies: Key Writings in the History of a Discipline* (New York: Routledge, 2013).
8 See Kate Daley Bailey's 2-part essay, "A is for Adjunct" at http://bulletin.equinoxpub.com/2014/04 /a-is-for-adjunct-part-1.

Response to Thesis 6

Tara Baldrick-Morrone

> Thesis 6: Although it is necessary, the doctoral degree alone is hardly a sufficient credential for being admitted to academia as a full-time employee because most of the other applicants also possess this credential (i.e., it is the level playing field onto which ABDs have yet to be admitted). There was a time, prior to the early 1970s, when the job market was such that merely possessing a Ph.D. would lead to multiple tenure-track job offers; in the humanities that time has long passed.

After reading this thesis again, I had three reactions, two of which can be defined as "knee-jerk" and perhaps not as insightful as the last one. Each is defined by a key phrase from the thesis:

1   The doctoral degree "is the level playing field ..."

Although I will not say too much about this because Drew Durdin addresses this in his comments on Thesis 7, this playing field is frequently uneven, as an institution that has awarded one applicant's degree can certainly carry more social capital than the institution of another applicant (e.g., an applicant who has received their doctoral degree from the University of Notre Dame may be given greater consideration for a tenure-track position in early Christianity than an applicant whose degree is from a state school like Florida State University). Though, to be sure, there are many factors at play besides the degree-granting institution when an applicant is considered for a particular position (the institution's need, letters of recommendation, number of publications, teaching experience, etc.).

2   "There was a time ... when the job market was such that merely possessing a Ph.D. would lead to multiple tenure-track job offers ..."

Although the narrative that we have been told is that tenure-track jobs are increasingly elusive, at the initial time of writing this piece the jobs report from the American Academy of Religion and the Society of Biblical Literature on academic year 2013/14, which was made available in November 2014, made it seem as if the tides had actually been turning.[1] Based on the number of job postings through AAR-SBL Employment Services, the report found "that over three-fourths (76.2%) of appointments were tenure-track positions."[2] However, before breaking out into celebration, the report was also quick to say that "it seems likely that a significant number of contingent positions and positions other than tenure-track faculty positions may exist in the field but are not posted with AAR and SBL."[3]

While some took solace in the supposed good news of the availability of tenure-track positions, at the time I was hesitant to deduce that the "crisis" was over. The most recent jobs report on academic year 2015–2016, released in January 2017, only seems to confirm that past suspicion. As the report indicated, out of the 302 positions posted through Employment Services, only 187 were confirmed tenure-track or tenured. Considering this in terms of larger trends, the report noted that the "numbers of tenure-track or tenured positions in AY14–AY16 are lower than at any point prior to the AY10–AY11 period."[4] At the same time, the number of contingent positions that have filled those "missing" tenure-track positions, as before, remains unclear given the absence of that data. The number of think pieces on and the visibility of issues affecting contingent faculty has greatly increased since my initial comments, but I still recommend reading Kelly J. Baker's "Contingency and Gender" and "What Can Learned Societies Do About Adjuncts?" for insight directly related to the academic study of religion.[5]

3   "[T]he doctoral degree alone is hardly a sufficient credential ..."

On my reading, this is the crux of the thesis. If we take the playing field as level, then it stands to reason that there are actions that we can/ought/must/are forced to take to set ourselves apart from one another. Thinking about this reminded me of a line in Frank Donoghue's *The Last Professors: The Corporate University and the Fate of the Humanities*. Donoghue writes, "We in the humanities have adapted to the conditions of our profession by developing a culture as steeped in the ethos of productivity and salesmanship as anyone might encounter in the business world."[6] This hyperprofessionalization, as Donoghue and others have termed it, has crept into the halls of the academy, especially for those of us in the trenches, that is, those of us who have not yet been validated by the academy to which many of us so desperately wish to belong. Those activities that we can engage in to legitimate our existence in the field of religious studies (e.g., being an instructor of record for undergraduate courses, writing essays for edited volumes, presenting at annual conferences, perhaps even writing a blog post or two, etc.) help us to make a name for ourselves, to network with more established scholars, to gain experience that we can use when we obtain the coveted prize that is a tenure-track job (or a job outside of academia, depending on your definition of achievement and success).

And yet this constant ratcheting-up of expectations does not guarantee us a thing, not even an interview with a third-tier institution. Performing any combination of the aforementioned tasks (or all of them, for that matter) does not always amount to a job. Donoghue makes a discomforting point in saying that hyperprofessionalization and other such developments in academia "seem to have caught professors by surprise, leaving them unprepared to deal with the very phenomena that directly affect their jobs."[7] It is for this reason that I cannot be as optimistic as some of my colleagues. Sure, perhaps steps have been taken to rein in what is required of graduate students, but until there is a sustained conversation that addresses the ever increasing demands placed upon us (especially in terms of the expectations of hiring committees), not much will change.

Tara Baldrick-Morrone is a Ph.D. candidate in Religions of Western Antiquity at Florida State University. Her research focuses on the ways in which the ancient world is reimagined and reconstructed in contemporary discourses, especially those addressing such topics as abortion and martyrdom.

Notes

1   All reports mentioned here can be found in either the Employment Services section of the AAR's website at www.aarweb.org/employment-services/employment-trends or the Data and Research section for the SBL's website at www.sbl-site.org/careercenter/dataresearch.aspx.
2   American Academy of Religion and Society of Biblical Literature, *Job Advertisement Data 2013–2014*, 2.
3   Ibid., 11.
4   American Academy of Religion and Society of Biblical Literature, *Job Advertisement Data 2015–2016*, 6.
5   Both of these pieces, written in 2015, were posted on *ChronicleVitae*'s website.
6   Frank Donoghue, *The Last Professors: The Corporate University and the Fate of the Humanities* (New York: Fordham University Press, 2008), 26.
7   Ibid., 134.

Response to Thesis 7

Andrew Durdin

Thesis 7: For some of those who will be judging candidates' credentials to determine their admission to the profession, the reputation of the school from which they have earned their Ph.D. plays a significant role in assessment of applicants' skills and future promise as colleagues. Although one's alma mater does communicate with whom one has trained and what traditions of scholarship one may pursue, for yet others the reputation of candidates' schools is secondary to the quality of their current research, the places where they have published their work, and the experience they have had in the classroom.

The academic job market is not a level playing field. This should not come as any surprise. But in my conversations and commiserations with other early-career scholars, I've frequently found that the full implications of this sentiment are rarely appreciated, nor are they taken as a potential point of empowerment to those facing the uphill battle for employment where the odds are increasingly stacked against them. In my view, embracing the fact of the uneven field and using it to adjust our expectations can help us avoid some of the negative dispositions that authors have raised in these posts during the past few weeks. It also frees us up to be strategic with those things we can control in potentially new and creative ways.

In Thesis 7 McCutcheon has pointed us to two criteria on which candidates for academic jobs might be assessed: "some" will weight a candidate on the reputation of her institutional affiliation while "others" might find this secondary to the quality of her scholarly work. My almost automatic response to this duality is to claim that things are far more complicated: as written, Thesis 7 is a false dichotomy. As Tara Baldrick-Morrone indicated in her Response to Thesis 6, many factors are at play when considering an applicant for a particular position. Even as I've perused the first job postings of the season, I'm struck by the list of qualifications (preferred and essential) that departments claim are relevant in judging applicants. In addition to the obvious qualities such as possessing a Ph.D., submitting letters of recommendation, and having an "active" and "competitive" research agenda as well as teaching qualifications, most job postings also contain administrative and "catch-all" language that point to a general desire for a candidate willing to act as an overall team player, a "good" colleague to work with. These latter qualities are much more intangible and interpersonal, less able to be assessed on paper, and must be navigated "in the room," i.e., in the interviews where both applicants and committee members can negotiate between explicit matters on the page and more implicit qualifications.

While a number of things can and likely do get factored into assessing candidates, in my experience—albeit limited—and based on my rather anecdotal and informal interactions with others on the job market, the two elements McCutcheon gives us here—institutional affiliation versus individual quality—often take on a specific relationship. Put plainly, the latter is often appealed to as a response to the frustration felt in relation to the former. In fact, these two criteria seem already morally coded. That is, it's not really a choice among equals: the quality of a candidate's work is almost intuitively preferable to said candidate's institutional affiliation. We're struck with a sense of injustice when we entertain the possibility that hiring committees might select job candidates based solely—or mostly—on the prestige of their degree. After all the years of work and financial hardship in graduate school, it is a disquieting thought that it all might come down to a question of affiliation. This disquiet is not helped by recent studies (which perhaps reinforce our intuitions) that show a small coterie of elite academic programs perpetuate themselves through hiring practices in a closed network.[1]

By contrast, we often hope that solid scholarly work will somehow allow us to punch through the inequalities of our field and the academy in general—that by sheer effort alone, we'll be able to transcend the disproportionate accumulations of social capital and end up being the exception to the bleak landscape testified to in article after article floating across our social media feeds. But merit—as a possible response to the inherent unevenness of the job market—simply defers the issue. In appealing to merit, we're acting as though long-entrenched status hierarchies don't exist or don't matter—at least not to "us." To plow ahead in a game rigged in advance, all the while acting as though this isn't the case, leads to burnout, frustration, and resentment. It results in the loss of confidence or the compulsive need to "do more," as other contributors have touched on in past weeks. To paraphrase a sentiment from Slavoj Žižek: many of us are fetishists in practice but not in theory when it comes to the job market. We know the general state of the academic job market—we've read the stats on the shrinking number of tenure positions, the indentured servitude of adjuncting, and the closing of religious studies departments as STEM fields reign supreme. And we know that the whole idea of meritocratic "bootstraps" is a myth often perpetuated by the most privileged. Yet, for all this, our own particular situation often remains mystified, and a latent conception of meritocracy lingers. We are perfectly content to commiserate over the abysmal state of the job market, in what can generally be understood as the antecedent to a future explanation of why we never made it or the beginnings of a triumph narrative, in which we succeeded against all odds (likely because of the quality of our work, not the prestige of our degree). Either way, we are perpetuating the idea that if one works hard enough and produces quality scholarship then one might breakthrough the entrenched hierarchies in our field and beat the house at its own game.

Of course this is not a call to give up and go get a "real job," nor is it to say that we shouldn't strive to produce quality scholarship or present ourselves as well-rounded applicants. On the contrary, as religious studies scholar Mike Altman put so nicely in a comment to a previous post in this series, we should embrace job market nihilism. We should put off notions that one can "game" the system and spend our energy instead on what we might have some control over. Acknowledging that the game is rigged might open us up to playing the game more skillfully and strategically and to resist hanging our potential success on any one factor, whether it's the reputation of our program or the quality of our work. We should accept that, despite our best efforts, we can't know or control most aspects of the job search in advance. Based on what we can know—through whatever channels and connections—of the preferences and priorities of those "some" and "others" who here represent the judges and gatekeepers of vocational academic work, we should carefully craft our self-representation and qualities for each application and interview, tailoring ourselves as best we can to each specific imagined audience who will read our application, conduct our interviews, and, with any luck, eventually become our colleagues.

Andrew Durdin (Ph.D.) is a lecturer in the humanities at the University of Michigan—Dearborn. His research focuses on ancient Roman religion, theories of magic and religion, and the modern historiography of ancient religion.

Note

1 See www.insidehighered.com/news/2015/02/13/study-suggests-insular-faculty-hiring-practices-elite-departments. While religious studies departments have not been included in these studies, a quick look at the websites of some "top" schools in our field and the degree-granting institutions of their faculty members suggests a provisional pattern.

Response to Thesis 8

Jeffrey Wheatley

> Thesis 8: Like all institutions, academia provides a case study in the complex relationship between structure and agency; for, although there are a variety of things that one can do to increase one's competitiveness, job candidates must recognize that there are also a host of factors of which they are unaware and which are therefore beyond their control (e.g., the unstated needs, interests, goals, and even insecurities of the hiring department; the number of other candidates qualified at any given time in your area of expertise; the impact of world events on the perceived need for scholars in your subject area, etc.). Success likely requires one to learn to live with the latter while taking control of the former.

Most of Russell McCutcheon's theses on professionalization provide important suggestions for how young scholars can develop their academic careers. The eighth thesis is a bit different. It suggests that we might do well to embrace on some level the vicissitudes of pursuing an academic career. McCutcheon writes that:

> [A]lthough there are a variety of things that one can do to increase one's competitiveness, job candidates must recognize that there are also a host of factors of which they are unaware and which are therefore beyond their control.

However deserving we might think ourselves to be and however much we professionalize and develop research that fulfills our particular field's current desires, the truth is that academia in all of its institutional, personal, financial, and political dimensions will in all likelihood defy any attempt on the part of young scholars to understand the academic job market fully, much less master it completely. There are always unknowns. The academy is a game of risks.

In some ways Thesis 8 resonates with Tara Baldrick-Morrone's Response to Thesis 6. Regarding the demands of professionalization, she writes that:

> [T]his constant ratcheting-up of expectations does not guarantee us a thing, not even an interview with a third-tier institution. Performing any combination of the aforementioned tasks (or all of them, for that matter) does not equate to a job.

Acknowledging the reality of these vicissitudes does, I think, contribute to the development of a healthier realistic mentality in young scholars. To put it one way: failure to get a secure job does not indicate a failure in effort. But as I consider

Thesis 8 and the "Theses on Professionalization" broadly, I am stuck thinking not about the "additional" skills, forms of consciousness, or exercises that will serve young scholars should they pursue an academic career (even if one of these skills is the acceptance of a *lack* of control), but, as Baldrick-Morrone notes at the end of her post, I am stuck thinking about the responsibilities that the field broadly has toward young scholars. Furthermore, Thesis 8 prompts me to consider the structural forces that are more harmful and open to challenge than the examples McCutcheon provides. So, even as I acknowledge the utility and intent of Thesis 8, I want to use this opportunity to pivot towards these issues.

As a graduate student in the early stages of a Ph.D. program, I cannot lay claim to any direct knowledge of the visceral realities of being on the job market—the ways in which the unknowns play into hiring; the ways in which the ideals of a meritocracy cannot capture the messiness of the whole process. In some ways the academic career market to me remains an abstraction, albeit one whose presence looms. Thankfully, I have been fortunate enough to have graduate colleagues and faculty members who have made frank discussions about the job market a part of academic training and central to my sense of being a member of an academic (and social) community. Furthermore, many scholars have utilized digital spaces to give priority to discussing #altac,[1] the future of tenure, contingent labor conditions, the presumptuous privileging of those trained at elite institutions (see Andrew Durdin's Response to Thesis 7 in this volume), and the ways in which gender and race structure academia today. We need to continue to examine and scrutinize these variables and how they influence our relationships, our hierarchies, and our scholarly production. Because of the efforts of these vocal scholars, I and many other young graduate students, it seems, are getting a much better sense of what awaits us and what the costs (*and the rewards!*) might be should we pursue an academic career.

Some of the persistent "unknowns" in academic hiring are inevitable. In truth, the phrase "the unspokens," rather than "unknowns," better captures what I mean in this post. We might do better to accept some of the academy's "unspokens" as they are. The latter two examples that McCutcheon provides in Thesis 8 qualify for this treatment. However, McCutcheon's first example—"*the unstated needs, interests, goals, and even insecurities of the hiring Department*" as factors beyond the control of applicants—deserves more criticism. I think hiring institutions have a responsibility to craft pointed and relevant job descriptions that provide as transparent a view as possible to their intentions. Surely, this is a burden on these hiring committees. But I care more about the burden placed on job applicants lured by job descriptions whose authors have not disclosed (or figured out) what or whom they are really looking for. Applying to jobs is a costly and time-consuming endeavor that often occurs during a period in which many young scholars have diminishing or no support from their graduate institutions. We should question and challenge such a damaging "unspoken" variable alongside the ones I list in the previous paragraph.

I use "we" in a broad sense. I use it normatively, with the hope of drawing in scholars at all levels of academia to openly engage these issues. Young scholars have the most reason to be vocal about some of the more problematic unspokens that structure the academy today. Young scholars also occupy a position of vulnerability, which might be exacerbated if they are vocal in challenging the structures of the academy, especially if they are alone in doing so and especially if their social positionality (e.g., gender, class, race) already weakens their placement in the academy. The critique of some of the academy's unspokens, I would like to think, should be the responsibility of our institutions, not just a burden placed upon young scholars as they navigate the complicated world of the academy. I make this claim not because I think religious studies is a site that, because of its objects of study (variously defined), creates a unique demand for ethical practices and responsibilities. I do not. I make this claim because I am invested in these institutions and fields. I care about the knowledges, methods, and theories we produce, and I care about the professional exercises and institutions that undergird this production.

Jeffrey Wheatley is a doctoral student in American religions at Northwestern University. He researches race, religion, empire, and state power in the United States, focusing on the categories of "superstition" and "fanaticism," especially in the late nineteenth and early twentieth centuries. Related focal points include pedagogy, theory and method, global Christianity, secularism, the history of the study of religion, and popular use of the octopus as an image for visualizing dangerous others.

Note

1   See https://twitter.com/search?q=%23altac&src=typd.

Response to Thesis 9

Barbara Krawcowicz

Thesis 9: A structural element that must be taken into account is that departmental search committees often fail to entertain the difficult questions in advance and, instead, go on "fishing expeditions" by defining their open positions far too broadly and vaguely, such as looking for "the best qualified" applicant (without ever articulating what counts as "qualified"). Making explicit their implicit and often competing preferences may strike members of a department as being too costly an exercise. It is into this mix of unstated disagreements and longstanding rivalries that job applicants can be thrust, affecting such things as how their letters of application are read, their credentials judged, and their performance during campus interviews measured. While one cannot control such factors, when representing oneself one at least ought to be aware of their potential presence and impact.

An interesting job advert appeared on the Higher Ed website in 2015. A department of religious studies of an American university was searching for an assistant professor. Following the Higher Ed advert form it stated that the position was open until filled and that it was full time. The rest was a mystery. Minimum education: no response. Minimum experience: no response. Field? Specialization? Blank. The plethora of information regarding the position contained in the advertisement took my breath away. There is no doubt whatsoever that the hiring department had spent a significant amount of time considering all the important factors before it went public with the search. Imagine those long discussions: we need someone to teach X but it would be great if they could teach Y and Z as well. We could use someone with an expertise in the field of A; that would greatly enhance our program. But it is also essential that the person we hire has experience in B and C because our department really needs that! And also ... But as well ... And let us not forget about ...

Alright, I know, this advertisement was obviously a mistake and thus it cannot serve as an illustration of McCutcheon's Thesis 9. However, every single one of us, (i.e. of people in the trenches of what is commonly known as the job search but feels much more like one of the protracted and exhausting battles of World War I), has seen more than one advertisement that was, to say the least, vague in its description of the vacant position, required qualifications, job's responsibilities, etc.

As a grad student at Indiana University Bloomington, I attended a workshop where several tenured faculty members shared some of the knowledge they gathered while serving on job search committees. Among many interesting things said, one in particular caught my attention. In response to a complaint that many job descriptions were formulated in such a way that it was quite impossible to decide whether or not one was qualified and should apply for the job, one of the professors replied: well, the truth of the matter is that oftentimes the search committee doesn't really know what it is looking for. The professor smiled saying this and his words were met with chuckles among the audience. I don't think I laughed. Somehow it did not seem funny.

On the *Chronicle of Higher Education* discussion board,[1] there is a long thread entitled "Apply For The Damn Job." Am I really qualified to apply for this position? AFTDJ! I'm not sure whether they're actually looking for someone doing this-and-that. AFTDJ! The description is so broad that I don't really know if ... AFTDJ! You are never going to know for sure. So just AFTDJ if it *seems* that you may be a good fit. *Seems*. Yes, that's all you're going to know because, sometimes, the search committee itself does not have a clear picture of the ideal candidate.

So we apply for those damn jobs. One problem we immediately encounter is this: how can one tailor application documents to a job description if the description happens to be hopelessly vague? How can I prove that I am the best qualified candidate if I don't know what counts as qualified (let alone best)? The advertisement says they want a person whose work is interdisciplinary. OK, great, but what exactly does that mean? Does it even mean anything? Or is only a convenient placeholder for what should actually say, "well, we don't really know what we want" or "we will make up our minds once we see the applications and know who is available?"

That is not all, however.

Not long ago I applied for a job in Europe. The job description in the advertisement was surprisingly detailed. Moreover, there was an even more informative package available through the institution's online application system. From what was called a job specification I could learn infinitely more than I ever had from any analogous advertisements in the U.S.

The description was divided into the following sections:

1 job purpose;

2 main responsibilities;

3 knowledge, skills and experience needed for the job;

4 key contacts/relationships;

5 dimensions; and

6 job context and any other relevant information.

The list of knowledge, skills, and experience was divided into two sections: essential and desirable. The former consisted of five points. The latter—of another three.

My goodness, I thought, could one ask for a better job description? Admittedly, parts of it did leave a bit too much room for interpretation. For example, one of the essentials was an "ability to plan and deliver excellent teaching." One could ask, rightfully, what exactly counts as excellent teaching. Or what is meant by "high level competence in university lecturing," but then we all know that there are things that are not easily captured within any definite rubric. Especially in a limited space of a job advert.

Either way, I thought I had all the information I needed to prepare an excellent application. And so I did. In my letter I highlighted how I met all the essential requirements and some of the desirable ones. I made sure it was clear that I am capable of successfully discharging the main responsibilities listed.

I was invited for the interview.

The last position on the list of the desirables was occupied by—and here I will allow myself to replace the actual content of the job specification with a bit of a metaphor—an ability to cook vichyssoise. Well, I said to myself, I've never actually made this particular soup but I am no stranger to cooking in general and to cooking soups in particular. Besides, it is the very last of the desirables. Obviously it is not as important as the others.

How surprised I was when the interviewing panel presented me with leeks, potatoes, chicken broth, and whipping cream and requested that I prepare a delicious vichyssoise right then and there!

Evidently the desirables were considerably more essential than they appeared given the advertisement.

How was that possible, I wondered? Why was making vichyssoise not listed among the essentials? It clearly should have been!

Well, a knowledgeable person told me, probably the committee members were not in agreement regarding this ability's importance. Or perhaps they changed their mind sometime between the advert's publication and the interviews. Additionally, you need to keep in mind that in the country where the institution is located, it is often the case that the advertisement is not created by people who later serve on the committee. It is possible that the vichyssoise advocate(s) had less impact on the job description content and more on the actual interview and decision-making.

It is not only that, as McCutcheon has written, "Departmental search committees often fail to entertain the difficult questions in advance and, instead, go on 'fishing expeditions' by defining their open positions far too broadly and vaguely." It is also the case that sometimes they define and redefine the position as the search unfolds.

"While one cannot control such factors" as nebulous job descriptions, "unstated disagreements and longstanding rivalries," McCutcheon writes, "when representing oneself one at least ought to be aware of their potential presence and impact." I'm not sure how this awareness should translate into action. Unless what McCutcheon is saying is simply: AFTDJ!

Barbara Krawcowicz received her Ph.D. in religious studies from Indiana University Bloomington and in philosophy from Warsaw University. Currently, she serves as a post-doctoral fellow at the Department of Philosophy and Religion, Norwegian University of Science and Technology in Trondheim. She's working on a book devoted to Jewish ultra-Orthodox responses to the Holocaust. Her research interests include modern and contemporary Jewish thought, religious radicalism, gender and religion, as well as method and theory in religious studies.

Notes

1   See www.chronicle.com/forums/index.php/topic,73013.0.html.

Response to Thesis 10

Emily D. Crews

Thesis 10: Whether working at a publicly or privately funded institution, professors are comparable to self-employed entrepreneurs inasmuch as they can increase their social capital (i.e., reputation) by seeking out new books to read and review, unique topics on which to research and write, novel and timely courses to develop and teach, and different professional service opportunities to provide them with additional experience as well as new national and international contacts. Graduate students are in much the same position and the additional qualifications that result from their entrepreneurial pre-professional activities can serve to distinguish one job applicant from another. Documentation from such activities, as recorded on one's CV, communicate to the hiring committee that one is already skilled at participating in the many aspects of the profession that will surely be required of a tenure-track assistant professor.

In Thesis 10, Russell McCutcheon writes that the young scholar entering the job market may distinguish herself from her peers by making evident that she possesses "additional qualifications that result from" her "entrepreneurial pre-professional activities."

For many graduate students, advice of the type offered in Thesis 10 is both helpful and frustrating. It is immensely useful for us to have any lamp in the dark of the academic job market, particularly one that clearly points us to a course of action. However, to some this particular course of action sounds eerily similar to the unrealistic suggestion shouted down from the ivory towers of our institutions: "Do everything and be good at it all." I know very few graduate students and early career scholars who are not already engaged in a dizzying array of more-than-dissertation activities. Many of us are teaching, advising, publishing, and working while also applying to fellowships and serving as workshop leaders or conference organizers, all as part of our professional development and in spite of a common pressure to reduce the overall time it takes us to obtain our degrees.

Thus, the advice in Thesis 10 can, for many, incite an overwhelming fatigue: "*This* again. How can we possibly do more than we already do? And how can we possibly be good at everything in a field that's littered with speed-reading, twelve-language-knowing demi-gods?" What's more, many might suggest that it is yet another example of a tenured faculty member perpetuating the crippling indentured servitude of academia through willful ignorance of the toll taken by such demands for hyper-involvement. I understand the impulse to approach recommendations of this type with a defensive posture, and am sympathetic to the perspective that academia continues to suffer from a multitude of crises.

However, I think that to read McCutcheon in this way misses the real point of his suggestion. Instead, it would be helpful to consider that McCutcheon has spent much of his career at large state schools, often serving as a department chair; at Alabama he has been responsible for the growth of a robust undergraduate program in religious studies in an era where many of its kind have shrunk or disappeared entirely.

It is out of this context that McCutcheon offers Thesis 10, which I would argue points us not toward a "do more, be more" philosophy, but instead toward the importance of using our graduate school experiences to indicate that we have been and will continue to be productive members of a community. As university budgets are slashed and the Humanities continue to take heavy fire, it is more crucial than ever that new hires are able to help overburdened departments tackle growing workloads. When there are dozens of things that any given department must be able to do—offer courses; advise students; produce original research; organize job searches, conferences, and publications—asking to join the team means that we must be willing and able to shoulder part of the burden. Candidates who are unprepared or uninterested in doing so would, I assume, be unappealing as future colleagues, and thus less likely to land a tenure track position.[1]

McCutcheon's thesis leaves me wondering, however: are all types of preparation created equal? If not, what types of preparation are most valuable? What indicates that we are "already skilled at participating in the many aspects of the profession that will surely be required of a tenure-track Assistant Professor?" Conversely, are there types of preparation that are a waste of time? Further, from the perspective of members of a hiring committee, where is the line between diversification and distraction? Which types of activities or contributions make candidates seem well-trained and which make them seem unfocused? In the *Sophie's Choice* of graduate school, where every moment is precious and each new commitment means the loss of another hour of sleep, what is the wisest investment of our time?

Take, for example, this very exercise. Were I to cite it on my CV, how would a hiring committee view my having participated in this discussion? Does a relatively casual post in an online forum say much at all? If so, what? Could it read as time I have wasted when I might have been working on my dissertation (suggesting, perhaps, that I might go off course on the road to tenure)? Does it indicate that I am interested in being an active part of a rich community of people and ideas (and that I would be an asset to a department for this reason)?

Or another example: book reviews, an oft-debated topic in my own program. Are book reviews a service to the academic community and an indication of our expertise in a given area, or are they lines on our CV's that potential employers skip over on the way to other, more relevant types of experience? Should graduate students write them or shouldn't we?

While there are certainly many answers to all these questions, each based on the idiosyncrasies of the particular institution and department holding the search, I wonder if some who are reading this post, particularly those who have experience on hiring committees, might be able to provide a general set of guidelines for reference.[2] This includes a hope for further suggestions from Professor McCutcheon who, both in writing his "Theses" and in so many other ways, has been immensely helpful and generous to early career scholars.

Emily D. Crews is a Ph.D. candidate in history of religions at the University of Chicago Divinity School. Her dissertation examines the role of religion in its many forms in the lives of Nigerian immigrants in Chicago.

Notes

1 It should be noted that McCutcheon's advice, written before the economic crisis and the dramatic shift in the landscape of the academic job market, is specifically geared toward those who are applying to tenure track positions. How this advice might have changed or lost its relevance in light of the increasingly limited availability of such positions is well worth further discussion, which limited space has prevented here. On this topic, however, I will offer one question: does it make sense to prepare so thoroughly to be part of a department when most of us—well over 70%, according to recent statistics at www.aaup.org/report/heres-news-annual-report-economic-status-profession-2012-13—will end up in jobs that might not even not come with an office, much less full membership in the faculty body?
2 For instance, I'm sure that the needs and priorities of a large, elite research university differ significantly from those of a small liberal arts college.

Response to Thesis 11

Jennifer Collins-Elliott

Thesis 11: While higher education is organized so as to train ever increasing specialists–a process that begins with surveys and broad course work, examines candidates on their knowledge in general areas, and then culminates in writing a dissertation on a highly technical topic–eventual full-time employment can just as easily depend upon one's ability to contribute lower-level, so-called core or general education introductory courses to a department's curriculum. Because many departments of religious studies justify their existence not simply by appealing to the number of their majors or graduates, but also the number of core or general education courses that they offer to students pursuing degrees in other areas of the university, gaining early experience in such courses as a teaching assistant is an important step toward being able to persuade future employers of one's ability to be a colleague who helps to teach their department's "bread and butter" courses.

I see in Thesis 11 the confluence of a few vexing and sometimes controversial strands in the modern university, particularly at research-one (R1) state universities like McCutcheon's home institution. First, Thesis 11 speaks to the ways in which the modern academy pulls graduate students and young faculty in two different, and sometimes competing, directions: that of specialization (research) and that of generalization (teaching). Woven into this are the concerns raised in Emily D. Crews's piece (Response to Thesis 10) and the reappearance of the Platonic form of "well-rounded job candidate"—the person who publishes original research that contributes to their specialization while also learning enough on far-flung subjects in their broader field to feel intellectually honest in the classroom while teaching survey courses. And second, McCutcheon presents here, though only in passing, an on-going conversation about the "usefulness" of the humanities, the rhetoric of which is consonant with the increasing corporatization of public universities, and what future employment in the humanities might look like.

Similar to Thesis 10, there is a call here to be able to demonstrate one's flexibility and range on their CV and throughout the hiring process. In a market awash with qualified candidates, institutions can, to some extent, afford to look for their unicorn. While McCutcheon recommends gaining experience as a teaching assistant, it is often not enough simply to have assisted in a course but rather is necessary to have been the instructor of record. To have the potential or educational training to teach such-and-such a course without having actually taught it can be a deal-breaker for a hiring committee. There is no time for on-the-job teacher training at research-one state institutions when the enrollment and numbers of majors is ever more used to justifying the existence of many Humanities departments. What increasingly appears to be the case, however, is not the lack of teaching experience before entering the job market, but rather an excess of teaching experience that, at a point, becomes less useful and more redundant—a point McCutcheon addresses in Thesis 5 and the struggles of which Matt Sheedy gives voice to in his post.

While demonstrating teaching experience in "gen ed" courses can help open the door, the axiom "publish or perish" remains as true as ever for those who are offered tenure-track positions. As a graduate student working on her dissertation who is also teaching "bread and butter" courses, I waver between appreciating and questioning the usefulness of the experience that I'm currently gaining. I, and others in my position, have the opportunity to learn how to balance research and teaching, which is a challenge that tenure-track professors face. How can those of us trained in universities that rely on graduate student labor protect our research time? How can we graduate students or young scholars in lecturer positions, tasked with teaching large survey-courses while also trying to establish a research and publication record, work "smarter, not harder"? How does one fight the teaching undertow? Years ago when McCutcheon was the keynote speaker at Florida State University's Department of Religion Annual Graduate Student Symposium,[1] he gave me two pieces of advice about teaching: he told me that I wasn't obligated to the textbook, and that every course should have a thesis statement. I found this advice to be a relief. With this in mind I found it much easier to craft a more cohesive world religions syllabus and one that would give me space to incorporate aspects of my own research. While I still think of this advice each time I write a syllabus, it has also led me to invest an inordinate amount of my time in my teaching—a danger addressed in Thesis 19. While McCutcheon is undoubtedly correct that having teaching experience for "bread and butter" courses on one's CV is crucial in the current job market, the process of gaining this experience in graduate school can feel a bit like trying to do a wheelie while you still have the training wheels on your bike.

With politicians like Florida Governor Rick Scott doing their best to marginalize the humanities[2] and as of 2007 at least 70 percent of faculty members being employed "off the tenure track,"[3] perhaps we should think about for whom these theses were written, or rather, what kind of future they imagine? When McCutcheon says that, "gaining early experience in such courses as a teaching assistant is an important step toward being able to persuade future employers of one's ability to be a colleague who helps to teach their department's 'bread and butter' courses," I think he's absolutely right. But then I find myself trying to imagine what these "future employers" might want me, and the majority of graduating Ph.D.s in the humanities, for, and what kind of positions might become more common in the next 5–10 years? The AAUP's report on tenure and teaching-intensive appointments[4] suggests that there is an emerging employment field between semester-to-semester lecture appointments and full-time tenure-track faculty. The language of these appointments vary, sometimes called "instructor tenure," "continuing lectureship," or "senior lectureship," but each of these positions is meant to offer greater stability, support, professionalization, and perhaps benefits than more traditional forms of contingency labor.

Thesis 11, read alongside the other 20, continues to provide a clear and concise framework for all levels of graduate students and young scholars. However, in light of increasing graduate student teaching and longer periods of lectureship between graduation and possible tenure-track employment, coupled with the emergence of a "middle class" of university teaching, we should be mindful of the ways in which the imagined audience for this advice as well as the imagined employment landscape has changed in the nearly 10 years since McCutcheon published his theses.

Jennifer Collins-Elliott is a doctoral candidate in the Department of Religion at Florida State University, writing her dissertation on sexual violence in early Christianity, tentatively titled "'Bespattered with the Mud of Another's Lust': Rape and Physical Embodiment in Christian Literature of the 4th–6th Centuries CE." She is also a lecturer in the Department of Religious Studies at the University of Tennessee, Knoxville.

Notes

1 See http://religion.fsu.acsitefactory.com/graduate-studies/graduate-student-symposium.
2 See http://politics.heraldtribune.com/2011/10/10/rick-scott-wants-to-shift-university-funding-away-from-some-majors.
3 See www.aaup.org/report/tenure-and-teaching-intensive-appointments.
4 Ibid.

Response to Thesis 12

Nickolas P. Roubekas

Thesis 12: Many doctoral students do not realize that finding authors willing to write book notes, book reviews, etc., is sometimes difficult for journal editors. As a first step in professionalizing themselves, graduate students should become aware of the journals in their field and write to their book review editors, suggesting that the journal allow them to write and submit a review (especially for books that they are already reading for their courses or research, thereby minimizing on work additional to their class and dissertation research). Besides providing experience in writing and a much needed line on one's CV, one never knows who will read the review or what other opportunities might follow upon it.

Most scholars tend to see book reviewing as a burdensome, tedious, and frankly pointless undertaking that diverts them from more important and creative projects. Add teaching workloads, administration work, grant applications, and personal obligations and one realizes that dedicating precious time to review a new book is, to say the least, unattractive. A line on one's CV or the enticement of a free book are often not enough to persuade scholars to review a new publication.

Ph.D. students or young scholars entering the job market do not face the same problems but they do deal with an even more stressful issue, namely, the dim and admittedly deterring possibilities of employability. When one needs to spend countless hours filling in applications, writing postdoctoral project proposals while at the same time finalizing a Ph.D. thesis or working on individual chapters followed by back-and-forth email exchanges with her/his supervisor, why should s/he spend time in reviewing a book? Is merely a free book or a line in one's CV enough to persuade young scholars to engage into such a time-consuming project?

I think that there are three important reasons why doctoral students and young scholars should consider book reviews as *a* step in professionalizing themselves, but certainly not merely the first one. I strongly believe that book reviewing is an academic exercise that is often neglected or even scorned among academics for several reasons. First, most journals simply ask for a mere presentation of the book under review without requiring (or, worse, sometimes, denying to accept) a critical approach by the reviewer. Second, some reviewers tend to request and evaluate books written by either 'friends' or 'enemies', with a specific agenda in mind, which in turn produces biased reviews that add little to the academic ongoing discussions and debates. Third, book review editors often assign books without considering the reviewer's field, expertise, and ability to submit something substantial. Fourth, the book reviews section in academic journals is often seen by scholars as a promotional one replacing publishers' catalogues. Fifth, editors tend to accept almost all submitted reviews. This, of course, reflects the difficulty they have in finding reviewers to begin with and, as one can imagine, the high acceptance rate is sometimes against the scholarly nature of the book reviews section and its service to the field.

So, why bother?

Here are three reasons why I think Ph.D. students and young scholars should consider book reviews beyond the given demand for reviewers, a free book, and a line on their CV's:

1 Academic reading of a book and reviewing a book serve different purposes. In the former, one goes through a particular text in search of important data or information for justifying theories, approaches, and conclusions promoted in a research output (be it a Ph.D. thesis, a journal article, a research proposal, etc.). In the latter, however, the stakes are higher. Reviewers are—ideally—required not only to present the structure and basic ideas of the book under review, but also to: identify problems; point out future developments that the reviewed book possibly promotes; parallel the text in question with previously published works and underline the scope and the location of the work in the wider academic setting; critically assess the methods and theories promoted and justify their potentiality within the specific field it belongs to.

2 Writing book reviews will help you do better in job interviews. This admittedly bizarre statement needs further reflection. It is almost sure that during an interview for an academic job no one will ask you something along the lines of "What do you think of Bruce Lincoln's approach to myth?" If your Ph.D. thesis was on myth, you are most likely aware of Lincoln's approach to the topic. But, in all honesty, no one cares about it. It is too specialized, narrowed, and people who decide whether you will get the job or not will want to see something beyond your ability to defend anew your Ph.D. thesis. It is more likely to be asked something like "What do you think a department of Religious Studies should offer to students?" Such a question virtually requires a broader and academically coherent answer. Your ability to know, apply, and evaluate Lincoln's definition of myth granted you a Ph.D. (or will soon do so). Your critical approach to Lincoln's work on myth and its placement in the field of Religious Studies with the simultaneous evaluation of how the discipline should or could function based on Lincoln's suggestions (which is the result of

a different reading of his work usually required when you review a book) will allow you to go beyond your Ph.D. thesis and, hopefully, impress your interviewers.

3   Writing book reviews will make you a better academic author. When reviewing a book keep in mind that you are working on a text that managed to survive going through various stages before being published. From the book proposal stage and the various anonymous reviews to series editors and copy editors and their suggestions, what you are working on is—most of the time—a polished and well-presented text. A careful and thorough reading of a book under review will give you a very good idea of what is the standard in academic writing regarding structure, style, referencing, and argumentation. If you are working on your thesis, this is an invaluable source; if you are working on a book proposal, you have at hand an example of what you should be aiming at. Given that for most—if not all—young scholars their Ph.D. thesis will constitute the topic of their first book proposal, having worked on book reviews gives them an advantage in presenting a project that is coherent, well thought-out, and has all the academic elements that will convince a publisher to offer a contract.

Nickolas P. Roubekas is assistant professor of religious studies at the University of Vienna, Austria. He is the author of *An Ancient Theory of Religion: Euhemerism from Antiquity to the Present* (Routledge, 2017), editor of the forthcoming *Theorizing 'Religion' in Antiquity* (Equinox, 2018), and managing editor of the *Journal of Cognitive Historiography*.

Response to Thesis 13

Vincent Burgess

Thesis 13: Because there is no direct relationship between seniority and the quality of one's writing, one's familiarity with the literature, or the novelty of one's ideas, graduate students ought never to refrain from submitting their work to a scholarly journal for possible peer review publication simply because they understand themselves to be novices. Even if rejected, the comments that result from the blind review process will be of benefit to students who have so far only received feedback from professors already familiar with their work.

Overall, this seems like great advice—and advice which is unlikely to be drastically affected by changing hiring paradigms, or even the potential shifting landscape of academic publishing. Unlike other authors in this series, I cannot draw upon any specific anecdotes or overt experiences when it comes to this topic. To be honest, aside from delivering a handful of conference papers, this is the first time I've come close to writing anything to be published. However, the imperative to publish, and to publish often, has been looming over my head for many years—even before I began graduate school.

In my first religious studies theory course at the Ohio State University we spent some time going over the biography and bibliography of Mircea Eliade. Eliade, it is said, had published 100 articles by the time he turned 18.[1] That's a relatively intimidating factoid to learn when one is just beginning to process what would be expected of them as a graduate student/scholar in academia. Now, I have since learned not to hold myself to Eliade's standards (for numerous reasons), but my understanding of the necessity to publish has never gone away.

There is, however, the inherent inferiority complex which seems to come along with being a graduate student (and much has recently been written on the notion of the "imposter syndrome"). Some of this is a result of one's own insecurities, but much of it has been institutionalized as a primary component of academia and the processes of educating and professionalizing graduate students—presumably as a means of preserving the various egos and hierarchies central to said process. That is, once one's academic authority has been established, one would be understandably hesitant to relinquish even an iota of it by either implying or flat out saying that a graduate student is capable of researching and writing with the same skill and expertise as a more experienced academic. Who knows what could happen? Hell, the whole system may come crashing down.

Relatedly, a graduate student's 'fear of screwing up' is especially appropriate when it can mean the difference between a highly sought-after job in academia or ... well ... nothing. For this reason, it's important to highlight the centrality of confidence to this thesis—being confident enough in your academic preparation to date, your research expertise regarding a particularly technical topic, the subsequent intervention that your research and writing can make to the field, and confident enough to withstand the inevitable criticisms which come along with the submission process (no matter how constructive they may be).

After all, in most cases a well-read graduate student who has spent a considerable amount of time researching a very specific topic, case study, or question will, in fact, be better versed on the subject than most other scholars in the discipline, whether they are a junior or senior scholar. They should therefore not be hesitant to share their findings with the broader scholastic community if and when they have something to contribute. As one never knows when a significant intervention into a field or sub-field might be made, nor by whom, I agree that McCutcheon is right here to encourage graduate students to challenge such hierarchical preconceptions vis-à-vis experience versus a potentially valuable contribution to the field. However, there are also broader issues to consider—such as the matter of one's time.

As has been pointed out repeatedly in this collection (particularly in the essays by Matt Sheedy and Emily D. Crews), one's time as a graduate student (and, of course, as an instructor, lecturer, and/or eventual professor) is invaluable, and any extra work must be approached with substantial consideration and cost-benefit analysis. Sending a paper off for consideration to a publisher can entail a considerable amount of time. There is the researching, writing, editing, sending it off to professors for notes and initial feedback, waiting, re-writing, sending it off to the publication, waiting, waiting, more waiting, more editing (if accepted), more editing (if not accepted), sending it off to a different publication, waiting, waiting, and repeat.

Since professionalization is the goal here, it is important to point out that this endeavor—in time management and beginning to traverse the world of publishing—is undoubtedly worthwhile, as it will begin to prepare one for a potential lifetime of such activities. Just as one would not wait to demonstrate an ability to serve one's department, and one would not wait to take every opportunity to develop their teaching skills, it would also, therefore, stand to reason that an ambitious graduate student should also not wait to begin publishing their work.

This, however, raises a question which is often the subject of much debate, especially when it comes to the hiring process: Should a graduate student take *every* opportunity to publish? Even though these theses are not necessarily about "how to get a job," but, rather, how to *prepare* oneself for an eventual position in academia, I cannot help but take such questions—and the broader issue of employability—into account while considering this particular thesis.

There seem to be two schools of thought on the subject:

1   All publications are good, and any is better than none.

2   It's better to publish less, more selectively, with higher quality work, in better journals—even if that means not publishing at all before one goes on the job market.

There is not space here to delve too deeply into this debate, but I will say that there does not seem to be a single scenario that is best for anyone, as there are many variables to consider—not least of which is the fickle nature of many hiring committees (as succinctly described in a 1997 piece written by Russell McCutcheon and Tim Murphy,[2] along with Jeffrey Wheatley's Response to Thesis 8 in this collection).

Even if publishing is neither a necessary nor sufficient condition for being hired, it probably won't hurt your chances. As long as it is quality work which has something of value to add to the conversation—that is, a significant intervention or contribution to the field. To return to McCutcheon's thesis, regardless of whether or not one is successful in their endeavor to publish their research, they will nonetheless come away with valuable feedback. Feedback which will help them hone their work as they move forward, therefore raising the overall quality of their writing and increasing the chances that they are more successful next time. And, perhaps equally important, one will gain valuable experience from beginning to negotiate the publishing arena, which will surely help her/him in the future.

Vincent Burgess is a Ph.D. candidate in the Asian Religions doctoral program of the Department of Asian Studies at Cornell University. His research is currently focused on discourses of renunciation and environmentalism among contemporary, North Indian religious traditions.

Notes

1   Daniel Pals, *Seven Theories of Religion* (Oxford: Oxford University Press, 1996), 159.
2   Russell McCutcheon and Tim Murphy, "Historic Artifact? An Open Letter to Department Search Committees," originally appeared in the now defunct *Bulletin of the Council of the Societies for the Study of Religion*, January 26, 1997. Reprinted in Russell McCutcheon, *The Discipline of Religion* (New York: Routledge, 2003). Currently available on the *Studying Religion in Culture* blog, https://religion.ua.edu/blog/2015/09/15/an-open-letter-to-department-search-committees.

Response to Thesis 14

Adrian Hermann

Thesis 14: Depending on the type of institution into which one is hired (i.e., its teaching load, service obligations, emphasis on research, sabbatical opportunities, etc.), the dissertation may constitute one of the few, or quite possibly even the last, opportunity a candidate has to devote an extended period of time to one, focused project, free from the many obligations routinely expected of an assistant professor. Given the pressure to publish that, for some time, has attended academic careers, graduate students would be wise to write their dissertations while keeping in mind their eventual submission for possible publication—whether as a monograph (which, depending on a department's "tenure and promotion" requirements, may be preferable) or as separate peer review essays.

In his fourteenth thesis on professionalization, McCutcheon alerts graduate students to the fact that the time spent working on their dissertation might be the only instance in their professional career in which they can completely focus on only one large research project. At the same time, he highlights the importance of thinking about one's own research in terms of publishability from the very start.

Reflecting on this thesis today as someone who received his degree from a university in Switzerland and is now working in Germany, a number of things come to mind.

In the current climate in which peer-reviewed publications are becoming more and more important for any substantial academic career, beginning to think early on about the possibilities of publishing one's work is not only sound but necessary advice. At the same time, the two parts of McCutcheon's thesis could also be read as slightly at odds with each other. Every young scholar faces the question of whether to treat the environment offered by a graduate program or graduate school as a chance to focus purely on one's own interests without necessarily taking into account employability, or to choose a topic which may be more fashionable and might promise "market success." Making this choice is complicated by the fact that as someone just starting out in a graduate program you might not be able to completely assess how your possible topic will fit into the current research climate and the priorities of the field as a whole. While the decision itself has to be taken by each student individually, advisors should discuss these issues with their Ph.D. students and both encourage them to follow their interests while also alerting them to the fact that not all topics might be similarly conducive to their subsequent applications to faculty positions.

In any case, even as a graduate student it is important to actively be looking for chances to publish the work one has decided to focus on. In Germany, most dissertations in the humanities have traditionally been published as books. While publishing online is now a possibility at almost all institutions, in most cases it is not yet advisable to do so, as many hiring committees are still paying close attention to the context (i.e. the publisher) in which a particular dissertation appears. At the same time, it seems to me that thinking about designing one's dissertation to facilitate publishing journal articles based on the manuscript is a good idea that many Ph.D. advisors do not yet think about enough. A closer focus on this issue might be one of the more important changes currently taking place in graduate programs in the humanities, at least in Germany. At the same time, if your advisor is a senior scholar, he or she might not be completely aware that young scholars today are facing new requirements for launching a professional career. Therefore, even in the context of the often more traditional German system, it seems advisable to prepare the dissertation in a way which still allows for publication as a book by one of the more recognized publishers, and at the same time attempt to publish one or more chapters as articles, possibly while still working towards the degree.

Another issue that seems to be insufficiently explored by graduate students and young scholars in the humanities is the idea of writing together with another person. As a graduate student, the chance to co-author an article or book chapter either with someone with more experience in the given field of research or with another graduate student or young scholar might offer an early chance to contribute something substantial to the scholarly conversation. Such a publication might also receive increased interest by readers already familiar with your co-author. While writing in pairs or groups is an established practice in the natural sciences or social sciences, it is not yet widespread in religious studies. Luckily, it looks like this is about to change.

This goes along with another suggestion about finding and identifying possibilities of getting work published even very early in graduate school. You might not be aware that editors of collections on a specific topic or even of conference volumes are often looking for a particular essay to fill a spot or deal with a specific topic which is still missing from their outline. If you hear about such a publication being prepared, it might be a good idea to ask the editor(s) about their plans and to propose contributing a chapter of your own. You might just end up with your first publication as a result.

The biggest difference between universities in the U.S. and the German (and larger European) context probably concerns the possibility of fully focusing on one large project. Traditionally, in Germany the completion of a "Habilitation thesis," a second focused and long-term book project after the dissertation, used to be a necessary requirement to apply to full professor positions. Therefore, it always has been expected and—as much as was feasible—was encouraged by universities and colleagues that a young scholar finds the necessary time and space to work on such a second large research project.

While many young scholars continue to work towards completing a "Habilitation," other career options have become available. Over the last decade and a half, new large-scale funding initiatives, especially in Germany, have led to a comparably longer post-doc period than before (at least in the humanities). A young scholar might for a couple of years—or even for up to six years (as, for example, in the Emmy-Noether-Program of the German Research Foundation)—continue to work on a clearly defined research project while also supervising a number of Ph.D. students, before moving on to a full-time faculty position. In such a position as a 'research group leader' the teaching load is not as high as for most other positions available to Ph.D. holders.

At the same time, the introduction of an assistant professor position ("Juniorprofessor") into the academic system in Germany has made the situation even more complex. Young scholars appointed to one of these positions are awarded all the rights and duties which traditionally were limited to full professors in the German system. They teach regular classes, participate in their departments' administrative work, and are also expected to bring in third-party funded grants and supervise Ph.D. students. At the same time, because they are demonstrating their potential as future full professors in these other ways, they are no longer expected to complete and submit a formal "Habilitation." Nevertheless, many of these young professors, especially in more traditional disciplines in the humanities (like History or German studies) are hedging their bets and try to write a formal habilitation thesis at the same time as they are attempting to fulfill all the other responsibilities their positions entail.

All of these career choices and possibilities are taking place in a context in which the rise of big research clusters and large collaborative research endeavors even in the humanities, as well as an increased pressure on all scholars to apply for a variety of small and large third-party funded research grants, make it difficult to find the time to focus on writing a second comprehensive monograph. Rather, every young scholar I know is constantly struggling with the challenge of keeping up with the various deadlines for essays, articles and book chapters which one has promised to funding institutions and colleagues in the context of one's own or other's research projects.

In regard to publishing, the academic world is changing rapidly, so that often your own mentors are unsure how to counsel you on which publications (books, journal articles etc.) you should focus on, and which types of publications are the most important. In this way, it becomes increasingly important to discuss such issues with other young scholars and colleagues to get an idea of how they are dealing with these different demands.

I find it important to reflect on these issues while I myself am moving from being a graduate student/post-doc to thinking about my own priorities in mentoring future Ph.D. students. As many aspects of how graduate students and young scholars should approach publishing in order to prepare for a successful professional career in the humanities are profoundly changing, these issues are only becoming more important.

Adrian Hermann is professor of religion and society at the Forum Internationale Wissenschaft, University of Bonn, Germany. In 2011 he graduated with a D.Phil. in the study of religion from the University of Basel, Switzerland. His work focuses on method and theory in the study of religion, non-Western Christianity (particularly in Southeast Asia), and the religious history of the globalized world.

Response to Thesis 15

Kelly J. Baker

Thesis 15: Having successfully defended the dissertation, the manuscript does candidates no good in their desk drawer. However, before making revisions (unless they are dissatisfied with its argument or quality), graduates should create a prospectus containing a brief cover letter, annotated table of contents, and sample chapter (e.g., the introduction) and submit it to a select number of top-tier publishers in their area of expertise. Obtaining an outside experts' assessment of the manuscript—a step often essential to a publisher's process of evaluation—provides the best place to begin one's revisions of a manuscript with which one is intimately familiar and, perhaps, too closely tied.

I must confess that I found Russell McCutcheon's "Theses on Professionalization" after I decided to take a break from the job market in 2013. I read each hastily, and I couldn't help but wonder how his theses applied to the dismal and dire job market that left me bruised and aching. I briefly contemplated writing a rousing response to each, but the idea floated away as I adjusted to life outside of academia. I was glad to reread these theses when Matt Sheedy invited me to respond to Thesis 15 on manuscripts and publishing.

"[T]he manuscript does candidates no good in their desk drawer" is one of those statements that compels response. When I reread this sentence, I reacted by shouting "of course, it doesn't!" This is likely not the response McCutcheon would have expected, but Thesis 15 offers sound, practical advice to job candidates on turning a dissertation into a monograph. It is true that your dissertation cannot become a book without yanking it out of your desk (or from the cloud) and shaping it into a manuscript worthy of peer review and press approval. Job candidates should create a prospectus, or proposal, and send it out to "top-tier publishers" in their respective fields. McCutcheon further suggests finding outside readers, who can provide expertise on what your dissertation *needs* to become a proper book in religious studies.

His advice is remarkably similar to the advice my advisor gave me as I was finishing my dissertation in 2008. My advisor also emphasized that our dissertations shouldn't read like dissertations. He had me rewrite the damn thing at least four times, so it read like a monograph. This proved to be very helpful advice as much I am still loath to admit. I sent the manuscript off to scholars who knew my general area of expertise, American religious history, but who would also be able to offer suggestions on what revisions it required and which ones would make it the book that I wanted it to be.

Three presses contacted me before my dissertation was filed. My topic, the 1920s Klan, intrigued them. The editors from each had either read blog posts that I had written on the topic or noticed papers I presented at academic conferences. Another editor from a different press emailed because one of the outside readers recommended my manuscript for her catalogue.

After I defended my dissertation, I sent off the proposals along with the full manuscript to one press after another. (Academic presses frown upon simultaneous submissions.) The publishers wanted the whole manuscript rather than sample chapters. After all, I was a junior scholar with some articles published and they wanted to assess the project in its entirety. I quickly learned that some presses wouldn't consider manuscripts from dissertations without substantial difference between the two. Editors sought manuscripts that read more like full-fledged monographs.

Before I graduated, I had a book contract and advance. My committee was convinced that I would have no problem getting a tenure track job. Any department, they assured, would be lucky to have me. I chose to believe them. I had four campus visits that year. Following my advisor's advice about publishing seemed to work.

However, no amount of advice mattered after the market crash in 2008. The job market for tenure-track positions in the humanities, which already wasn't good, became worse. The common lament was "there are no jobs," but this wasn't true. There were still jobs, but they were not tenure track. Contingent positions, those part-time and full-time jobs re-upped every semester or year, were readily available. I had no problem securing temporary lecturer gigs. My book contract might have helped. Yet, I'm not sure it mattered much when departments just need bodies in front of classrooms to teach students. I finished my book while teaching part-time and applying for tenure track jobs. I got a contract for another book after getting a full-time lecturer job.

I imagined that if I just worked hard enough and published more that I could cajole search committees into hiring me. I didn't get a tenure track job.

So, while I agree that your manuscript does you no good in your desk drawer, I'm not entirely convinced that it does you any good out of the drawer either. A book contract likely makes a candidate look better to search committees. A completed manuscript possibly looks better. Neither the contract nor the manuscript are a guarantee that you'll do well on the job market and score one of those elusive tenure track jobs. They might help. They might not. (It is even possible to publish too much for assistant professor jobs.)

You can do everything right and still not get a tenure track job because there are fewer and fewer of these positions. This is not a reflection on you, but the reality of humanities job market now. Are job candidates professionalizing for a job that they might never attain? What kind of advice can we offer if the positions that largely await job candidates are low-paying, temporary work?

Turn the manuscript into a book if you want to. Abandon it if you don't. I can't advise writing a book, a long, arduous task, because you are searching for a tenure track job. Clearing the drawer in the hope of being a model candidate feels risky in ways that it maybe didn't in 2007. Write a book and seek a contract because you want to. Realize that the secure employment in academia is getting harder to come by. And be ready to walk away if you don't like your options.

Kelly J. Baker is the author of the award-winning *Gospel According to the Klan: The KKK's Appeal to Protestant America, 1915-1930* (University Press of Kansas, 2011); *The Zombies Are Coming!: The Realities of the Zombie Apocalypse in American Culture* (Bondfire Books, 2013); *Grace Period: A Memoir in Pieces* (Raven Books, 2017); and *Sexism Ed: Essays on Gender and Labor in Academia* (Raven Books, 2018). She's also the editor of *Women in Higher Education*.

Response to Thesis 16

Lauren E. Osborne

Thesis 16: Apart from professionalizing themselves through research and publication, candidates should consider the cost of regularly attending regional and national scholarly conferences simply as the price of being a graduate student. Waiting until one is on the job market is therefore too late to consider attending and trying to participate in such conferences—especially when one learns that being placed on the program of such annual meetings often comes about gradually, over the course of several (or more) years. Whereas regional meetings are often useful places to try out one's research, become accustomed to speaking in public, and learn the rituals of the question/answer sessions that follow the presentation of papers (knowledge especially important during on-campus interviews), national meetings play a crucial role in efforts to integrate oneself into networks of colleagues at other institutions who share one's interests.

Is this thesis still relevant? As my students often hear me say, "yes and no." I am reluctant to agree with McCutcheon that graduate students "should consider the cost of regularly attending regional and national scholarly conferences simply as the price of being a graduate student"; while I do think that conference attendance may be valuable (for reasons that I will describe below), it should not be understood as a financial obligation necessary for advancement of one's career.

For many, the cost of attending a national meeting is prohibitive. There's the membership fee, the registration fee, the airfare, the hotel, ground transportation between airport and conference, any food or drinks consumed while traveling (always more expensive than what one would eat at home)—these costs are out of reach for many graduate students, most especially those from working class backgrounds who may not have a financial "cushion" or family members who are able to help. Thankfully, some professional organizations now offer some financial assistance for graduate students, non-tenure track faculty members, and unemployed people to attend annual meetings (in addition to the standard of scaling membership and registration fees by employment status). The American Academy of Religion[1] and the Society of Biblical Literature[2] both offer travel grants for those who may need support in order to make attending and participating in an annual meeting possible. Additionally, many institutions now offer financial assistance for their graduate students to attend conferences, although the details of these programs differ depending on the institutional context. If you are a graduate student who would like to attend a conference, *always* ask if your institution provides support for such activities.

But in many ways, national conferences are not all they're cracked up to be. Many associations are so large that the chances of rubbing elbows with "famous" senior scholars in one's field are slim to none; in many cases, those senior scholars might not even be attending the conferences anymore. The programs are so bloated that you may end up moving in a small pack from one panel to the next of similarly minded people in your area of specialty, rarely or never encountering anyone from a different area of specialization (ironic, considered that you're constantly surrounded by thousands of people). Competition for inclusion on the program is fierce. And should you be lucky enough to get to present, you may receive little to no feedback. I'm not the first to point out these shortcomings of the meetings of national associations. In his piece in *Inside Higher Ed*,[3] Rob Weir argues that large humanities conferences are, as he puts it, "past their sell-by date." Why? He cites, among other points, the abominable practice of reading written papers aloud and the financial hardship of attendance.

So why do we still do this? Fear of change and force of habit, yes, but I might dare to suggest there are some benefits to attending conferences. Close readers of McCutcheon's thesis have probably noticed that I have thus far considered the thesis primarily in light of national conferences, while he in fact refers to regional conferences as well. He notes, "national meetings play a crucial role in efforts to integrate oneself into networks of colleagues at other institutions who share one's interests." I disagree. While a graduate student, I found regional and similarly small conferences to be considerable more hospitable environments for integrating myself into a network. The national meetings were simply too large for this. It was through participation in regional and other small conferences that I actually came to speak with colleagues across a range of areas of interest and career stages, and even to keep in touch with those people after the conference. When we consider the substantially lower (but not nonexistent) financial obligation of attending regional or other small meetings, in terms of forming a network, this is a no-brainer. Small conferences are absolutely the way to go.

But even here, I offer an additional word of caution: do not feel that, as a graduate student, you must submit to or attend every conference that appears in your inbox. You do not even need to consider most. This is not to say that most conferences are not worthwhile. Rather, this is a point about quantity of conferences. There is a point at which attendance can become burdensome (both in terms of expense and use of one's time). You can keep up with what's current just as easily by following a few academic journals; this is easily accomplished via RSS feed, email updates, or even by flipping through the current periodical section in your institution's library.

Before ending this, it is worth mentioning the conference interview, which is probably looming large on the minds of many graduate student readers. If you are able to, it is likely worth attending one national meeting before entering onto the job market. The conference interview is an awkward format. Thankfully, many institutions now mention directly in job ads that interviews via Skype or telephone are possible for applicants not attending national meetings. And also thankfully, some have recently pointed to the unjust system that is perpetuated by conference interviews;[4] interviews via Skype or phone aren't perfect, but they at least don't cost applicants thousands of dollars, nor do they require that search committees spend days on end sitting in cubicles in the middle of a convention center—a dehumanizing experience for everyone involved.

I will close by noting the one major benefit of attending, and when possible, participating in, conferences small and large: cultural literacy. Conferences have their own culture, and familiarizing oneself with the workings of that culture, as a graduate student, is important. It is not, however, worth thousands of dollars, nor is it worth extensive time away from your research. It is a benefit that may be gained through targeted attendance of and participation in conferences that are most likely to sustain and reinvigorate your excitement about the field, with minimal impact on your wallets.

Lauren E. Osborne is assistant professor of religion at Whitman College in Walla Walla, Washington. Her first book (in progress) is an aesthetic study of the recited Qur'an.

Notes

1   See www.aarweb.org/programs-services/annual-meeting-travel-grant-program.
2   See www.sbl-site.org/membership/AMtravelgrant.aspx.
3   See www.insidehighered.com/views/2011/07/05/end-large-conferences.
4   See https://chroniclevitae.com/news/718-end-the-conference-interview.

Response to Thesis 17

Aldea Mulhern

Thesis 17: National scholarly conferences and professional associations often host on-site job placement services and publish employment periodicals. Becoming thoroughly aware of such services and resources, long before actually being on the job market, may not only assist one's decision-making when it comes time to select an area of expertise (i.e., judging national employment trends over time may shed light on areas likely to require staffing in the coming years) but also prepare one for the eventual time when one is on the market and seeking campus interviews.

Too many graduate students seem unprepared for what awaits them once they complete their dissertations.[1]

So opens Russell McCutcheon's short work, featuring twenty-one theses that aim to redress the problem stated in that first sentence: grad students who are looking for full-time academic employment don't know what they're in for. And in one sense, that's a problem that we can't fix. Applying for that first academic job is a process of imagining the sort of scholar that we aren't yet, but that we can be, if given the institutional support necessary to take those next steps after earning the Ph.D. It is a process of persuading a department to invest its resources in us, and asking them to believe that together we can have, and will have, a symbiotic and mutually productive relationship over perhaps thirty years or more, assuming that we candidates are in our mid-thirties, that the average age of retirement is around sixty-five, that the first job is tenure-track, and that the first job works out. These are wildly optimistic assumptions. Even with the help of McCutcheon's theses, and the other forms of advice we get from across the religious studies spectrum, candidates are journeying into a particular kind of uncertainty: the relational kind, that asks us to stretch toward our future selves, to bring that future scholar into being, before the eyes of a search committee, before they eyes of a department of students and professional colleagues; before our own eyes.

In Thesis 17, which inspires my reflection here, McCutcheon tells us that employment information exists, and tells us to look at it, early. We should look, and look early, it is written, because doing so may help us pick a specialization that will work for the market, and prepare us, in some way, for our future interviews. Surely, this is sound advice. How can it hurt, to look down the road and see what's coming? Yet there is a tension in this advice, the same tension that runs through the job application process and the degree process itself, which merits discussion: we're still busy becoming. The trick of becoming, I think, is reaching toward what we think will be required of us, and toward what we require. Academic jobs need us to fill the departmental niche their history has grown for them, but also need us to stand on our own talents, skills, and intellectual networks in order to do that. Similarly, we need our own center of intellectual gravity, and we also need scholarly jousting, intellectual community, and institutional support inside which to conduct the work.

A few things should be acknowledged at this point. McCutcheon wrote his theses in 2007, and intended them to be a reality check. In 2008, the academic job market, which had been in decline in Canada and the U.S. since the 1990s and perhaps earlier, crashed when the larger economy crashed. An already unfavorable market became even more tenuous. The employment landscape has thus undergone important shifts since the time McCutcheon was writing. The AAR/SBL's Employment Services, for example, do not currently involve a job fair by any conventional understanding of the term. Instead, job applicants, who can outnumber the positions they apply for by two orders of magnitude, pay for access to employment listings, and for the ability to upload their CVs to be viewed by prospective employers.[2] Those prospective employers pay to post job ads, and to use the employment center's physical location as a dedicated area for rapid-fire interviews with potential candidates during the annual meeting. Some of my colleagues speak about the anxiety-ridden "bullpen" of the employment center's curtained interview areas as an improvement over the discomfort of interviewing ad hoc in hotel rooms during the conference; however, the employment center also continues the practice by organizing hotel-room interviewing.

The benefits and pitfalls of the AAR/SBL employment center have been discussed by other scholars, some of whom are already visible in the *Bulletin* community.[3] I will not reproduce what these commentators have said, but rather will confine myself to two observations about the employment center, speaking as one ABD Ph.D. candidate[4] joining the job market, at whom the center (and the advice) is directed: on the one hand, the center's usefulness is limited, the costs associated with participating in it are quite significant, and many of those costs accrue to a vulnerable population.[5] On the other hand, limited utility is still utility: although only few Canadian institutions use the AAR/SBL employment center, American institutions continue to conduct interviews there, and there remains an expectation that engaged scholars will already be in attendance at the meeting and will be available to interview there.

I can respond to McCutcheon's Thesis 17 in one way simply, then, by saying that the job fair model ain't what it used to be, but that we're still using it, in a particular way. The 2013/14 AAR/SBL report[6] shows that candidates who are more than one calendar year away from graduation don't stand a chance of getting work. Given the services offered, I find it doubtful that a very young scholar would learn much from participating in the current job service, except perhaps to worry (not worth the price tag) or to avoid the problem by dropping out to look for a different kind of job (possibly a substantial net saving). The job service is much less a showing, and much more a doing: an exercise in bureaucratization that imperfectly, but still usefully, connects prospective employees and prospective employers across an atomized, pressurized, and idiosyncratic landscape of too few jobs and too many applicants.

The core of McCutcheon's advice, though, was not that job services are in all times and places key locations of information to which we are otherwise oblivious. Rather, I take him and other scholars to be pushing graduate students to be more aware of the water they are swimming in, and the difficult choices they will face. That advice is good. However, anyone who's had an advisor knows that very good advice is sometimes impossible to follow, until you're on the threshold of the place where you no longer need it. When Rod Stewart sang "I wish that I knew what I know now / when I was younger" the problem wasn't that someone had failed to tell him. The problem remains that it's un-simple to know what you don't already know, and to use foresight to manifest courage and grace while you stumble around figuring things out.

Ph.D. programs are advertised as four to five years long in Canada and the U.S., and they typically take longer than that to complete. When I arrived at the University of Toronto as a newly minted M.A. in religion and culture keen for a Ph.D. in religious studies, looking at job ads offered me only the muddiest impression of *what the work of a professor of religious studies might actually be.* Job ads, things which I could hardly contextualize and which I could only view piecemeal, did not have much to do with my formation. I hardly saw them. They existed as multiple overlapping lists, updated erratically and staggered over months, sometimes behind pay-walls, struggling to express the needs of departments and in a vexed relationship to the field as a whole. What formed me, my project, and my scholarly identity, was my network.

Above all, I was busy trying to grow into a quality academic. A Ph.D. is a credential, certainly, but it is also an opportunity to craft oneself, to practice thinking well and writing well on topics that fascinate us, and that's why many of us undertake one. I did not come to this degree because I anticipated that San Diego State University would want a sociocultural anthropologist of religion to teach three courses about food politics in Toronto (they do not). I came to it the same way many of us do. I had been inspired. I'd taken classes that opened me in some way. I'd read work that helped me understand the world around me in new light, and I'd met scholars who were open and erudite and who welcomed my thinking and my questions. I dimly saw that the training could sculpt me into a certain kind of person, like going to the gym, but for my mind. I thought I could test and grow what I was capable of, alongside people who were better than me at a craft I admired, and continue to be in dialogue with them. More than wanting a job, I wanted to become the person alongside whom members of that community would want to work.

When I selected my project, I tried hard to pick one that would *work* on the job market, as well as one that I would love to do. I tried to pick one that showed breadth, that would allow me to develop expertise that was demonstrable and translatable, that would allow me to go as deep as was necessary without driving me all the way into an enclave. But those goals were highly impressionistic, and impressed on me by mentors: by my committee and above all my supervisor, by my departmental directors, my upper-year colleagues and the community of advisors I'd collected from conferences, including the writer of the theses on professionalization that I read in my first year as a Ph.D. student. My project came from my method and theory classes, from the books I loved and hated, from my clumsy early attempts to represent my goals to a persistently patient and faithful committee, and from their encouragement to check out the world and to do my homework, and find a project where those two things intersected.

I am glad we talk about professionalization. It would be a waste, and cruel, not to, and it is central to the health of our discipline to mitigate the cruelty of current waste. But I am also hopeful that the discourse of professionalization doesn't overreach the process of cultivating oneself as an academic, or as a person.[7] The need to plug in to the job market early is real, but that need is tied to a failure of the community, including its graduate students, to imagine what an academic is: by definition, a member of a department and an institution of education. The job market can be read, by a novice, as asking a number of things of us (to be a social scientist; to be confessional; to deconstruct religion as a category; to reproduce religion as a category; to abandon hope, all ye who enter here). I think what McCutcheon and others want us to read in it is this: departments need academics who can be trusted to think responsibly, reliably, and well, who will carry out inquiry and share what they find usefully, who will cultivate learning in students and maintain productive relationships with colleagues and take care of their academic area and show up for meetings and *be constructive*.

By virtue of attaining the credential, we demonstrate the necessary aptitude and skill. At that point, the thing we're selling is hope, specifically the hope of our future selves as scholar-colleagues. The job doesn't go to the "best" human. The job goes to the best apparent *fit*. So I think the root piece of advice to be found here is to think deeply, in an ongoing way and at every stage, about fit. Aim to be fit, look for a fit, show them the fit, and then, ideally, go where there's a fit.

Aldea Mulhern is visiting assistant professor of cultural diversity and intercultural communication at Grand Valley State University in Michigan, U.S.A. When the above essay first appeared as a blog post on the *Bulletin*'s website, she was a Ph.D. candidate at the Department for the Study of Religion at the University of Toronto, Canada. Aldea works at the intersection of food and religion, and her first book is a comparative ethnography of Jewish and Muslim communities' involvement in Toronto's food movement.

Notes

1   From the preamble to McCutcheon's "Theses on Professionalization" as it appears on the website of The Religious Studies Project (February 29, 2012), www.religiousstudies project.com/2012/02/29/russell-mccutcheon-theses-on-professionalization.
        The theses first appeared without preamble in the collection of essays edited by Mathieu E. Courville, *The Next Step in Studying Religion: A Graduate's Guide* (London: Continuum, 2007).

2   The searchable CV-hosting service used to cost the applicant, and as of 2015 is now free to applicants, but see note 4.

3   For example, see http://bulletin.equinoxpub.com/2011/11/speed-date-interviews-at-the-aarsbl-a-look-at-the-high-costs-of-the-academic-job-hunt and http://bulletin.equinoxpub.com/2012/06/a-bit-of-relief-for-independent-scholars-in-the-pacific-northwest.

4   At the time of the original writing, in 2015. The author is glad to report that at the time of this re-write in 2017, she holds a Ph.D. and is, for the moment at least, academically employed.

5   While the CV-hosting service is now free, and while the job listings are not behind a dedicated pay-wall, these facts are deceptive. It is not sufficient to be an active paid member of the AAR or SBL to access these services: one must be a member, and have registered and paid to attend the annual meeting. This means that job seekers must register and pay for the annual meeting in order to access the online job listings and to upload a CV, even if they have not been invited to interview at the meeting, and even if they do not actually plan to attend.

6   See www.aarweb.org/sites/default/files/pdfs/Career_Services/AARSBLJobsReport2013-2014.pdf.

7   Not all of us will get jobs in this field, but we will all be people. This fact is not missed by McCutcheon, but pervades his theses, and much other good advice from compassionate and responsible academics.

Response to Thesis 18

Thomas J. Whitley

Thesis 18: Despite the dissertation being the primary, and sometimes even the exclusive, focus of candidates' attention during the last years of their Ph.D., once hired into a tenure-track position a variety of other just as time consuming tasks compete for their attention. Learning to juggle many balls simultaneously—knowing which will bounce if dropped and which will break—is therefore an essential skill for early career professors who wish to continue carrying out original research while also teaching a full course load and serving the needs of their departments and the profession at large.

Time management is at the heart of Thesis 18. This is not something that all academics think regularly about; graduate students seem to be especially poor at cultivating this skill. Academics can be (read: seem) heroic when it comes to just getting done what needs to be done, not allowing evenings, weekends, or vacations to get in the way. This type of living on the edge may provide an adrenaline rush for graduate students, but it is only setting them up for failure. Yet, many graduate students, I fear, simply do not realize what will be expected of them when (read: if) they get that elusive tenure-track job. Taking three classes is simply not the same as preparing and teaching three classes. And while graduate students do understand this, even those who have only been given the opportunity to be a teaching assistant and have not been instructor of record, their ability to realistically imagine what being a professional academic looks like is hampered by the fact that ours is a profession that holds its cards close to the chest. Very few graduate advisors talk to their graduate students about what service to the department, service to the university, and service to the field actually look like. And so graduate students prepare for a career in academia with a vision that is only as broad as their previous experience in academia, an experience that has been largely limited to the classroom.

The value in Thesis 18 can only be realized if graduate students heed McCutcheon's advice. The best way to prepare for "juggling many balls simultaneously" is to juggle many balls simultaneously. As such, I encourage graduate students to not only learn more about time management techniques that work for them, but to get involved, as they are able, in their department, in their university, and in their field. Can you help organize a conference? Can you organize and propose a panel for your regional or national conference? Are there committees that you can serve on that will give you a glimpse into what the life of an academic really looks like?

In case you're wondering, I followed my own advice here. I served on a departmental committee, co-directed and then directed a graduate student conference, chaired a section of my region's professional/academic society, and served on a national board for one of the major national professional/academic societies. All of this while being a doctoral student, writing my dissertation, writing regularly for online audiences, and working on peer-reviewed publications. While some of my (graduate student) colleagues thought this was impressive, those who are already working in the field know that it is simply what life as an academic looks like. It is, as McCutcheon said, a juggling act, and the only way to get better at juggling is to juggle.

Thomas J. Whitley has a Ph.D. in religion from Florida State University and writes about religion, politics, and culture. His work has appeared in *Marginalia Review of Books, Religious Studies News, Ancient Jew Review, Perspectives in Religious Studies,* and *Dead Sea Discoveries.*

Response to Thesis 19

Sarah Lynn Kleeb

> Thesis 19: Although it can be intellectually stimulating, developing new courses is time consuming. Depending on the needs of their department, teaching multiple sections of the same course provides early career professors with fewer course preparations, helps them to quickly establish their area of expertise in the curriculum and among students, and allows them to gain teaching competencies far quicker, thereby enabling them to devote more time to their research and writing.

In his Thesis 19, McCutcheon reminds us of the often substantial weight that comes with developing new courses term after term, and encourages teaching multiple sections of one course, in order to refine teaching skills while still leaving time for one's own research and writing. Developing new courses is indeed time consuming, and doing so can potentially feel overwhelming, depending on how many courses one is developing at the same time; each course can easily become a substantial research project in and of itself. These multiple sections, however, are entirely dependent "on the needs of [the] department," and there, I fear, is the proverbial rub. Are multiple sections of religion courses even a thing anymore? Because I, for one, am not seeing much evidence of that. Only the obligatory 1st-year "World Religions" course at my university had multiple sections—and by "multiple," I mean two: one day section and one evening section, with one of these generally taught by regular faculty, the other by a sessional lecturer.

I can only speak from experience (having just defended in August), but perhaps my perplexity is due to the idiosyncrasies of my former home department, where ABD students are rarely hired to teach the same course twice (in the admittedly admirable interest of giving as many opportunities for development to as many students as possible). In such an environment, I never found myself in the position to teach multiple sections of a religion course, and only once was I able to teach the same course twice. Even then, it was at a year's remove—it was our "Study of Religion" course (a method and theory primer for undergrads), for which they had trouble recruiting an instructor during a summer term. I'd taught the course the previous summer. That said, upon attaining a permanent position, or even a "stable" adjunct position (an oxymoron, perhaps), it may be possible to teach the same course within or across different terms, but it's also worth considering how much time is actually saved in doing so.

First, though, some background: while I only had the opportunity to teach one of my religion courses twice, I also spent the last few years of my doctoral work teaching a general humanities course. It was an introductory survey course that functioned as an academic writing "boot camp" for 1st year students. This was a course that I just kind of fell into, and I was in the fortunate position of being hired to teach this course for multiple terms, over multiple years. In this role, I was able to teach two sections per year (one in the fall and one in the winter, on a semester model), but never multiple sections in the same term. While this meant that I didn't have to build from the ground up every term, it also never saved as much time as I thought it would.

In my experience, very few courses can be run verbatim multiple times. Perhaps that is the case if one is teaching multiple sections during the same term, but, again, if anyone sees that actually happening with great frequency, please let me know. Even my twice-taught "Study of Religion" course underwent significant changes from one year to the next, despite the subject matter being essentially the same. Every course I teach is as much a learning experience for myself as it is for my students, and there are many reasons to tweak courses from term to term, year to year. Some ideas, approaches, or theories that I think will be really engaging for students end up flopping, and I'm often surprised by students' enthusiasm regarding concepts that I fear will be too weighty or abstract for them. Each time either of those things happen, a revision is necessary. Of course, that's not even taking into account the need to keep current with the scholarship I bring into the classroom, nor the need to re-work and re-structure readings and assignments each term to help curb plagiarism, particularly with the increasing access students have to purchasing work submitted in previous terms. None of this is to suggest that lectures, readings, and general content can never be recycled. When this is possible, it is undoubtedly a time-saver. But a one-size-fits-all approach to courses taught across multiple terms or years isn't necessarily realistic. The recycling I've done has always been partial, at best.

While assembling the academic content of courses and lectures admittedly takes the most time, we shouldn't disregard how much time is gobbled up by the basic ins and outs of course development: establishing course timelines, late policies, general assignment structures, methods of evaluation, and grading rubrics; creating generic and reusable blurbs regarding academic integrity, accessibility, lecture notes policies, and useful campus resources; constructing explanations of intended learning outcomes and general expectations for students in our courses, etc. While content may need to shift somewhat (or, sometimes, considerably) from term to term, these little things are often relative constants, and, particularly as early career scholars, developing a firm understanding these fundamentals of putting a course together will likely save time in the long run. These are foundations that are generally reusable, regardless of the content or approach of a course.

As such, I'd recommend honing general and widely applicable course construction skills and refining your pedagogical approach, particularly while in the final years of graduate school or the first couple of years after graduation. Consider creating "stock" syllabi for 1st, 2nd, 3rd, and 4th year courses—general frameworks with clear parameters that take into consideration the needs of these different groups of students (i.e., 1st year students will generally need more specific direction than 3rd or 4th year students), into which specific readings and topics can be inserted later. Take advantage of pedagogical development and instructional skills workshops on campus to learn "best practices" for such things. While the content of courses tends to be our primary focus—that, after all, is what gets our juices flowing and excitement levels elevated—having a consistent, comprehensive, and transparent set of policies in place will not only save you time, it will improve the learning environment for your students.

I would also recommend familiarizing yourself with the resources available to undergraduate students (e.g., writing centers, language resources, research librarians, etc.), and doing so as early as possible. Solidifying relationships with such departments can help take the pressure off some of the more tedious, but still time consuming, aspects of running a course. Resources available through campus writing centers, for example, can help keep us from feeling like we have to "reinvent the wheel" each term, as we assign our students essays and other writing assignments. Librarians are often happy to hold research skill development clinics for undergrads, allowing us to devote our attention to course content, rather than telling students over and over again what a "peer reviewed" source is, and why it matters. I always encourage students to take full advantage of all the campus resources available to them (and for which they're paying, via their tuition, whether or not they use them), but am often surprised at how little we instructors and professors ourselves are encouraged to make use of these same resources in our classes, aside from simply telling students that they exist. While the applicability of such things may depend on the kinds of work you plan to assign in your courses, when they are relevant, they are invaluable, and they absolutely free up time that can be used in other ways. All those little emails about acceptable sources and essay formatting really add up, especially if you have hundreds of students per term, all with the same sets of questions.

So, while McCutcheon's advice here isn't necessarily unsound, the ideal and reality don't always match up quite so tidily, in my experience. Recycled courses don't require the same time commitment as newly developed courses, but they still often require significant reworking (again, unless the "multiple sections" fall in the same term, which seems an increasingly distant possibility). Taking time early on to develop expertise in the fundamentals of course construction benefits your students by your knowledge of pedagogical best practices, it benefits campus programs by encouraging students to utilize them, and it benefits scholars by making course development second nature, which opens up time that can be used for research and writing.

Moreover, in an academic world that relies heavily on adjuncts and sessional lecturers, and in a context in which humanities disciplines face ever more cutbacks, McCutcheon's advice might not be as widely applicable as it once was. As more scholars end up taking on sessional or adjunct positions in which they are at the mercy of the market, the hope of reducing one's workload by teaching multiple sections of a course may not be realistic. As pessimistic or defeatist as this may sound, to fill and maintain the kinds of positions increasingly available to many scholars, we may just have to do more for less.

Sarah Lynn Kleeb received her Ph.D. from the University of Toronto in 2015, with a dissertation exploring the legacy of Gustavo Gutierrez's theory of liberation, through the lens of Frankfurt School critical theory. She is currently director of education at ALPHA Education, a social justice education non-profit in Toronto. She continues to teach academic writing, media studies, and humanities courses at the University of Toronto, Scarborough.

Response to Thesis 20

Charles McCrary

> Thesis 20: Despite what some maintain, teaching and research are complementary activities, inasmuch as teaching, somewhat like publication, constitutes the dissemination of information gained by means of prior research. Based on one's strengths, candidates can understandably emphasize one over the over, but declining always to carry out both, integrating them together when possible, is to shirk one's responsibilities as a scholar.

Among graduate students who teach, teaching is often discussed as if it were a distraction from the "real" work: coursework and, more importantly, writing (articles and dissertations, not blogs). Your advisor might tell you this. Other students will tell you this. Even one presenter at Florida State University's Program for Instructional Excellence Teaching Conference and TA Orientation,[1] which was mandatory for all graduate instructors and TAs, acknowledged that teaching is not "what you're here to do." Graduate students teach about two-thirds of all undergraduates who take FSU religion classes, and yet certain faculty members (not all) advise graduate students to spend only as much time teaching as absolutely necessary. Now, there are of course all sorts of institutional issues, and we could talk about the exploitation of graduate student labor or the quality of undergraduate education. As the university becomes increasingly bureaucratic, courses are becoming standardized. The discretion and expertise of the instructor are sacrificed to mandated language and assignments designed by committees of non-educators. I could point out that while what I'm "here to do" is to write a dissertation, the university's interest in me extends only so far as I facilitate the instruction of seventy customer-students per semester, at a pay rate of about a tenth my advisor's. But instead I want to think about that disconnect between teaching and our "real" work and how, practically, we might bridge the gulf between the two.

Almost no one would say that teaching is ipso facto a waste of time. But plenty of us, I think, do understand it as a very different activity from research—and often a distraction from it (for better or worse). We are all busy, and as Russell McCutcheon's eighteenth thesis recognizes, we must juggle many balls, "knowing which will bounce if dropped and which will break." The teaching ball hits the ground first for many of us, especially those of us for whom teaching is not a part of our evaluation and/or those whose sole teaching evaluations come from our students. Quality teaching is not "incentivized," to adopt the parlance of the corporate university.

If research is indeed our main focus, how can our teaching enhance, inform, or otherwise complement that research? Of course they are both important in their own right, and they are both scholarship. But, at least for graduate students, one is our "job" and the other is the thing we get paid to do in order to fund our "job." (This situation obviously is different for adjunct lecturers, VAPs, post-docs, assistant professors, and tenured professors, respectively, and it varies among institutions and contracts. But I'll "write what I know.") How can teaching be something better than a distraction, waste of time, or side job? It is probably obvious how research can contribute to teaching, but how might teaching improve our research?

In his Thesis 20, Russell McCutcheon suggests one way in which teaching and research are "complementary": they both constitute "the dissemination of information gained by means of prior research." I hate to quibble over word choice, but I want to raise two issues here. First, I think teaching and research both *involve* disseminating information, but they don't *constitute* it. This is especially the case with teaching, which ideally should be a collaborative experience, which of course involves knowledge-dissemination but also includes discussion, feedback, and other collaborative means to produce new knowledge. Second, in the thesis McCutcheon argues that teaching and research are similar, related, or analogous, but not really *complementary*. It's true that teaching and research employ some of the same skills, and by practicing one you might hone both. In the remainder of this piece, though, I want to consider the ways that teaching—preparation, planning, designing courses, facilitating discussion, delivering lectures, creating assignments, even grading papers—can make your conference papers, articles, chapters, dissertations, and books better.

As much as I might agree with McCutcheon's appeal to one's "responsibilities as a scholar" and the internalized shame I do feel for "shirking" them, teaching is not just about ideals or principles. It's also about what you do with your hours. When you have to write an article or dissertation but you also must plan a lesson for your World Religions class, what do you do? What follows is, I suppose, advice. (Ugh. First I dissect word choices, and then I dole out advice. I swear I'm not normally this pedantic.) Quick caveat: my "advice" is based only on my particular and limited experience. It might or might not be helpful or applicable to you. [End of disclaimer/confession.]

I believe that teaching has improved the quality, if not always the rate, of my scholarship.[2] Here are a few ways that teaching can complement, and even enhance and improve, your research.

Test your themes and frameworks. Find some similar case study and design a lesson about it. "Classification," to quote J. Z. Smith, "often produces surprise, the condition which calls forth efforts of explanation."[3] If you research religion and colonial governance in one place, prepare a lesson on the same topic in a totally different place. The similarities and differences will demand explanation, and those explanations might help sharpen your understanding of your own research.

Try out some new themes and frameworks. If you are intrigued by a somewhat unfamiliar framework around which a body of scholarship (or an AAR program unit) is already organized, plan a few lessons on that theme and read a few books on it. Then, you can see if it's useful or applicable, and if it is, you have a head start on joining those conversations.

Find new models for scholarship. As I write I keep models in mind. These are the works that I want mine to resemble in style, organization, use of sources, conceptual framing, or method. I think the most important works we read are those to which we say, "I want to do it like that." One such book for me is Jason Josephson's *The Invention of Religion in Japan* (University of Chicago Press, 2012). But I never would have read it had I not scheduled a World Religions lesson on "religion in Japan." Now, each semester I find at least three or four monographs I'd like to read (podcasts, such as those from the New Books Network,[4] are a great way to find these), and then I schedule new lessons about those topics. I force myself to read the books, since I need to design the lessons.

See what your students notice. If possible, teach something from your research materials. Students will bring a set of questions that you might not expect. They think "outside of the box" because they are not trained in specific sub-disciplines. They ask the foundational questions that sometimes we have skipped past.

In these ways and more, teaching has been enjoyable, intellectually gratifying, and even productive of research, if indirectly. It might seem odd to say it—and I never would have anticipated this a few years ago—but my dissertation will be much better because I teach World Religions. This is only because I readjusted my outlook to think of teaching and research as truly complementary.

Charles McCrary is a scholar of American religions. He received his Ph.D. from Florida State University in 2018, and his dissertation was titled "Sincerely Held Religious Belief: A History."

Notes

1   See   http://pie.fsu.edu/sites/g/files/imported/storage/original/application/1363f60c2921c52c24bc13963ed61f40.pdf.
2   Please forgive the crass calculations going on here. Really, I think teaching is worth doing because it is important, and I value students as people and have an ethical obligation to help them and do as good a job as possible. So, I'm uncomfortable with the line of argument I'm advancing because it reminds me of corporate mindfulness retreats where they tell you that taking breaks actually makes you *more productive* and thus is "worth it" and acceptable. I suppose that is what I'm trying to argue about teaching.
3   Jonathan Z. Smith, "A Matter of Class," in *Relating Religion: Essays in the Study of Religion* (Chicago, IL: University of Chicago Press, 2004), 175.
4   See http://newbooksnetwork.com.

Response to Thesis 21

Katelyn Dykstra

Thesis 21: As with the effort to enter any profession, a price must inevitably be paid—economic as well as social—in terms of the other activities and goals one might instead have worked toward and possibly attained. Candidates must therefore not only be as deliberate as possible in determining which costs they are willing to pay and which they are not, but they must also learn to trust their own judgments when, regardless how their job search turns out, they someday look back on the decisions they once made.

I have started writing this blog post no less than four times. Each time I look at the completed piece and despair that I have not said exactly what I wanted to. I think the trouble is because this thesis is perhaps the most challenging one to get right: how to maintain balance in graduate school so that when we leave we (1) do not regret the decision to do it in the first place; and (2) we do not look around us and discover we have lost friends, alienated family members, and missed out on a lot of "life" we wanted to have. Given that I have not yet completed my Ph.D., I am not sure that I am qualified to say what I do and do not regret. But what I can say is that I have taken on a lot during my Ph.D. and am still standing. Along the way, I have learned a few things.

Since I started my Ph.D., I have had the sneaking suspicion that no one really wanted me to do it (with the few exceptions of me, my Master's advisor, and my grandfather who is still stuck in the world in which a Ph.D. in the humanities was as amazing as being a "real" doctor). I received a slew of emails from professors, family members, and friends discouraging the decision(s). Some in the form of serious articles,[1] and some humorous, such as the animated clip "So you Want to Get a Ph.D. in the Humanities."[2] The consensus seemed to be, why not get a "real" job with your already challenging Master's degree. Or, better yet, go to law school and have a job assured.[3]

Certainly, a Ph.D. would only make me overqualified for jobs in the "real" world, and I have a family to feed. I couldn't possibly put the financial burden solely on my partner to support us and our two children while I wiled away my time in the stacks of the library. (I will refrain from bursting with distain at the privileging of law and medicine over a Ph.D. in the humanities, but let it just stand here that while I do not understate the importance of doctors and lawyers in this world—we need them—we also need professors who are passionate, and respected for what they do. We do save lives, in our own way.) So, the question stands: three years in, do I regret it? The answer is unequivocally no. And trust me, my answer is a fully aware one. With a number of friends currently on the job hunt, I am no stranger to the bleak job market. Nor am I enchanted with the idea of becoming a professor.

Moreover, as you all likely know, a Ph.D. is really hard work. Since I began my Ph.D. I have really tried to treat it like a "regular" nine-to-five job. This is something that I noticed in my Honors advisor that I envied, and thought was smart. I start working once my children go off to school, and usually I quit once they come home. Occasionally, I pick it up again after they are in bed. And, rarely, I will spend a Saturday in the stacks, or making endless pots of coffee in the graduate student office in my department. Lately, it has been more frequent to see me in the office late at night, or bleary-eyed pouring over theory on a Saturday afternoon, because I recently wrote my second, and final, candidacy exam (applause). But, studying is not all there is to a Ph.D., no no. These days it means proving you can BE a professor, which means service and publications as well. It means working other paid and unpaid jobs, not just to boost the CV, but to find out if you actually want to spend the rest of your life in the hallways of the university. For me, I have had as many as three paid positions at one time while working on my MA and Ph.D., as well as numerous unpaid positions, committee appointments, and volunteer jobs, including the president of my department's student association. Even so, I cannot be sure that any of this will secure me a tenure-track position, ever. While I am one of those hopeful grad students who dream equally of an academic job and another unnamed position doing something in my field, I cannot be assured of that either. The conclusion here is that I spend a lot of time away from my family, both in mind and in body. I struggle to be present in both, but often find my mind drifting to Djuna Barnes,[4] grant applications, or the last department meeting instead of hockey practice. And so, I feel guilty. Really guilty. All the time.

All of this said, I do think graduate school is worth it, if for no other reason than it allows Ph.D.s some years to do exactly what they dreamed of doing—reading books, thinking deeply about a question, hanging out with really smart people, living in the queer time of graduate school just that little bit longer—before heading off to "the real world." So, I have six tips for how to get through a Ph.D. in the humanities, because I like lists:

1   We will never not feel guilty, so measure the amount of guilt you can manage. How many hours can you spend at the library before the guilt of leaving your dog at home alone begins to outweigh your productivity? Go home. Walk the dog. And while you do, try your utmost not to feel like you should be working. Compartmentalize. When you work, work. When you quit to watch *Buffy*, relish it.

2   Do not be afraid to prioritize your graduate student friendships. Someone once told me that the friends you make in grad school are the ones you will keep forever, because not only did you survive a

grueling process together, you also get each other's passions, and that is a rare thing indeed. You need them, and they need you too.

3   Get involved on campus. Sit on committees. Get involved in your Graduate Student Association, and with your department council. It will not only expose you to the kind of service work you will be required to do should you land an academic job, but it will show you what other skills you have, and what you enjoy doing and what you do not within a pretty non-threatening environment in which people are very excited to mentor you.

4   BUT! Write your thesis. Study. You will not regret spending time working on your dissertation. But you will not remember the fifth committee you did not spend time on, and no one will hold it against you that you do not come to a meeting because you were writing. That is what you are ultimately in grad school to do.

5   Exercise and eat well. I once came upon one of my brilliant colleagues on the elliptical while reading Faulkner. I was astonished (and still am) that she did not motion-sick puke all over the machines. But, it is worth the risk to make sure it happens. You will not be able to get back the damage you did to your body (especially your liver) in grad school. Mitigate that damage by biking to campus, or by reading on the bike in the gym, or making time to go with a friend to a yoga class. Whatever it takes. Take a page out of Taryn Hine's book,[5] and publically announce your plans on the internet, so that someone holds you accountable.

6   I believe what I, what we, do is important. And I refuse to lose sight of that. I believe academic labor is a kind of activism, and that combined with community based activism and work, what we do has, can, and will change the world. I believe teaching undergraduates to critically think about the world around them is a beautiful thing. A necessary thing. Perhaps even a life-saving thing. Having attended The University of Prince Edward Island, a small teaching-university, for my undergraduate degree, I spent a lot of time with my professors. They shaped me. They taught me how to make my anger productive, how to take my emotions into the community, how to turn theory into a theatre performance. Now, I know this sounds like idealism, and it is. But, does that necessarily make it less important? Idealism is, I argue, the only straw we have to hang onto through this process, because the rest of it is designed to sink us.

Addendum: It has been almost two years since I wrote this blog post, and I admit that my idealism has dwindled. I miss the pluckiness I read in my words here. (I also miss the encouraging presence of my grandfather, who has since passed away. His absence has undoubtedly made it harder for me to see the light in the darkness.)

As graduate students, our labor is vastly undervalued. Our passion for our work is exploited, so we take any work that is offered to us, and we are given little guidance on how to do it, in all but rare circumstances. Mental illness for graduate students is disproportionate to the general population, and we have no assurances of any reliable work when we are done. While I still think there is value in getting a Ph.D. because we need people in this rapidly changing world who can think through issues in a thorough and meaningful way, universities need to find a better way of supporting Ph.D.s as they go through the process. It is no shock that the university as an institution is in crisis, and those that are most vulnerable within it are feeling it most acutely. In this critical moment, my advice has not changed much, but as I approach the (hopefully) last months of my Ph.D. program, I want to emphasize this: Find your people. Find a community of people inside and outside the university that can nourish and support you. Work on those relationships. Find scholarly work and texts that inspire you and return to them often. Don't spend too much time alone. And, finally, advocate for your-self. Don't let the system steam roll you. If something feels exploitative, it likely is. In the face of these moments of exploitation, get loud. Take this opportunity to learn how to use your voice. In this topsy-turvy world, this skill is more necessary than ever.

Katelyn Dykstra is a Ph.D. candidate in the Department of English, Film, and Theatre at the University of Manitoba. Her dissertation project explores contemporary representations of intersex in literature and film.

Notes

1   E.g. www.theguardian.com/careers/Ph.D.-right-career-option.
2   See www.youtube.com/watch?v=obTNwPJvOI8.
3   A fallacy, as is asserted by the *HuffPost* piece at www.huffingtonpost.ca/2012/09/04/ becoming-a-lawyer_n_1663150.html.
4   E.g. *Nightwood* (New York: New Directions, 1946).
5   See www.facebook.com/pg/tarynfitness/about/?tab=page_info .

Index

Lightning Source UK Ltd.
Milton Keynes UK
UKHW011021301118
333249UK00002B/73/P